John Capgrave's Lives of
St. Augustine
and
St. Gilbert of Sempringham,
And a Sermon.

EDITED BY

J. J. MUNRO, F.R.Hist.S.,

EDITOR OF 'ROMEUS AND JULIET,' 'THE
SHAKSPEARE ALLUSION BOOK' AND AUTHOR WITH
DR. FURNIVALL OF 'SHAKESPEARE : LIFE AND WORK.'

LONDON:
PUBLISHED FOR THE EARLY ENGLISH TEXT SOCIETY
BY KEGAN PAUL, TRENCH, TRÜBNER & CO., Ltd.,
DRYDEN HOUSE, 43 GERRARD STREET, SOHO, W.
AND BY HENRY FROWDE, OXFORD UNIVERSITY PRESS,
AMEN CORNER, E.C.

———

1910

TO

DR. HENRY BRADLEY

OF THE OXFORD DICTIONARY

THIS BOOK IS DEDICATED
IN ADMIRATION FOR HIS LEARNING
AND GRATITUDE FOR HIS ENCOURAGEMENT

O my wel-beloued in our lord god ij. nicholas
mayster of ye ordre of sempyngham — By Sy -
vhech ordre is entytled on to ye
name of seynt gilbert / frer J. C.   John
a mougl doctourrs left fende ye Capgraue.
nerens as to fluch dignyte deſiryng clenesse
to your soule and helth to your body noſt
wuth inne felba dayes thas notyfied on
to me pat ye lyf of our fader seynt auguſ
tyn vhech yat I tranſlat in to our tuge
at inſtance of a cteyn thona thas broubt
to your preſens vhech lyked you thel as it
is told faue ʒe bold / I ſchul adde yto alle
yno religyous pat lyue vndyr his reule
but to ʒis I anſwerd yat it thas not my char
ge but if men like for to bnothe yis mater
diffuſely yei may lerne it in a ſmo paſſed
at ambrug ye ʒer be for myn oppoſicion
vhech fmon implatji vhil ſette in engliſh
in ye lyſt endʒ of ye thorſ than aftir ʒe
had red yis lyf of seynt auguſty ʒe ſayde
to on of my freudes yat ʒe deſired gretly
ye lyf of seynt gilbert ſchuld be tranſlat
in the ſame forme Thus mad he inſtance
to me and I graunted both ʒour petycyon for, Efia
I bold not fruſtrate hym of his medicacion
Do ye honour of god and of all ſeyntis yia
thil be begynne yis tretys namelich for the
ſoltarye thoene of ʒour religion vhech un-

INTRODUCTION

John Capgrave. In his Introduction to Capgrave's *Chronicle of England* the Rev. Francis Hingeston-Randolph expresses his approval of 'the singular honesty and straightforwardness of character, which must have belonged to the writer,'—on the model, may be, of Barham—'Thomas Ingoldsby, Esq., of Tappington Everard'—who speaks in a note to his *Blasphemer's Warning* of 'Honest John Capgrave, the veracious biographer of "English Saints".' To this eulogy, enounced under the authority of Bale, who writes of Capgrave's 'thunder against the wanton and arbitrary acts of prelates'—inaudible thunder to us in these after days—to all of this, Dr. Furnivall, with scripture authentic, in his Forewords to Capgrave's *Katharine* (xv, xxii), protests in fervent opposition. 'Capgrave, being an Englishman, was of course by race and nature a flunkey, and had an inordinate reverence for kings and rank,' says this Edwardian Elizabethan in his whole-hearted way. For the Augustinian friar had meted out unstinted praise to Henry IV, who 'gained the crown, by the providence, as we believe, of God'; had registered his encomium of that felicitous shatterer of heretics, as he termed Henry V, the victor of Agincourt; and had declared himself the devoted servant of his lord, that weak and pious youth, Henry VI; but as Pope says:—

> Manners with fortunes, humours turn with climes,
> Tenets with books, and principles with times,

and so, when Edward IV of York is crowned, the virtues of Lancaster are forgotten; he, in his turn, enters 'by Goddis provision', to redress the evils begun by Henry IV; and Prior and Provincial Capgrave dedicates his *Chronicle* to him. Like the nameless foe of Browning's Brother Lawrence,[1] Capgrave hated with an intensity almost feroçious, but reserved his hatred for the heretic. To his virulent attack on Wyclif, 'the organ of the devil, the enemy of the church, the confusion of men, the idol of heresy, the mirror of hypocrisy,' he turns again in our own text with libidinous insinuation (31/15). He approved of the torture and destruction, even at the stake and the gallows, of those whose nice tenets were not his own. Throughout his *Chronicle* we may see exhibited an intense love of the marvellous, and an amazing credulity in accepting legendary material, nowadays mostly relegated to the realm of myth and wonder.

But let us not forget that in many of these things he was but of his time. Long generations of controversy, turmoil, and bloodshed were yet to pass before man could allow his neighbour freedom to think, to speak, to live. We are yet but emerging, in Capgrave's day, from the long middle ages, when the roseate dawn of the Renascence is only discernible on the horizon; and little indeed of its light steals into our Lynn scriptorium, and falls upon our black-lettered page. Round about us are war, rebellion, executions, the fall of a dynasty, heresy, hunger, drought, pestilence, and angry thunder. Wonders are and have long been in the air, and find record in our books of history; the heavens fulminate, and stars fall. Some time before 1361, the storm beats down men, beasts, trees, and housing, and the devil appears in man's likeness; in 1361 itself, the sun is eclipsed, rain like blood falls, and a cross of blood moves in the air, and finally falls in the sea at Boulogne; while at the same time in France, England, and elsewhere, two mysterious castles appear, black and white hosts issue therefrom and fight; and all at last, castles and hosts, melt into thin air, and vanish.[2] These things are in our histories.

Small wonder then that this first among the lettered men of his day abuses Oldcastle and vilifies Wyclif; looks out somewhat severely on this strifeful England, and labors in saintly legend; sees much of the marvellous and supernatural in history, and

---

[1] *Soliloquy of the Spanish Cloister.*

[2] *The Brut or The Chronicles of England,* ed. Brie, 1908, vol. ii, pp. 313, 314.

changes in these changeful times from the old patron to the new. Yet he loved England, too; rejoiced in the beauty of her green and fertile lands, in the grandeur of her cities, in the 'wonderful and angelic splendor', both in countenance and in costume, in courage and vigor of mind, of her people.

Capgrave's biography has already been briefly sketched by Hingeston-Randolph in the *Chronicle*, and told at greater length by Dr. Furnivall in the *Katharine*, and is given in the *Dictionary of National Biography*. Our volume can add very little to the information given in these three productions. *The Life of St. Augustine* is not dated, but must have been finished little prior to the *Life of St. Gilbert*, from the fact that Nicholas Reysby's notice of the former led him to request the latter (61/6), and the *Gilbert* is dated at its conclusion, 1451. The Sermon is dated 1422, and Capgrave tells us he preached it the year before his opposition at Cambridge. His Latin *Concordia*, written for the Abbot of St. James's in Northampton and perhaps identical with the *De Sequacibus Augustini* mentioned by Bale,[1] is referred to in the Sermon, as is also the English *Augustine* and the *Gilbert* (146/5, 6, 34, 147/27). *The Life of St. Norbert*, composed for Abbot John Wyngale of West Dereham, was written in 1440 (*Introduction*, p. xi), and is also mentioned in the Sermon (147/34). The Sermon itself was written down at the end of the *Gilbert*, according to a promise made at the beginning to do so, in 1451 (61/13). It mentions, moreover, the appropriation of Peterston to Walsingham, which took place in 1449.

The Life of St. Augustine. This life was written by Capgrave at the request of an unnamed gentlewoman born on St. Augustine's Day. The writer tells us it was translated 'treuly oute of Latyn'; in the *Gilbert* he speaks of it as 'translat in-to our tunge'; and in the Sermon he refers to it as 'þe book wheeh I mad to a gentil woman in Englisch'.

It looks at first sight as though Capgrave had merely translated an older Latin text, as he did in the *Life of Gilbert*; but no Latin life corresponding to our text has been discovered, and as Capgrave never refers to 'myn auctour', and always alludes to himself as handling the material, I incline to conclude that he is himself the

---

[1] *Chronicle*, pp. 323, note 3, 326.

original composer, and that his reference to translation from Latin signifies his use of Augustine's books, from which he translates whole passages. He speaks, in the first person, of knowing an old copy of the pseudo-Aristotelian *Predicaments* (4/3), and refers once more to his knowledge of the book (11/28). He cites his own supposition regarding *De Beata Vita*, speaks in the first person concerning the name of Augustine's sister, and refers to himself, all in one half-page (5/2, 9, 16). He decides to limit his description of the contents of *De Beata Vita*, and of Augustine's complaint at the death of Monica (24/15, 33/33). He refers to his reading in Augustine's books, and to his opinion regarding regular and secular Augustinian canons (34/6, 44/17), and he makes insinuations against the followers of Wyclif. While it is still possible that a Latin life may have been used, I incline, for these reasons, to the opinion that Capgrave is the composer.

The first twenty-four chapters of the life are based on the *Confessions*, and xx, xxi to some extent on Sermons. The remainder of the life, except the conclusion, is based on Augustine's Sermons and on *De Civitate Dei*, and others of his books ; or is an account of the composition of the Saint's writings, *De Immortalitate Animae*, *De Quantitate Animae*, &c., and of the invasion of northern Africa by the Vandals, and the Saint's death. Some of the material to be found in the *Confessions* is not used. Of Augustine's youthful studies of classical poets, and thefts from his parents' table, we hear nothing (Book I). Of his consultation of astrologers (Book II), of Monica's desire to see Augustine wed (Book VI), of Vindicianus and Firminus, of almost the whole of the beautiful seventh Book, no mention is made. The attention given to Augustine's writings and to the frustration of heretics is greatly due, if the work is original, to Capgrave's theological propensities and extreme orthodoxy.

Hermes, in the text (12/19), is Capgrave's misreading of the original Hierius. References to the Augustinian text are given in the Notes.

Capgrave himself wrote a Latin *Vita S. Augustini* [1]; it is improbable, as he does not mention the fact, that this could have been his original for the English text.

---

[1] *Katharine*, xv.

Life of St. Gilbert. This life was written for the nuns of Sempringham, who could read little Latin, for their perusal in vacant times. It is founded on the Latin life of the Saint written at the direction of Roger, Gilbert's successor, and dedicated to Hubert, Archbishop of Canterbury. This life exists in two manuscripts in the British Museum, Cotton Cleopatra B. I, and Harley 468; and in one Bodleian MS., Digby 36. Of these MSS., the Cotton, of the thirteenth century, is the oldest, and from it Dugdale printed long passages in the *Monasticon*, vi. II. pp. v*–xxix*, after p. 945, suppressing the detailed account of the miracles, and the fuller account of the insurrection of the lay brothers. Passages from the Cotton MS., printed by Dugdale, are given in the Notes, to show how literally Capgrave followed it in the main. He reserved to himself the right to add, however, anything he learnt from the Gilbertine monks, or anything pertinent to the matter which occurred to him (62/26). An instance of this 'pertinent' addition occurs in p. 63, in which Capgrave recounts the merits and fusion of Norman and Saxon, and his acquaintance with John, Lord Beaumont. He breaks in again later, p. 91, l. 23, and p. 103, l. 19.

The Sermon. Capgrave's text can only be regarded as an abstract of his original sermon, preached in Cambridge, the year before his opposition, 1422. He refers in it to other works written since that date, *The Life of St. Augustine, Concordia, The Life of St. Gilbert, The Life of St. Norbert*, and to the appropriation of Peterston to Walsingham, 1449. He also alludes to two famous theologians, Hugo and Richard de St. Victor.

The contents of this sermon were known from an account of it given in Harley MS. 980, p. 231 (see notes, p. 159). The Harley account describes the abstract as from 'vii sermon.'

Manuscripts.

1. *Additional MS.* 36704. This manuscript is in Capgrave's own hand, with his characteristic orthography, and contains the author's corrections in the text. It appears to be holograph. It does not, however, contain Capgrave's peculiar monogram, ⅋, which Dr. Furnivall discusses in his Introduction to *The Life of St. Katharine* (p. xiv), and which occurs at the end of *The Life of*

St. Norbert in the Phillipps Collection at Cheltenham.   Nor does
it contain the characteristic 'Feliciter', which also occurs at the
conclusion of the *Norbert*, and of the *Exodus*, and of the Corpus
MS. of the *Liber de Illustribus Henricis*.   The monogram itself
is not infallible, nor is the 'Feliciter', for both of these were liable
to be copied by scribes.[1]

Additional MS. 36704 is $8\frac{1}{4} \times 5\frac{3}{4}$ inches, and contains 123
folios of paper.   It is bound in oak boards covered with vellum,
and is fastened, when shut, by two leather straps and clasps.
It was formerly impressed on its front with a coat of arms,
evidently a shield quartered, which it is now impossible to identify.

The fly-leaves 1–4 *b* and 122–123 *b* are from an early fifteenth-
century MS. of the Digest, containing Lib. xlvi, tit. 1.

On the fly-leaf, fol. 2, is a cypher: ' Opnstbbbt sfmfi sprfl Thpmf',
which reads: 'Constabat semel sorel Thotne' (*Brit. Mus. Cat.*,
1900–5, p. 192).

On the fly-leaf, fol. 3, is written: 'M*agister* Joh*annes* Capgraue
co*nventus* Linn fec*it* istu*m* lib*rum* ex præcepto vni*us* generose.'

On the fly-leaf, fol. 4 *b*, in a late hand is written : 'Joȟn Capgrave A Monke of Bury translated this Booke out of Latin into
English. Nᵒ. 25.'

Folio 120 is signed: 'Andrew Fountaine, Sepʳ 25 1817.'

Fly-leaf, fol. 121 *b*, is inscribed : 'Reydun Joȟ Kewe & Matild*is*
ux*or* Joȟ. Payn. · Tunsted pro a*n*ima Alicie Curteys Will*elmus*
Pays & q*ui*b*us* tenet*ur* (?)' (*Brit. Mus. Cat.*, p. 192).

Fly-leaf, fol. 122 *b*, is signed: 'R. Barn.'

From fly-leaf, fol. 123, has been erased: 'Liber sancte . . .'

The capitals are illuminated in red, and the numbers of the
chapters and initial capitals are also in red.   Evidently the text
was first written in black, and small letters were sometimes put
to indicate the chapter capitals, and small Arabic figures were
put in the margin to indicate the chapter numbers.   Then the
illumination in red was done, and as the writer read through
his text he made corrections in his red ink.   Sometimes he missed
a page in illuminating.

---

[1] The monogram, apparently, was so copied in All Souls MS. 17, the *Guide
to the Antiquities of Rome.* See *Katharine*, xxiv–v. The monogram might,
of course, be affixed by an author to a scribe's copy, as a warrant of
authorization.

The manuscript was purchased for the British Museum at the Fountaine Sale at Sotheby's, June 11–14, 1902, where it was numbered Lot 167.

2. *Cotton Vitellius*, D. XV. Of this manuscript only seven small fragments were saved from the Cotton fire of 1731. These are now mounted on paper and constitute folios 29–35. I have been able to identify all of them, and find them somewhat disarranged. They run as follows :—

Cotton.	Additional.	Our Text.
29	48 *b*	p. 64
29 *b*	49	p. 65
30	49 *b*	p. 65
30 *b*	50	p. 66
31 } misplaced	59 *b*–60	p. 78
31 *b* }	60 *b*–61	p. 78
32	56–56 *b*	p. 73
32 *b*	56 *b*–57	pp. 73–4
33 } reversed	89	pp. 111–12
33 *b* }	88 *b* ·	p. 111
34 } reversed	90	p. 113
34 *b* }	89 *b*	p. 112
35 } misplaced	50 *b*	p. 66
35 *b* }	?	? (illegible)

From this it will be seen that two fragments are reversed and two misplaced.

The Cotton MS. was inferior, of course, to our original. In monosyllabic words, so far as we can tell, it has the Capgravian avoidance of *gh* spellings for O.E. *h* before *t*, gives *myth* for our *myth* on 32 *b* and 33 *b* (our 73/33, 111/14), *nyth* for our *nyth*, and *þoute* for our *þoute*, 33 *b* ; but has *tawht* for our *taute*, 29, and *ryghtfull* for our *rithful*, fol. 31.

The Life of St. Norbert. On p. 147 of our text, Capgrave remarks of the Premonstratensians that they 'be-gan in Fraunce vndir a holy man þei cleped Norbertus, . . . and be-cause þat I mad his lyf in Englisch to þe abbot of Derham þat deyid last þerfor as now I wil no lenger tarie in þat fundacion.' Capgrave's own MS., dated 1440, with his characteristic orthography and avoidance of the *gh* spelling, and with his monogram, is in the

Phillipps Collection at Cheltenham, having been purchased at Sotheby's in 1861 at the Savile Sale for £150. To my friend, Dr. H. N. MacCracken, who was at Cheltenham working on his valuable Lydgate Canon, I am indebted for the following account of it.

The MS. is a quarto in vellum, in oak boards covered with vellum; it has 58 folios,[1] with xxxvii chapters, and 5 stanzas to a page. The numbers of chapters are marked in the margins, and the chapters are separated by capitals in color.

The first folio is illuminated. In the letter ' J ' (see below) is a monk in black, kneeling, presenting his book to a monk (abbot ?) in white, seated.

On fol. 1 is written: Newington. fadbrooke.

12 : Richard Clarke est verus possessor huius libri.

13 *b* : [a note of Sums.]

26 : Rev. Ai. Hubbard.

27 *b* : france barnard.

44 : Epping Essex. ffordman Newington his booke 1670.

50 *b* : Indenture made yere. . Edw. sent Jan 23. [year not stated.] There are other scribblings.

The following are the first four stanzas of *Norbert* :—

Joye, grace, in pees, loue, feith, & charite,
Euyr rest up-on ȝour goodly religious breest,
To whom þat I, with moost humylite,
Euyr recomende lowly as ȝouꝛ preest.
And þouȝ I be of rymeris now þe leest,
ȝet wil I now, obeying ȝouꝛ comaundment,
Put me in daungeꝛ in þis werk present.

Who schal þese dayis make now ony þing,
But it schal be tosed & pulled as wolle ?
Summe schul sey all þis is flateryng;
Summe of charite schul preise it at þe fulle.
Now lete hem rende, lete hem hale & pulle,
Swech maner puple, for I haue myn entent,
So I plese him þat ȝaue me comaundment,

---

[1] Sotheby's Catalogue says a folio and 59 leaves. See Dr. Furnivall's Forewords to *Katharine*, xliv.

To make þis werk of þat noble with,
Norbert called, wich, with ful hye grace,
Made a ordr̄ þat schewith now very lith
Of good ensaumple to men in euery place.
Ʒe noble men, if þat ʒe list to race,
Or rende my leuys þat I to ʒou write,
Ʒe may weel doo it; I schal ʒou neuer wite.

In ʒour̄ correccion̄ put I þis mater̄,
ffor I wil sewe & translate þis story.
And wele I wote ʒour̄ hertis be so cler̄
So ful of charite with-outen trechery;
Ʒe will not put on me no vyleny
But I deserue it, and þat schal I nowt,
As I hope, neythir in speche ne þowt.

These are the last two stanzas :—

Go litel book, to hem þat wil ye rede
Sey you were made to þe abbot of Derham [1]:
Fast be Stoke it staut, witʒouten drede;
It is to lordes and gentilys all in sam,
And eke to for men a very Iulianes ham.
The abbotes name was called at þat tyde,
The good Ion Wygnale, þat neuer wold him hide

ffor no gestis, but rather he wold hem seke.
The freris name þat translate þis story
Thei called Ion Capgraue, whech in assumpcion weke
Made a ende of all his rymyng cry,
The ʒer of Crist our Lord, witʒouten ly,
A thousand four hundred & fourty euene.
Aftyr þis lyf I pray God send us heuene.

ffeliciter.

---

[1] 'This is, of course, not Durham, but West Dereham, on the Stoke or
Wissey, three miles from Stoke Ferry in Norfolk, where an abbey of Premonstratensians from Welbeck had been founded in 1188. East Dereham,
famous for Borrow, Cowper, &c., is some distance from Stoke, and on another
stream. There was a monastery there too. H. N. M. ffeliciter!'

Other characteristic lines written down by Dr. MacCracken are:

Fol. 3.   On-to our Lord rith þus men may suppose, etc.
         On-to my counceles witȝ whech I enspired þe, etc.
         Turne aȝen lest þat þou be schent.

   9.   Was wroutȝ in þat cuntre rith for heŕ sake.

In all this we have the genuine Capgravian manner and orthography: the plural and genitive in *is, ys*, and *es*; the avoidance
of *gh* spellings for O.E. *h, with*, wight, *lith*, light; the forms *puple,
ordŕ, witȝ, wroutȝ*; the curled final *r*; the final *e* for *ie* or *y* in
humylite, charite, &c.; the only unusual form being the *wich* of
l. 16. For the 'ffreŕ I. C. amongis doctouris lest' of the *Gilbert*,
61/3, we have the author, 'of rymeris now the leest,' l. 5, and the
same care in giving the book's date, and the name of its receiver
and 'commander'. Above all there is the monogram, with the
' ffeliciter '.

The unusual import of the opening stanzas calls for some remark.
The author puts himself in danger in his work: for no work is
done at this time, 'but it schal be tosed and pulled as wolle.'
Some will say his book is flattery. But he does not mind, so long
as he pleases him who commanded it. And if certain 'noble men'
list to raze or rend his leaves, they may do it; he will never blame
them. He leaves it to them, and thinks their hearts are charitable
enough, and lacking in treachery enough, not to do him any
villainy unless he deserves it; and that, he hopes, he shall not,
either in speech or thought.

All this looks as though Capgrave's book was not certain of
a very favourable audience whither it was going. Possibly those
'noble men', the good monks of Dereham, were not inclined to
welcome the life of their Norbertus by an Austin friar of Lynn,
and had rather that the 'litel book' had been composed in their
own scriptorium.

The Language of the MS.

The value of our MS. is that it is holograph, definitely dated,
and definitely located as to its origin in Lynn, Norfolk. In these
respects it is as decisive a record of Middle English as the

Ormulum (Bodl. Junius MS. I). It was written when the vernacular was appreciably making headway in supplanting Latin as the language of the erudite and official—a process, nevertheless, not to be accomplished for many a day,—when standard English was developing from the East Midland speech. It precedes the establishment of the Caxton Press at Westminster—the chief instrument of standardization—by some twenty-five years, and it was written by the most learned prose-writer of the time.

By Capgrave's time the breakdown of the Old English inflexional system was complete, and its office was filled by numerous prepositions, &c. The nouns, with a few minor exceptions, were reduced to a single declension based on the O.E. strong masculines. The old dative singular in *e* had disappeared, only two regular forms remaining in the singular, the nominative, and the genitive in *is* (*ys, es*). One general form alone remained for the plural, *is* (*ys, es*). The breakdown of the inflexional system with the disappearance of unstressed final *e* had annihilated all trace of grammatical gender. Several nouns, specified hereafter, remained uninflected in the genitive singular, some few had no ending in the plural, and a few form the plural by mutation or by the addition of *n*. Proper names were sometimes uninflected.

Capgrave never uses ʒ for O.E. *h* before *t*, as in *kniʒt*, no trace of this sound remaining in his speech. ʒ is used initially for *y*, as in *ʒe, ʒeꝛ, ʒet, ʒaf*; for a sibilant replacing the *thorn* in the third person singular, present of some verbs, *hatʒ, vsetʒ*, and *tellʒ*, with syncopation of *e*, and for the thorn sound in *with—witʒ*; and for *z* in *ʒel*, &c. Its use in *þouʒ* is probably to distinguish the word from *þou*.

The *thorn*, þ, is written with an open top like *y*, *th* being used generally after a stop, for capitalization, and at the end of words.

For the guttural stop Capgrave uses *g—gestis, gessed, gilty*, where modern spelling has *gu*. *g* also serves for the *j* sound, *gelous, gayleꝛ, gendres*, &c.

For O.E. *cw*, French *qu*, and rarely for O.E. *hw*, Capgrave uses *qw*. For O.E. *hw* in *who* (*hwa*), &c., we have generally *wh*, as in modern English. Modern *how* (O.E. *hu*) is spelt *who*.

th is used for the *thorn* where an initial capital is required; often for the thorn also at the end of words, *vnneth, both*, and sometimes in the middle, *anothir*.　*th* also replaces *ht* at the end of words in which the O.E. *h* is lost, as *lith, rith*, the spelling alternating with *lite, rite*.

This latter use of the *th* does not indicate that any trace of the old pronunciation remained in Capgrave's speech.　Firstly, the *th* spelling alternates in the old *ht* words with *t* or *te*, as noted above; secondly, it so alternates in words, which had no *h*, *profith*, *profite, parfith, parfite, parfit*.[1]　The device of employing the *th* for the *ht* spelling is found also in the Northeast Midland *Havelok* (Oxford Laud MS. 108).　Here such forms as *brouth, nouth, douther, rith, nith, lith, knith* are common.　*cht* and *ct* forms are also abundant; but *th* is used for final *t* in such words as *leth, woth, neth* (let, wot, neat).　For the *te* ending to old *ht*, we have *aute* ryming with *laute* (*aute* possessed, *laute* caught, received).　This looks to me as though the O.E. *h* sound tended to disappear fairly early in Northeast Midland.　(Laud MS. 108 sometimes suffers from its editors in connexion with these spellings. Emerson, for instance, *Middle English Reader*, 1909, consistently transposes *h* and *t*, and reads *riht, niht, mouht* in his text, and makes *auhte* and *lauhte*.　He also destroys the *th* ending where it is used for *t*, printing *let, wot, net*.　Kluge, *Mittelenglisches Lesebuch*, 1904, consistently retains the *th* forms, but has *au[ch]te, lau[ch]te*.)　Other instances of the early disappearance of O.E. *h* spellings are given by Dr. Furnivall in the Forewords to *Katharine*, and are found elsewhere in the Midland dialect, *nyt* ryming with *syt* (night, sight) in *The Debate of the Body and the Soul*; *lyt, lythe, rythe* (light, right, Emerson, 117, 118) occur in *Gild of St. William of Norwich*; and compare the *broute* of the Digby MS. of *The Harrowing of Hell* ryming with *biþoute*, ll. 5, 6.

An intermediate form to the *th* and *te* endings of the old *ht* words is seen in the *siȝth, untiȝth*, &c., of the *Debate*, the *knicth, knict, ricth, nicth* of *Havelok*, the *þouȝth, briȝth*, &c., of *Adam Davy's Five Dreams about Edward II*, and in other texts.　That the *gh* and *ȝ* forms were sometimes wrongly used is seen in the *yghe, lyghe, dyghe, syghe*, &c. (eye, lie, die, saw) of the *Pearl*;

---

[1] 'These two words,' says Dr. Bradley, 'are poor evidence, for *-fiȝt* represented a French intermediate stage between *-fect* and *-feit*.'

in the *clouʒt, ouʒt* (clout, out) of the *Debate*; and in the *whyʒte* (white) of the *West Midland Prose Psalter*, &c.

cc is used for *tch* in *cacch, fecch, wicches, wecch, wrecched*.

Nouns.—The genitive singular is formed in *is* (*ys, es*), the plural in *is* (*ys, es*).

To these forms there are common exceptions:—

(*a*) In the case of O.E. neuters, with unchanged plural forms, *schep, vnch* (from O.E. *ynce*), *þing, wepun, ʒere, god* (goods).

(*b*) In the case of words retaining the plural in *n* from O.E. weak declension: *eyne, hosyn, schon, childyrn* (also *childyr*, O.E. *cildru*).

(*c*) Those forming the plural by mutation: *toth, teth*; *man,* gen. *mannes*, pl. and gen. pl. *mennys*; *foot, feet.*

(*d*) Certain words from the French, ending in a sibilant and unchanged in the plural: *sciens, vers, passe, insolens* (126/8); or ending in a vowel, *vertu* (67/6).

(*e*) A few words unchanged in the genitive singular: *fader, moder*, though we find also *faderis, moderis*. Proper names are sometimes uninflected.

(*f*) Anomalous: *peticyoñ*, plural (61/17).

The infinitive present of the verb is sometimes used as a noun, as *tary* (113/16). A number of Anglicized Latin words in the text come from Capgrave's originals: *fluctuatioñ, vomite, rectractationes, transumpciones, disceptatioñ,* &c. *Statua, subucula, acrisia*, and *orarium* are quoted as Latin words. *Idus* and *nonas* (see the word in note, p. 158, and glossary) retain their Latin forms.

Verbs.—The verbs in Capgrave are rather irregular in their forms. The present and past indicative are as follows:—

	Present.	Past.	
	Weak and Strong.	Weak.	Strong.
S. 1.	—	*id* (*ed*)	—
2.	*ist* (*est*)	[*idest*]	—
3.	*iþ* (*ith, eth*), *th, etʒ, ʒ*	*id, t*	—
Pl. 1, 2, 3.	— *en* (*in, yn*)	*id* (*ed*)	[— *e*]

The third person singular contains the greatest variety of forms. The commonest ending, *ith*, is often found as *eth*, and these, with syncopation of the vowel, appear as *th*, as in *comth* and *lith*. In such forms as *vset3* and *tell3* we have the supplanting of the thorn by the ȝ, mentioned above. *Tell* provides the whole variety, and one form in which the thorn is represented by a dental: *tellith, telletȝ, tellȝ*, and *tellit*. Other interesting spellings are *hatȝ, makitȝ*, and *poutȝ* (used, however, for the past, with *pout*, for the singular and plural). The *en* ending for the plural forms in the present tense are common: for the first person we have *lakkyn*; for the third, *defenden, obeyen, proferen, beren*, &c.

For the imperative of the second person singular we have the *here, forgif, entyr, lete*, &c. of p. 33. The ordinary *ep* ending for imperative of the second person plural is seen in the *beth* of 16/3 and 52/10; but *praisen*, 77/22, gives the unusual *en* ending.

In the third person of the past tense of weak verbs the *id* is weakened to *t* after the liquids: *delt, dwelt, filt, sempt*, &c. The past participle was sometimes likewise. *clipt, girt, filt. Teld* and *seld* appear for *told* and *sold* in the singular third person.

Infinitives in *en* (*in, yn*) are very common in Capgrave, as *aretten, asken, crien, fytyn, girdin, hydyn, pleten, heyne*, &c.

The present participle is formed in *ing* (*yng*), with numerous examples of *and*, generally characteristic of more northern texts. Examples are *brennaund, folowand, comand, kepand, herand, stodiand*, and other words all of O.E. origin.

The past participle of weak verbs is formed in *id* (*ed*); or exists in shortened forms, such as *alienat, implicat, infect, interrupt* (adoptions of Latin participles), *wasch* (representing the strong form), *rest* (wrested). In the strong verbs the past participle is formed by mutation, and sometimes the addition of the *en* ending, liable to loss of *n* (as *falle*). Relics of the O.E. *ge* prefix are seen in the *i-* of *i-schake, i-qwenchid, i-knowe*, and *i-goo*.

In the hands of Capgrave past participles, due to occasional weakening and use of similar vowels, assume a variety of forms. *Written* assumes *wretyn, writin, writyn, wrytin*; *wound* has *wounde, wounden, woundyn*; *found* has likewise *found, founde, founden*; *held* has *hald, halden, hold, holden*; and *done* has *do, don, doo*, &c.

Pronouns.—As the inflexion of adjectives has disappeared in Capgrave, the adjectival pronoun is not distinguished in the plural from its singular form. There is no example of the weakening of *pu* into *tu* by assimilation, but *of hem* seems in one case to be compounded into *on* (7/7). The personal pronouns are inflected thus :—

	First Person.		Second Person.	
	S.	Pl.	S.	Pl.
N.	*I*	*we*	*þou*	*ȝe*
Ac. and Dat.	*me*	*us*	*þe*	*ȝou, ȝow*
Gen.	*my, myn (mynͭ)*	*our (ourͭ)*	*þi, þin (þinͭ)*	*ȝour (ȝourͭ)*

my is sometimes used before a vowel-beginning word, as *my auctorͭ* (125/30). *þin* is used before vowels, *þin entente*.

The third personal pronoun is as follows :—

	M.	Neut.	F.	Plural.
N.	*he*	*it (he)*	*sche*	*þei*
Ac.	*him*	*it*	*hir (hirͭ), hire*	*hem* (once *þem*)
Dat.	*him*	*him*	*hir (hirͭ), hire*	*hem*
Gen.	*his, hise*	*his*	*hir (hirͭ), hire*	*her (herͭ), here*

This pronoun in Capgrave is quite regular except for occasional use of *he* for *it*, and the occurrence once of *þem* for the accusative *hem*. Reflexive forms with *self* are common. *himself* occurs for *itself* (97/30). The substantival possessive *our* is given (18/20).

The relative pronouns are *þat* and *whech (qwech)*, and very rarely *who (Katharine*, 24/116). The genitive *whos* and dative *whom (quome)* are commoner. Combination of *whech þat* is also common.

The interrogative pronouns are *who* (rare) with accusative *whom* for masculine and feminine, and a neuter *what*, nominative and accusative. The genitive and dative forms are *whos* and *whome (quome)*. *eþir, neþir, swech, all, many, on*, &c., are common indefinite pronouns.

The demonstrative pronouns are *þe*, undeclined, and singular forms *þat* and *þis* with plurals *þo* and *þese*.

Adverbs.—The commonest form is given in those based on adjectives, *besily, boystously, dirkly*, &c. These assume *ly*, from O.E. *lice* and identical with the *ly* ending of adjectives from O.E. *lic*. In one case, *namelych* (61/19), however, we have *lych*.

Of the genitival adverb we have several examples: *nedis, onys, twyes, þries, eft-sones*.

Of the datival adverb *seldom* is an example. *seld*, like *rith, scharp, soͭ*, and *stille*, are flat adverbs.

The pronominal adverbs are represented by *who* (how), *whan* (*whanne*), *þo*, and *þan, þanne* (then), and *who*. Other adverbs of place are *þidir* and *ʒondir, þenne* (thence), *whens*; and of time, *whilt, sone, sith, til,* and *afore.* Compound adverbs are *sumtyme, vndir-fote, ouyr̄-nyth, ferforth,* and *often-tyme.*

Adjectives.—No distinction is made between strong and weak adjectives, nor between singular and plural.

(*a*) A number of adjectives are formed from the verb, as past participles like *onlerned, croked,* or present participles like *chater-yng, grucching, folowand,* and *comand.*

The commonest class are those distinguished by formatives.

(*b*) Saxon formatives provide :—

    (-*ful*) *schalful*—for *schandful* or *schendful*; *wilful.*
    (-*fast*) *stedfast.*
    (*ward*) *homeward*—used, however, adverbially, but adjectival in form.
    (*sum*) *buxum, holsom.*
    (*ly* from *lig*) *bodely, dedly, goostly, fremanly.*
    (*w*) *ʒelow.*
    (*en*) *hethen, wollen.*
    (*ir*) *bittir, fayr.*
    (*isch* from *isc*) *lyuysch.*
    (*y* from *ig*) *besi, heuy, redy.*

(*c*) French formatives provide :—

    (*ous, ious*) *licorous, greuous, obliuious, ambicius.*
    (*al, il*) *gentill, simpil, sotil.*
    (*able*) *merciable, mesurable, delectable.*
    (*ik*) *autentik.*
    (*ant*) *poynaunt.* Noun provided by this adjectival form : *seruaunt.*
    (*ain*) *sodeyn, souereyn.*

(*d*) Latin formatives provide :—

    (*if, ive*) *commendatyf.*
    (*er* from *aris*) *seculer, reguler.*
    (*ary*) *exemplary* (noun in text).
    (*al*) *accidental, conuentual, matrimonial.*
    (*ate*) *desolate, approximate.*

The comparative of the adjective was formed in *er* : *hyer, redyer* ; the superlative in *est* : *hattest.* Otherwise *mor* or *moost* is prefixed.

While Capgrave's vocabulary marks the tendency of the time in its incorporation of new words, obsolescent words are numerous. For the *progenitouris* of *Augustine* we have the *forth-bringer* of the *Katharine*. *Morer* and *moring* in our text are used with *encreser* and *encresing*. *buxum* is not yet entirely displaced by *obedient*, nor *heyne* by *exalt*, nor *clepe* or *hite* by *call*. *lowed* and *meked* are both used for *humbled*. Capgrave also gives a number of interesting dual forms: *schone or ellis schyned* (83/19), *cloystir or clauser* (83/28), *witnesses or witnesseres* (110/9), *wasch . . . or ellis water* (112/27), *graue or elles þe sepultur* (119/3), *lendes or buttokkes* (120/2), *preisable or praysid* (136/18), and *signes or ellis myracles* (138/9).

Capgrave has a habit of losing the dentals at the end of his monosyllabics: *and* appears as *an* ; *saint* as *sain* ; *but* as *be*. *ragyn* and *euyr-lestyn* loose final *g*. *of hem* appears to be compressed into *on* and *aught* to be reduced to *or*.

And lastly a word of thanks. When the Globe editors dedicated their *Chaucer*, and Robert Steele his *Huon of Bordeaux*, and others at home and abroad, too numerous to mention, their books, to Dr. Furnivall, they made some expression of the debt we all owe to this friend and guide and pioneer. I am grateful to him for advice and help on many difficult points in this book. To Dr. Bradley I am also grateful for instruction on various grammatical points where I should otherwise have gone wrong.

J. J. M.

SEVEN-KINGS,
February, 1910.

LIVES OF
ST. AUGUSTINE AND ST. GILBERT

LIFE OF ST. AUGUSTINE

[CAPGRAVE'S PROLOG.]

A GRETE reule to all lerned men was sette be Seint Paule in
þe first capitle Ad Romanos, where he saide þat he was
dettouᵽ on-to wise men and onwise. Wise men clepid he men
4 gretly lerned, and onwise, simple ydiotis, to whom longith þe
blisse of heuene, and of whom ouᵽ Lord Ihesu spak in þe gospell,
and seid þat her aungellis see euyr þe face of þe Fadir whech is in
heuene. To þese both þe holy apostell saide he was dettouᵽ, to
8 paye ech of hem aftir þat he sauoured. And þouȝ I þat write now
þis be a man sumwhat endewid in lettiruᵽ, ȝet daᵽ I not take
up-on me for to be dettouᵽ on-to hem þat be endewid in sciens
moᵽ þan I, but I daᵽ sauely seye þat I am detouᵽ to oþir simpil
12 creatures þat be not lerned so mech as I. Wherfor my dettis wil
I pay of swech tresouᵽ as I haue in possessioñ, with moᵽ esy
labouᵽ þan euyr I receyued hem. The cause of þis writyng whech
meued me moost now will I telle. A noble creatuᵽ, a gentill
16 woman, desired of me with ful grete instauns to write on-to hiᵽ,
þat is to sey, to translate hir treuly oute of Latyn, þe lif of Seynt
Augustyn, grete doctouᵽ of þe cherch. Sche desired þis þing of me
rather þan of a-noþer man be-cause þat I am of his profession, for
20 sche supposed veryly þat I wold do it with þe bettir wil. Sche
desired eke þis lif of þis Seynt more þañ of ony oþir ¹ for sche was
browt forth in-to þis world in his solempne feste. Than wil I, in
þe name of ouᵽ Lord Ihesu, beginne þis werk, to þe worchip of þis
24 glorious doctouᵽ, and to þe plesauns and consolatioñ ² of þis gentil
woman þat hath so willed me with sundry [r]etribucione[s] ‖ þat
I coude not disobeye hir desiᵽ. This glorious name Augustinus is
mad comendable a-mongis ouᵽ auctouris for iij þingis. On is for
28 þe excellens of þe man. The secund for þe brennyng loue of
charite with whech his hert was fyred. The þird for þe noble

¹ MS. *part of a word commencing* b *crossed out.*
² *corner of leaf faded.*

1

ethimilogie whech longeth to þe name. Ethimilogie is cleped
in gramer þe trewe exposicioñ of a word. As touching þe first,
þat is to sey, þe excellens of þis Seint, it acordith ful wel on-to
his name, for þis word Augustus was first ʒoue on-to þe emperouŕ 4
Octauiane, as to þe moost honorable and excellent prince þat euyr
regned in þe empiŕ. For it soundith in ouŕ langage as a morer
of þe lordchip, and þis same Octauiane engrosed neŕ al þe lordchip
of þe world on-to þe empiŕ of Rome. So sey we of þis glorious 8
‹doctouŕ þat he berith þis[1] name for excellens aboue aĺ oþir.
Therfor þe oþir doctouris be likned[2] on-to þe sterres and he on-to
þe sunne, as it is pleynly conteyned in the epistil red in his feest,
wheŕ he seith þat lich as þe sunne schynyth in heuene, so schynyth 12
he in þe temple of ouŕ Lord. As touching þe secund diuisioñ, þat
is to seye, his feruent loue whech he had on-to ouŕ Lord, þis
acordeth eke on-to his name. For Augustus is þat month in
heruest whech is þe hattest month and moost ripening of frutes 16
þorw-oute aĺ þe ʒere. So þis man, brennyng in charite, wrote
on-to þe cristen puple swech swete exhortaciones of loue þat he is
cause[3] next God, daŕ I sey, þat many a soule hath ripeŕ frutes of

deuocioñ be-cause of his labour. Off þis brennyng charite whech 20
þis noble clerk ᴴ had is spoken be his owne mouth in þe ix book
of his Confessiones, where he seith þus of him & his felawis neuly ᵥ
conuerted on-to God: Thou Lord, he saide, hast hitte ouŕ hertis
with þe hote arowys[4] of charite, and eke we receyued þi wordis 24
in-to ouŕ hertis as þouʒ þei had be scharp arowys. Eke touching
þe ethimologie of his name, it berith witnesse of his grete excellens, ●

for þis name, as auctouris sey, is compownyd of augeo auges, þat
is as mech to sey as to make þing moŕ þan it was; it is eke 28
compowned of ana, þat is as mech to sey as a-boue; it is eke
compowned of astim, whech is as mech to sey as a cite. So for
to putte aĺ þese parties to-gidir[5], þe name of þis glorious Seynt is
þus browt on-to þis reson, a morer of þe cite a-boue, a gret 32
encreser of þe blis of heuene, for he was cause whil he lyued with
his tonge and aftir his deth with his bokis þat many a soule is
ledde þe rith weye to heuene.

[1] b *crossed through.*
[2] kilned *in text crossed out and* likned *written in margin.*
[3] *corner of leaf faded.*   [4] MS. harowys, h *dotted underneath in red.*
[5] ast *in MS. crossed through.*

[CHAPTER I.]

Of þe cuntṛ & þe town where he was bore. cap*itulum* I.

cap. 1.

AT ouṛ begi*nn*yng ȝe schul undirstand þat þis world is departed in-to iij *par*ties, and it was þus depa*r*ted as ouṛ auc- touris seye be ouṛ fadeṛ Noe. For in þe flood were saued[1] he and his iij sones, and to þese iij sones was aḻ þe world departed. Thei þat ca*m* of Sem were sette in þe est side of þe world, cleped now Asia. Thei [þat] cam of Iaphet were sette in þat partye of þe world cleped now Europa. And þei þat cam of Cam were sette to dwelle[2] in þat partie whech is cleped Affrica, where ‖ þis glorious man was bore. Asia is iu þe est side of þe world, and it conteyneth as mech in space as do þe othir too parties. In þis Asia stant Ynde and Pers, Mede, Mesopothamia, Surry, Araby, Capadoce, Comagene, Palestine, Iude, Galile, & many mo *pro-*uy*n*ces. Europe *con*teyneth Scithie, Nussie[3], Hu*n*garye, Achay, Macedony, Dalmacy, Ytaile, and aḻ þe Duche tonge, with France, Ynglond, Spayn, & many moo. Affrica hath p*r*incipali þe *pro*uy*n*ce of ȝeugis where grete Cartage stant. It hath eke anoþir *pro*uy*n*ce clepid Tripolitane, Getuly, Byȝance, Numedye, Mauritania. In þis Numedie stant þat cite where Seynt Austyn was bischop, cleped Ypone, and in þis same Numedie stant þat same cyte cleped Tagatens*es*, where þis doctouṛ was bore, sum-what upward moṛ on-to Cartage. Thus haue I schewid ȝou in what partie of þe world[4] he was bore,[4]—nowt in þe Greke tonge ne in þe Latyn tonge, but in þe Barbaṛ tonge. Neuyrþelasse we rede of hym þat whan he cam to lerne dyuers sciens, whech were þan most in Greke tonge, þat he hated þe Greke lett*er*is and loued weel þe Laty*n*, be whech inclynacio*n* we vndirstand þat þat same langage in whech he was bore was moṛ approximat on-to þe Latyn tonge þan on-to þe Grek tong. For, in very treuth, he had so grete knòwlech of both tongis þat aḻ his bokys

Marginal notes:
The three divisions of the world are
1. Asia;
2. Europe;
3. Africa.
Leaf 6, back.
The countries of Asia:
of Europe;
and of Africa.
At Hippo in Numidia Augustine was bishop;
at Tagaste he was born,
where the language was more akin to Latin than Greek.

---

[1] *final* d *inserted above.* [3] *So in* MS.

[2] *corner of leaf faded.* [4]—[4] *In margin.*

1-2

Augustine
wrote in
Latin and
translated
Aristotle's
'Categories,'
and the

Leaf 7.

author knows
of a copy in
an old hand.

he mad in Latyn, and oute of[1] þe Greke tonge he hym-selue
translate in-to Latyn a grete book whech Aristotle mad, cleped
his Cathegories, for I wot who hath þis book of ful eld hand.
This is seid[2] to my entent to proue þat he was bore a-mongis 4
☙ hem þat speke þe Barbaȓ tonge. The Barbaȓ tonge is euery tonge
in þe world whech is fer fro þe iij principall tongis, Hebrew,
Grek, & Latyn.

[Chapter II.]

Off þe progenitouris and þe kynrod of þis man.   o͞m ij.   8

Augustine's
parents were
noble and
rich,

❡

and sent him
to school in
Carthage.

His father's
name was
Patrick, a
heathen till
near death.

His mother
was Monica,
a Christian,
who had
other child-
ren besides
him.

In his book
' De Beata
Vita' he tells
of his brother.
He was born
on St. Brice's
Day.

Leaf 7,
back.

O F his progenitoures þus we rede þat þei were not of þe despect laboureres in þe puple, but born of good and rich
kynrod aftir þe fame of þe world, for þis man aftir heȓ deth had
sufficient possessioñ for to lyue by. And he him-self seith in his 12
Confessiones þat whan he was sent to skole to Cartage, because
þei herd sey þat heȓ child had a grete corage to lernyng, þat
he was[3] founde as wel and with as grete cost as ony[4] lordis son
þat went to skole. This myth not be do with-outen þat þei had 16
substauns of possessioñ. The name of his fader was clepid
Patrik, whech was a hethen man on-to þe tyme þat he schuld deye,
for þan, be labouȓ of his modir, he was mad cristen man, and so
deyed newly baptiȝed. His modir hith Monica; sche was a 20
cristen woman fro hir childhold, and norchid in þe best condiciones and moost plesaunt to God and to man. Sche had moo
childyrn þan him, as it semeth be his writing in his Confessiones.
And þouȝ þat he telle not heȓ names þere, we haue sout hem 24
oute of oþir of his bokis. For in þat book whech is cleped De
Beata Vita, þere tellith he of his broþir whech at þat festfull day
was[5] with him and with his modir in an hothous whech þei clepe
a stewe, þe day of his birth. Fore he was bore on Seynt Brices[6] 28
day, as þat ❡ same book makith mencion, and custumablely he
used whil he was paynem to make a gret fest on þat day, but aftir

---

[1] a character crossed out.   [2] corner of leaf faded.
[3] þei crossed out and he was written in margin.   [4] n crossed out.
[5] in margin.   [6] corner of leaf faded.

he was mad bischop he turned þis bodely fest[1] in-to spiritual Augustine must have written this book before he became bischop.
talkyng, and as I suppose þis bok was mad þat first day þat he
mad þis chaunge or he was bischop, for his moder was at þis fest
4 and sche deyid befor þat he was preest. This mannes name of His brother's name was Navigius and he had two cousins, Latridianus and Rusticus. The author does not know his sister's name, but he dedicated a book to her. His cousin Patricius was a canon in his third monastery.
whom we talk of her, whech, as we saide, was his broþir, was
cleped Nauigius. He spekith here eke in þis same book of too
cosynes of his ; on of hem hith Latridianus, þe othir hith Rusticus.
8 Thei both were at his feest, of whom he seith þat þei were trewe
cristen but not lettered. He had a sistir, but I haue not herd hir
name, and to hir he wrote a book whech he clepéd þe book of
cristen mannes lyf; it begynnyth þus : Et ego peccator. The
12 rubrich be-for þe bok is writyn þus : The book of Seynt Augustin,
þe bischop, on-to his sistir, a widow. Eke he had a-noþir cosyn
þat hith Patricius, as his fader hith, and þis man was on of þe
chanones þat lyued with him in þe þird monsterie aftir he was
16 bischop. In þe þird monasterye, seid I, for be-cause þat he mad
iij,—on or he was preest, a-noþir whil he was preest vndir bischop
Valerie. And who long he dwelt þer, and who dwelt þere with
him, schal be touchid aftir whan it comth in his place.

[CHAPTER III.]

20 Of þe condiciones of his fader and ‖ his modir. capitulum Leaf 8.
tercium.

O F þis mater spekith þis glorious man in þe ix book of his The character of Augustine's father,
Confessiones, wher he seith of his fader þat he was of nature
24 ful frendly and goodly and redy eke on-to ire as many men be,
kynde and fre of hert and sone meued to malencolie. This holi
woman weddid on-to hym, whan sche had aspied his hasti condicioñ, sche had swech gouernauns in hir dedis and swech moderacion
28 in hir wordes þat he coude neuyr cacch no hold to be wroth with and of his mother. How gently she rebuked her husband, reproved other wives, and by her example
hir in all his lyf. Sche wold, if he excedid, as Augustinus tellith,
abide til his ir were goo ; þan wold sche reherse on-to him þe euel
a-vised wordes whech he had spoke, or þe onresonable werkis
32 whech he had do. Sumtyme it happed þat sche sat a-mong oþir

---

[1] MS. *estyn with* yn *crossed out.*

matrones of hir knowlech, of whech women summe had merkys in
her face whech heꝛ husbandis had mad only for þei wold speke
a-geyn whaɳ heꝛ husbandis weꝛ wroth, and þan wold þese women
say on-to Monicha : We haue grete wondir of þe and þin husband ₄
þat þou briɳggist neuyr no merk of his strokys, ne non of us haue
herd þat euyr þeꝛ was ony strif be-twix ȝou too, not-withstand þat
he is an irous man and hasty as ony dwellith amongꭜ us. Sche
wold answeꝛ on-to hem on þis maneꝛ : Iff ȝe haue mynde[1] of ȝouꝛ ₈
tables matrimonial þat weꝛ mad be-twix ȝou and ȝouꝛ husbandis at
ȝouꝛ weddyɳg; ǁ ȝe wold not þan haue meruayle whi þat I suffir my
husband, þouȝ þat I haue wrong. For þere is it writyn þat þouȝ
wyuyꭜ[2] and husbandis be o flesch and o blood, ȝet ar wyuyꭜ[3] put ₁₂
in swech maneꝛ of subieccioɳ þat þei be bounde to do dew seruyse
on-to men ; wherfor, as me þinkith, þe best seruyse þat þei may doo
is to kepe pes in honshold and suffir wrong rather þan peꭜ schuld
be broke. For hir wordis many of þese women were stered to moꝛ ₁₆
paciens and leued in more rest þan þei dede be-foꝛ. Theꝛ was
with hir þe modir of hir husband dwellyng in houshold, and as
often is sene þei make sumtyme debate betwyx wif and husband,
namely wheꝛ ȝong damesellis be with chateryng tongis. Swech ₂₀
seruauntis were in Patrik hous, but for no tales of hem ne no
suspicioɳ of þe elde modir, Monicha was neuyr put in no blame,
so redy was hir paciens, so besi was hir plesauns. The elde moder,
seing þe good disposicioɳ of hir doutir, was compelled be consciens ₂₄
to compleyne of hir seruauntis on-to hir son, desiryng of him þat
he schuld snybbe þe maydenes þat þei schuld not be redy to telle
swech tales with whech peꭜ mith be broke[4] in Patrik hous.
Many mo noble condiciones rehersith þis man of his modir whech ₂₈
as now schul not be touched, for in þe orisoɳ, or ellis, þe compleynt, whech he mad aftir hir deth, it schal be talked moꝛ largely
aftir þe form of his Confessiones. ǁ O þing he touchith heꝛ gretly
longing to hiꝛ comendacioɳ in norching of hir childyrn ; he seith ₃₂
þat sche[5] trauayled[6] for hem neuly a-geyn as often as sche say
hem do ony þing whech was a-geyn þe plesauns of our Lord ; þat

---

[1] *inserted above.*   [2] wyuys *written in margin* ; wifis *in text.*
[3] wyuys *written in margin* ; wifys *in text.*   [4] MS. bebroke.
[5] *inserted in small writing above.*   [6] d *added afterwards.*

is to sey it greued hir as mech whan sche say hir childyrn trespas she was hurt when her
on-to our [1] Lord as euyr it greued whan sche bare hem bodyly. children sinned.

[Chapter IV.]

Of þe age of Seint Augustin whech is clepid Infancia. iiij.

4 INfancia is on of þe vij. ages, as our auctores say, whech We usually say that there
lestith fro þe birth on-to þe tyme þat þe child [2] is come to þe is no sin in infancy, but
age of vij 3ere, and þou3 it be soo þat we sey comouly þat St. Gregory tells of a
childyrn synne not in þis age, þat is to sey, dedly, 3et in sum on or child torn by the devil
8 to haue be seyn þe reuers, as Seint [3] Gregorie tellet3 in his Dialoges from its father's arme,
li. 4, þat a child of þis age was sodeynly be þe deuele rawt from and Augustine says he
his faderes armes. Not-withstanding þis or oþir whech myth be too must have
rehersed, as we said, comouly childyrn of þis age be clepid sinned in his childhood.
12 innocentis, for þei lak vse of reson for to discerne vice fro vertu.
But of þis age, and of synnes do in þis age, Seynt Augustyn
makit3 open confession in þe first book of þat mater, wher he seith
þat sum childyr þat can not speke, þei can loke angrily on hem þat
16 greue hem [4], and with handes and teth proferen in maner of a
veniauns. Nowt had þis doctour mynde þat he ded soo, but for
he say oþir childyrn do þus, þerfor supposed he þat he ded soo. ‖
Mech more þing he rehersith of þis mater in his first book of his Leaf 9,
20 Confessiones, whech is now not gretly nedful to be rityn. back.

[Chapter V.]

¶ Of þat age of him whech þei clepe Puericia. v.

PVericia also is þe secund age, and þat lestith fro seuene Boyhood is
3ere to xiiij 3ere. It is as mech to say in Englisch as þe the age of cleanness.
24 age of clennesse, for þis age is not mech defiled with dedis of Augustine in his 'Con-
leccherie or onclennesse. What defautes þat be in þis age of whech fessions' tells of his sins
our maystir had ful grete consciens, is writin in þe same book. At done then.
þis age, he saith, he was put to skole, and whan he schuld be bete,

---

[1] *inserted in small writing above.*   [2] *a character crossed out.*
[3] *a single g crossed out.*   [4] *bem inserted above.*

he prayed God þat he myth skape it, but ouꝛ Lord herd him nowt,
and þat displesed him, for he knew not þat tyme who profitable it
was to his soule to be bete for lernyng. With sad men and eld
men whech mad a game whan he was laschid, he was in partie 4
wroth. He lerned lesse þat he schuld or myth a lerne. He loued
bettir veyn games þan skole. The smale elementis of lernyng
receyued he first in þe same cite where he was bore. His gramer
lerned he in a cite be-side, whech is cleped Mandauris. He loued 8
bettir, as we sayde be-fore, þe Latyn letteris þan þe Grek, not-
withstand þat he lerned first þe Grek letteres. In þis age he had
grete [1] sekenesse in his stomake, and euyr was his modir bisi þat he
schuld be baptized, but þe fader wold not suffir it. And þis was 12
þe cause, as men ꝶ suppose, whi ouꝛ Lord wold not suffir him to be
baptized, for it was lesse greuauns to his soule [2] þat þe filth of
heresie schuld be in him rather be-foꝛ his baptem þan aftir his
baptem. Thus lerned he þe smale scienses, as spellyng, reding and 16
constrewyng in his ȝong age.

[CHAPTER VI.]

¶ Who he was sent to Cartage to lerne gretter sciens. vj.

VHanne he was fully xvj ȝeꝛ old his frendis sent him to
Cartage, a grete cite whech helde batayle with Rome & alle 20
Itaile many ȝeres. There lerned he rethorik and eloquens oute of
Tullius bokes, and oþir rethoricianes whech weꝛ be-fore him. But
in þis first ȝere þat he cam to Cartage, he a-bod litil at his study,
but rood to and fro, now to his fader, now to Cartage, for what for 24
euel felauchip þat he was falle in, what for insolens of his wauntown
age, he used tauernes and stewis and swech sory gouernauns as þei
vse whech haue no men to vndirtake heꝛ defautes. For his fadeꝛ
low at his gouernauns & rebuked him of no defaute. But his 28
modeꝛ, with ful sad countenauns, forbade him [3] all suspecious
cumpany, and he took ful litil heed at hiꝛ wordis. In þis same
tyme [4] was his fadeꝛ conuerted on-to þe feith, and mad a cathe-

---

[1] *sike crossed through.*   [2] *in margin.*

[3] *written in red in small writing above.*

[4] *written in red in small writing above.*

cume ; a cathecume is as mech to seye as a newe receyuo*ur* of þe and became a catechumen.
feith, for in elde tyme men had certeyn dayes assined be-twix heꝛ
conuercion and here baptem þat þei myth lerne wel þe articules of
4 ouꝛ feith or þei weꝛ boun*de* þerto. And so schuld men do[1] now,
as I suppose, if þei schuld be bap‖tiȝed at þat age. He schryuyth Leaf 10, back.
him[2] also þat in þis age he ded many insolens, more for vanite
þa*n* for nede, and in *special* of an appil-tre[3] þat stood fast by his Augustine robbed an apple-tree.
8 faderes vyne on a-noþir man*nes lond, of whech he makith grete
consciens, be-cause þat he myth haue had bettir appillis in his
faderes possession, and eke for when he had þese appelles, he ete
hem nawt, but þrew hem on-to hoggis. In all þis vanyte of his
12 lif he happed to fynde a book þat Tulli*us* Cicero mad, þe grete He read Cicero,
rhetorician of Rome, whech book þe maker clepid Hortenci*us*,
be-cause it[4] exhorted men gretly to fle þe vanite of þe world, and
to folow þe noble study of philosophie. This book chau*n*ged his
16 hert gretly, & mad him þat he had not so gret ioye in þoo vanites
as he had be-fore. But for al þat þe book plesed him not fully, for but liked no book without Christ's name in it.
he fond not þe name of Crist i*n* al þis book. This name was
couchid in his hert fro his moder tete, þat what book he red, weꝛ[5]
20 it neuyr so wys ne so wel i-spoke, weꝛ it neuyr so trew, he was not
fully plesed with it but if Cristis name weꝛ þe*re*. Than purposed he
for to rede holy scriptuꝛ, but be-cause þat, as Seint Paule seith, He began to read Scripture,
cun*nyng with-oute charite makith a man proude, and þis sciens but turned from it and
24 requirith meke disciplens, þerfor þe[6] eye of his mynde was followed the
I-qwenchid with þe grete lith of sotil vndyrstandi*ng* whech is Manichaean
conteyned in scr*i*ptuꝛ, and þus left he þis holy study. Tho felle heresy, and abode in it
he in-to þe grete errouꝛ of þe Maniches, for þei saide þat Goddis nine years.
28 son of heuene was not bore of a may ‖ de, ne he had not very flesch Leaf 11.
and blood as oþir men haue, but rather a fantastical body mad of þe
eyr, in whech he semed for [to] deye, but deth was þe*re* non, for very
body was þe*re* non. In þis fals heresie, whech avoideth þe most
32 substau*ns of ouꝛ feith, [7]fell he[7]. Many mo heresies held þei whech
were ful *perilous* to be rehersed, *specialy* in ouꝛ tonge. In þis

---

[1] *written in red in small writing above.*
[2] *writ*ten in small writing above.*
[3] *tre written in margin and mark of insertion made.*   [4] *h crossed through.*
[5] *it writ*ten in margin.*   [6] *þ written again and crossed through.*
[7-7] *in margin.*

heresie abood Augustin ny ix ʒere, inqwiring and sekyng groundes
and treuthis, or ellis resones, for to defende þis heresie, but he fond
non.

[CHAPTER VII.]

¶ Of the sorow þat his modir had for his[1] errour.   caᵐ. vij.   4

Monica was greatly grieved at Augustine's heresy, but God comforted her by a vision,

His modir, whan sche herd þat he was falle on-to þis heresie,
sche wept and sorowid more hertly þan women do þat folow
heꝛ childyrn to þe graue, and witʒ many menes and many exhortaciones was bisi nyth and day to bring him fro þis mischef.   In 8
all þis tribulacioñ and weping, ouꝛ Lord[2] wold not suffer hir to
go fully desolat, but schewed hir a consolacioñ be an aungel in hir
sleep.   Sche þoutʒ þat sche stood on a faiꝛ tre, planed al rith lich
a reule, and a faiꝛ ʒong man stood be-side hiꝛ with rich cloþis and 12
a mery chere, whech inqwired of hiꝛ what was þe cause of hir
weping.   Sche answered on-to him with ful heuy cher[3]: The
losse of my son Augustin, I wepe.   Tho þe ʒong man bad hir be of
good coumfort, and loke wel a-boute hir, for þere þat sche was hir 16
son schuld be, as he seide.   Tho loked sche, and say Augustin hir

Leaf 11, back.

son stand in þe same reule ‖ where-as sche stood.   The wise woman,
and vsed to swech reuelaciones, took of þis a gret coumfort, vndirstanding herby þat sumtyme sche schuld se him standing in þe 20

which she imparted to her son, who tried unsuccessfully to convince her that she misconstrued it,

same feith where þat sche stood.   Aftir þis not longe sche comound
þis visioñ with hir son, and seyd[4] on-to him þat sche hoped for to
se him a trewe cristen man or sche deyid, for þis consolacion had
sche fro heuene, and þis voys proporcioned to hir ioye, wher þat 24
þou art þere schal he be.   Nay, quod Augustin to his modir, ʒe
vndyrstand þe wordis a-mys; he seide, þere þat I am þere schulde
[5]ʒe be[5].   Nay, son, nay, quod sche, I vndirstod ful and noted his
wordes; he seid not, þere þat he is þere schal þou be, but, þere 28
þat þou art þer schal he be.   Thus was þe woman in her consolacioñ stabil[6] and coude not be led oute fro hir trewe beleue with
no sophisticacion þat hir son coude make.   Sche receuyed a-noþir

---

[1] *a character crossed through.*   [2] *in margin.*
[3] c *added afterwards.*   [4] ont *crossed through.*
[5—5] *in margin.*   [6] *added in margin.*

consolacion be an holy bischop þat was gretly lerned in holy
scriptur and gretly excersised to lede men fro errour. To þis
man went sche, oft desiring of him þat he wold speke with hir son
4 and comoun with him in þat heresie, and schew [1] þe fals [1] and þe
onresonable doctrine whech þat heresie susteyned. The bischop
answerd to hir a-geyn and seide: For soth, þi son as ȝet is not
disposed for to be led any bettir weye, for he is neuly come on-to
8 þis doctrine, and mech redyer for to purpos questiones þan to
receyue ony doctrine. Wherfore, be my councel, suffir him for
a tyme & pray to God for him with-oute ony letting, and þou
schal [2] se þat he in his redyng and in his stodie schal aspie ful wel
12 in what errour he is falle, and who many horible þingis þat it
techith. For I was sumtyme deceyued with þe same doctrine and
had ful grete corage to lerne þe noueltes þerof, but þorw þe mercy
of our Lord, with long redyng of her bokes, I aspied þat it was
16 a secte rather to be fled þan [3] folowid. This answere myth not
suffise to þe woman, so grete desire was in hir hert þat he schuld
speke with hir son, so þat þe bischop was compelled to voyde hir
with swech wordys: Go fro me, woman, go fro me with þis
20 sikyrnesse. It is impossible that a child whech hath so many
teres wept for him schuld perisch. These wordis [4] of þe bischop
imprended sche in hir mynde as þouȝ an aungell had spoke
hem from heuene.

[CHAPTER VIII.]

24 ¶ What þat he ded fro þe tyme þat he was xx ȝer on-to xxix.

ca^m. viij.

AT þe age of xx ȝere he dwelt stille at Cartage, and þe maystires
þat were redde him, þe book of Aristotle cleped his Cathe-
28 gories, we clepe hem at þese dayes þe Predicamentis. Augustinus
gat þis book of his maystir, and hom to his chambir he went, red
it, vndirstood it, with-oute ony techer. For in the iiij book of his
Confessiones he is a-knowe þat alle þe bokes of philosophie, or
32 gemetrie, or arsmetrik, or any of þe vij sciens whech he myth

[Side notes right margin:]
Monica asked a bishop to lead Augustine in the right way, but he refused, knowing would not be led, and dismissed her with words of comfort.

Leaf 12.

Augustine studied and understood Aristotle and the seven sciences without a teacher.

---

[1] MS. schewid þe falshed; id *and* hed *crossed through in red.*
[2] a *not clear and afterwards written above in red.*   [3] MS. þat.
[4] MS. This word*is*; *is* added in red.

haue at leyser, he vndirstood hem, with-outen maystir, ¶ or with-oute ony techer. Aftir he was þus lerned in philosophie and oþir dyuers sciens, he cam first hom in-to þe cite where he was bore,

and þer taute he gramer, meruelyng all þe cuntre of þe noble 4 reules þat he [1] had founde to redinesse of childirn þat schuld lerne. Whan he had kept þis exersise longe in his owne cite, tho he resorted a-geyn [2] on-to Cartage, and þere taute he retorik [3] on the moost excellent wise. In þe xxvj ȝere of his age he wrote iij 8 bokes on-to a rethorician of Rome; þei cleped him Hermes [4]: þese bokes be intituled De Pulcro & Apto, þat is to sey in Englisch, of þing whech is fayre and able; þei are not in hand now. I coude neuyr speke with man þat sey hem, for his bokes which he mad aftir he 12 was cristen be more in deynte þan þoo whech he mad be-fore. In

þe xxix ȝere of his age spak he with Faustus, a grete snare of þe deuele, for þis man was þe moost famous heretik of all þe Manicheis, but he was ful famous in fayre endytyng. For he mad a ful cursed 16 book a-geyn oure feith, to qwech book þis same Augustin mad notable answeres in [5] a grete volume whech conteynyth xxxiij [6] bokes. The cause whi Faustus was desired for to cum speke with Augustin is þis: Augustin had many questiones with þe Manicheis 20 of her feith and of here lawe [7], and aspied so many notable errouris in her bokes þat he, ne non of hem, coude make no answer to his resones. Tho seid þei whan þei were concluded with argumentis

on all sides þat Faustus schuld come and he schuld make ‖ answere 24 on-to all þese motyues. For Faustus was in swech opinion amongis hem þat who-so [8]-euer folowid him and was conuersaunt with him, þei saide þat he folowid no man, but rather the Holy Goost. So Faustus is come to Cartage; a-non as he was come 28 Augustin with certeyn of his felawschip went on-to him. Ther had þei too grete comunicacion of þoo questiones for whech þei

were in trouble be-fore. And with-inne fewe dayes Augustin aspied wel what Faustus was, a mery man and a iocunde, a fayr- 32 spoke man eke, but not gretly grounded [9] in sciens. Tho be-gan

---

[1] he *inserted in small writing above.*   [2] *a word or part of a word erased.*
[3] gramer *crossed through and dotted underneath, and* retorik *written in margin with insertion mark.*   [4] Hermes *inserted in margin.*
[5] *inserted in small writing above.*   [6] iij *inserted above.*
[7] lawe *inserted in small writing above.*   [8] MS. se.
[9] groundes *crossed through in red and dotted underneath.*

Augustin to reherse on-to him þe doutes and þe articules comou*n*d
afore & writyn in billis a-geyn Manicheis lawe. Faustus, whan *Faustus,*
seeing his
he had aspied þe grete cu*n*nyng of Augusti*n* and þe sotil inuec- *own*
inferiority,
4 ciones whech he mad he durst not dispute with him, but be-for *submitted.*
hem alle he was fayn to sey þat he coude not answere to þo
motiues. Fro þis day forward had Augusti*n* no deynte in her *Augustine*
was then free
bokes whan þat he say her grete maystir and here p*r*ince coude *from secte.*
8 not[1] satisfie his resones. Thus lyued he[2] with suspense mynde, in
grete doute what secte he schuld hold or what wey he schuld take.
Al þis is touched in þe v. book of his Co*n*fessiones.

[CHAPTER IX.]

¶ Who Augustin aftir þis went to Rome.   c^m. ix.

12 CErteyn frendis þat he had at þat tyme, seing þe grete desir of *His friends,*
knowing of
lernyng in him, ȝoue him cou*n*cel þat he schulde go to *his reveis at*
Carthage,
Rome, and þis was her cause. For at Cartage both he and his *sent him to*
Rome.
disciples were lettid gretly with felauchip and reuel, and as þei
16 herd sey, and summe ǁ of hem knew it be exp*er*iens, at Rome was *Leaf 13,*
back.
more liberte ȝoue on-to skoleres and more quiete þa*n* was at
Cartage. This same desire þat was in his hert was the dispen-
sacion of our Lord. For our Lord[3] knew ful[4] wel where he schuld
20 be conuerted and what tyme, and had ordeyned be-fore þe menes
and þe mi*n*istres and þe places, as he wold dispose. Thus he disposed him fully for to saile to Rome. His modir folowid him to *Monica*
wanted to go
þe se-side, for sikirly sche wil go with him. And he disseyued *with him,*
24 hir in þis maner. He feyned first þat þei had no wynd ne likly *but he*
deceived her,
non for to haue many day, wherfor he desired þat sche schuld goo *and sailed*
without her.
to hir in a-geyn, and wha*n* tyme cam he wold clepe hir. To þis
wold not sche consent, for fro his presens wold sche not. Tho with
28 grete bisinesse he cou*n*celled hire for to a-bide as for þat nyth in a
oratorie þat was consecrat in þe name of Seint Cip*r*iane, for it
was ny þe schip, and sikirly, he told hir, þat þe next day þei wold
saile. Thus deceyued he his modir, for þat same nyth þei pulled

---

[1] not *inserted in small writing above.*   [2] he *written in red in margin.*
[3] lord *inserted in margin in red.*   [4] wl *crossed through.*

up sail & stale þe schip from hir. All þat nyth lay sche praying
and sobbing, desiring of ouꝛ Lord[1] þat þei schulde no wynd haue
til þat sche cam. In þe morow whan sche cam to þe brynk and
say þe schip goo, than wept sche intollerablely[2], and filt þe eres of 4
God with grete compleintis, and ȝet wist sche not what ioye God
wold cause hiꝛ of his absens. Thus went sche hom a-geyn and
prayed for him deuly, and he went forth to Rome. Whan he was

com þidir he feÌÌ ‖ in greuous seknesse & his moder knew not þat, 8
but þouȝ[3] he were absent sche prayed for him deuly þat ouꝛ Lord
schuld send her ioye of hir son, for in þis mater sche had moꝛ sorow
for him þan euyr sche had to bryng him forth on-to þe world.

Euery day sche offered for him at þe auteꝛ; euery day sche gaf 12
elmesse. Twyes on þe day went she to cherch, not for to telle
veyn tales, but for to bere tydyngis of ouꝛ Lord of heuene in
deuoute sermones, or elles for heꝛ diuine seruyse that God schuld
accept hir prayeres, whech weꝛ principali for þe goostly helth of 16
hir son Augustin. Be hir prayeres Austyn is now rered fro his
seknesse and hath begunne for to do þing for whech he was come,
þat is to seye, to tech rethorik; many disciples be gadered on-to
his skole, and his fame be-gan fast to spriuge.   20

[CHAPTER X.]

¶ Who Austin eke was sent to Melan to lerne hem rethorik. x.

AT þis tyme þe cyte of Melan, wher Seynt Ambrose was
bischop, sent on-to þe meyꝛ of Rome, whech hith
Symachus, praying him þat he wold sende on-to hem a weel 24
lerned man for to teche heꝛ inuent rethorik. And he, with ful
good a-vise, sent hem Austyn, a proued maystir, as he wrote, and
a man of grete cunnyng. Thus be þe prouidens of God cam
Austyn to Melan, and þere feÌÌ in knowlech of Seynt Ambrose þe 28
bischop[4], a noble man and a holy, knowyn þorw aÌÌ þe world.
Ambrose receyued Augustin ful faderly, and cherisched him in þe
best maneꝛ. Augustin went oft on-to cherch for to heꝛ Ambrose

---

[1] lord *added in margin.*   [2] r *inserted above.*
[3] þouȝ *in margin.*
[4] MS. and *with* nd *crossed out in red and dotted underneath.*

preche, not for [to] lerne ‖ treuthes of ouꝛ feith, ne nowt to amende Leaf 14, back.
þe erroures of his soule, but only to aspie wheithir his fame and his
speche acorded.   For he was noted þorw-oute Itaile a fayꝛ-spoke Augustine went to hear Ambrose's rhetoric,
4 man, and gretly roted in rethorik.   Thus went ouꝛ Augustin day
be day, only to reporte þe wordis; for þe sentens had he smal
delite; and Ꝫet, as he is a-know in his Confessiones, þe wordes of
Seynt Ambrose abiden in his soule magꝛ his hed, and were dayly
8 grucching a-geyn swech lif as he had.   Happed on a day ouꝛ fadeꝛ
Ambrose prechid of þe incarnacioñ of ouꝛ Lord Ihesu Crist, who
þat for þe special loue whech he had to mankynde he disdeyned
not to take þe flesch and blood of man with all þe infirmites, saue
12 synne.   Augustin stood in þe puple and sodeyn fere fell up-on
him, so þat þe þoutes whech weꝛ pryuy with-inne him mad his face and one day his words turned him to the true faith,
pale and his body for to tremel þat all þe puple myth aspie it.
Aftir þe sermon was ended he went on-to Ambrose, and told him
16 of his new chaunge, and who longe he had ben in þe Manicheis
heresie, and who sith þat tyme þat he spak with Faustus þat secte
was ferre fro his plesauns.   Whan Ambrose herd þat he had no
trost ne no confidens in [1] þe heresie of þese Manicheis, he þankid
20 God heyly, and be-cause he knew wel be inspiracion of þe Holy
Gost [2] what Augustin schuld be, he treted him ful fadirly with
swete exhortaciones, þinking with swech menes to brynge him to
þe trew be-leue.   Tho Augustin cast in his hert fully to ‖ despise þe Leaf 15.
24 Manicheis heresi, for euyr þe feith of Crist he purposed for to take, but he would not yet be baptized.
but baptiꝪed wold he not be on-to þe tyme þat he myth know þe
treuthis of Cristis feith.

[CHAPTER XI.]

¶ [3] In what maner his moder sowt him. [3]   cap. xi.

28 IN þis same tyme Monicha, his modir, took þe se, and put hir- Monica took ship after her son.
selue to grete perel for to se hir son.   Hir grete feith and
hope þat sche had in God, hiꝛ grete charite þat sche had to
conuercioñ of hir son, mad þe womannes hert bold, and in maner

---

[1] in *inserted above in small writing.*
[2] gost *written in red in margin replacing* God *in text, and a mark of insertion made.*   [2–3] *Inserted in margin.*

She calmed the frightened shipmen, and met her son, who told her he had left the Manichaean sect.

turned it to a mannes hert, þat not only sche wanted [1] feer or dred
in þe se, but þe schipmen whech weꝛ aferd sche coumforted in þe
best maner, saying on-to hem in þis maneꝛ: Beth of good coumfort, seres, for treuly I had a visioñ fro heuene þat we schul skape 4
þis iornay ful weel. Sche is come to lond and to þe speche of
hir son, and after longe daliauns he told hiꝛ pleynly þat out of
Manicheis skole was he go for euyr, but on-to Cristis skole, whech
sche desired him to come, was he not parfithly entred. ȝet whan 8
sche herd him sey þis sche hopped with ful mery chere [2] þat sche
had o part of [3] hiꝛ desire, for too þingis desired sche, on þat he
weꝛ delyuered fro þat fals heresie of þe Manichees, and þat was
fulfilt, þe oþir þat sche schuld se him a trew Cristen man, and þis 12
sche hoped. With a grete spirith and a merie chere sche cried and

She con-tinued to pray for his soul,

seide: Now beleue I in my Lord God, þat or my soule passe out
of þis world I schal se him a trew Cristen man. Than sent sche
praieres on-to heuene [4] with gretter bisinesse þan euyr sche ded 16

Leaf 15, back.

þat ouꝛ Lord schuld hast þis mateꝛ, ‖ & make brith þe þirknesse
of Augustines soule. Sche loued Ambrose as an aungel of God,
for be him sche wist weel þat hir son was brout þus to swech
fluctuacioñ. Fluctuacioñ calle we heꝛ whan a man is broute fro 20
an euel entent, and ȝet þe same man stand in study wheithir he
schal to þe good wey or nowt. In þis plith stood ouꝛ Austyn.

and made offerings at the altars where saints were buried, as she had in Africa, but ceased on the advice of Ambrose. Augustine says she fasted on Saturdays, as was the custom in Rome.

The custom of his moder and eke of þe cuntꝛ whilles sche dwelt
in Affrik, was [5] to offer bred and potage and wyne at the aucteris 24
where martires were byried. And þis custom was for-bode hiꝛ
be þe kepeꝛ of þe cherch at Melane, seying on-to hir þat it was þe
bischoppis wil, Ambrose, þat swech mete and drynk sche schuld ȝeue
to pore men, and to þe memories of the martires sche schuld 28
brynge, he seid, a deuoute soule ful of holy prayeres. Whan
sche herd þis deuoutely sche chaunged hir vse aftir þat informacioñ. Seynt Augustin, hir son, tellith of hire þat sche used to fast
þe Satirday, as deuoute folk ded þan at Rome, and þo persones þat 32
ete and dronk with hiꝛ continuely at Melane saide þat it was not
þe vsage þere at Melane, wher-for hir dynersite was in maner of
a slaundir to þe cumpany. In þis mateꝛ sche took councell of

---

[1] feꝛ *crossed through.*   [2] chere *inserted above in red.*
[3] MS. o part of part of *with second* part *crossed through.*
[4] *final* ne *inserted in red above.*
[5] *inserted in margin in red.*

Seyn Ambrose, and he sette hir[1] þis reule, þat wheᵽ-so-euyr sche
cam sche schuld do aftir þe custom of þe felauchip whech sche
dwelt in.   In þis same tyme come too of Augustin grete frendis *Augustine's friends,*
4 on-to him[2], Alipius and Nebridius.   This Alipius was bore in þe *Alypius and Nebridius,*
same town wheᵽ Augustin was bore, and Nebridius bore fast be
Cartage, ‖ where he had faiᵽ possession, but it likid him bettir *Leaf 16.*
to forsake alł þat he had and com to dwelł with Augustin.
8 These iij men to-gidir at Melane had grete councelł and grete *seek with him*
stody what maner secte þei schuld chese, and what lyf þei schuld *what sect they should*
hald.   At þese dayes was Augustin xxx ȝeᵽ of age.   So alł iij *follow, propose to*
were acorded first to chese hem wyues, and all sex dwelł in on *take wives,∨ and study,*
12 hous, and þei for to stody swech bokes as þei wold haue and do *and dwell together.*
non oþir bisinesse.   Than was alleggid a-mongis hem what sorrow
þere schuld be if þei acorded not, [3] & specialy for h[er] wyuys, who
þe[i] schuld lyue, if dista[uns] fel betwix[3].   God ouᵽ Lord had
16 ordeyned a-noþir wey, and for þat cause he put a delay in þat
mateᵽ, for he suffered þe hert of Augustin to be sette on swech *Augustine's maid.*
a mayde, and of so ȝong age, that he must nede abyde tyl sche
were able.

[CHAPTER XII.]

20   ¶ On what maner ouᵽ Lord suffered Alipius to be appechid of
theft.   xij.

THIS processe telȝ Augustin in þe vj book of his Confessiones
in þis maner.   Alipius, he seith, was at Cartage, stodying *Alypius studied*
24 in rethorik.   It was þe vsage at þoo dayes þa[t] þe rethoricianes *rhetoric at Carthage,*
schuld pleten in court for euery cause whech was litigious.   This
Alipius, a litil be-foᵽ þe court schuld be hold, walkyd a-lone with *and, on a day before he*
his reporting tables in his hand, stodying ful bysily, for it was his *should have pleaded,*
28 cours þat day for to plete.   Be-neth þat hous where he walked
was housyng be þe ground, in whech dwelt coynoures of siluyr,
and wroute þere ful bisily.   Owt of þe strete comth a ȝong child, *passed a*
a theef, with an ex in his hand, and went on-to a certeyn roof *coiner's house where a boy*
32 whech was cured with leed, and euene ouyr þe coynouris hous *was stealing lead.*
he be-gan for to hewe. ‖ The coynouris herd þe noyse and sent *Leaf 16,*
up too or thre of heᵽ felauchip to loke what theef was so bold *back.*

---

[1] MS. his *with* r *written above in red.*   [2] MS. hinn.
[3-3] *written in margin and part of end words cut away at edge of leaf.*

The boy
heard a noise
and ran
away,
and men
coming,
Alypius was
arrested.
þat tyme of þe day and so ny þe dome-place to stele þe metall of
þe houses. The boy herd men com with grete noyse; he left his
exe þere, and ran hom in grete hast. Thus com þe men and se no
persone þere but Alipius alone; þei [1] se þe led broke, þei fynde þe 4
ex by, and on him þei go all and areste him for þis dede. Alipius,
þat was innocent, and be-cause of his study took non hed at þe
boy, neythir whan he cam ne whan he went, is þus led forth as
a theef on-to þe iuge. Happed a man þat knew him and knew 8
what vertue he was of for to mete him with þese tormentouris.
He pulled him o side and inqwired of him who þis myth be.
A man of swech birth and swech kunnyng þat he schuld be take
in swech defaute, he seid, it was grete merueile. Alipius answerd 12
on-to him and told him þat he was ongilty in þis mateř, but he

But a friend
tricked the
boy into con-
fessing the
abandoned
axe was his,
had mynde þat he say a boy renne fro þe place and leue þere his
ex. The man caused [2] þat þei turned all a-geyn in-to þe same
strete, and as it happed, þe same boy stood in þe dore þat had doo 16
þe dede. This man whech ȝaue [3] so grete fauouř on-to Alipius took
þe ex in hand; rith þus he seide on-to þe boy: Heř haue we
founde an exe; knowest þou owt to whom it schuld longe? ȝa,

and so was
Alypius
saved.
forsoth, seř, seide he, þat same ex is ouř. Thus was Allipius 20
wrongfully attached and meruelously delyuered. God Almyty

Leaf 17.
suffered þis, as Augustin writith ‖ in his Confessiones, for to lerne
him whech schuld be aftirward a iuge of mennes soules in þe
cherch þat he schuld not deme ouyr sone of signes owtward.   24

[CHAPTER XIII.]

¶ Who he went to Simpliciane. xiij.

Augustine
finally con-
sents to
become a
Christian,
NOW is Augustin dryuyn so ferř þat he is fully consentid to go
be þe wey of Crist, but be-cause of þe hardnesse of it, he
was ful loth þerto. But ouř merciable Lord put a new coumfort 28
in his hert þat he schuld go to an hermyte in þe desert fast by
Melan, whech hermyte hith Simpliciane. Augustin had herd
mech þing of him þat he had serued God in ful vertuous lyf, and

and goes to
Simplician,
the hermit,
who dwelt by
Milan,
þe fame was trewe in-dede. This man Simpliciane lyued in 32
a monastery fast by Melan with othir heremites of holy lyf

[1] *final i added in red.*   [2] *final d inserted above.*
                    [3] *to crossed through.*

at þe costis & expens of Seynt Ambrose. For Seint Ambrose at the expense of Ambrose.
had Simpliciane in so grete reuerens þat he worchipid him as
his fader, and aftir his deth asined on-to his clerkis and his
4 puple to be chose bischop successour on-to him, and so it was
in-dede. To þis Simpliciane teld Augustin þe besinesse of Augustine told him his history,
his hert, in who many errouris he had falle an[d] what dowte
he stood in to what lyf he schuld drawe. The good fader
8 Simpliciane gaf him exhortacion to folow þe meknesse of our and was advised,
Lord Ihesu and despise þe fals delectacionis of þis world. He
rehersed on-to him eke a grete exaumple of[1] þe conuercion of on,
Victorine, a worthi man, a grete rethorician, a famous philisophr, and told of the example
12 whech man for grete sciens had a statua rered to his liknesse in of Victorine,
þe markette at Rome. This same man cam to Simpliciane often-
tyme and inqwired of him many þingis, and oft-tyme wold
say ‖ on-to Sympliciane : Knowe now wel þat I wil be a cristen Leaf 17,
16 man. Simplician wold say a-gayn on-to him : I wil not be-leue it back.
til þat I se þe withinne þe kirk. And Victorine wold þanne in
scorne conclude be maner of an argument : Ergo, þe wallis of þe
cherch make a cristen man. This iteration of wordis was oft- how he was converted to real Christianity.
20 tyme vsed be-twix þese too men, but at þe last our Lord enspired
soo Victorines hert þat sodeynly he seid to Simpliciane : Go we to
þe cherch, for in very treuth, I wil be a cristen man. Thus was
þis worthi man conuerted to þe feith ; and al þis told Simpliciane
24 to Augustin þat he schulde folow his steppis. Be þis holy fader
Simpliciane was Augustin brovt on-to þis desire, þat al maner Augustine came thus to despise the world, but had not yet chosen his way of life.
worldly delectacion displesed him, for þe loue of his hert is now
only sette to serue God. He say many men in þe cherch lyuyng
28 in sundry maner, summe þus & summe þus, wherfor he hatȝ not
chose as ȝet þe lyf whech he wil lede.

[CHAPTER XIV.]

¶ Off þe comyng of Poncian on-to Augustin and of what þingis
þei talked of. capitulum xiiij.

32 IN þis tyme was Augustin & Alipius dwellyng to-gidyr, for Augustine and Alypius dwelt to-gether,
Nebridius was not with hem at þat tyme. So happed it þat
a man of court whech was dwellyng in þe paleys at Rome whos

---

[1] *inserted above in red.*

2–2

andPonciane, their fellow countryman, came to them, name was Ponciane, be-cause he was bore in Affrica, rith as þei were, cam on-to hem to se her welfaȝ, as þe maner of men is whech be bore in straunge cuntre & dwelle fer fro hom. He fonde hem sittyng in a hous and be-for hem a bord on whech þei vsed to 4

Leaf 18. pleye certeyn games ‖ to refresch with þe sadnesse of her study. Vpon þis bord lay a book whech book Ponciane supposed had be of sum seculeȝ sciens whech as þei vsed. Poncian vnsperd þe bok

and found the 'Epistles' of St. Paul before them. and say wel þat it was a bok longing to cristen feith, whech bok 8 we clepe þe Epistoles of Seynt Paule. This Ponciane with myry cheȝ mad in maneȝ of a þankyng to God þat Augustin his cuntreman was falle in-to studye of swech holy bokes, for þis same Ponciane had neuly take cristendham and was a stedfast and 12 a trewe cristen man. Augustin sayde on-to him þan þat al þe felicite of his study was only ȝoue to rede swech bokes. Tho

They talked of the holy hermits, be-gunne þei to speke of þe dyuers cumpanyes of holy heremites whech dwelled in wildyrnesse, both in Itale and in Egipt, and in 16 special of grete Antonie whos name was ful famous to alȝ þe seruauntes of God, but to Augustin and his felawes it was on-knowyn on-to þat houȝ. For whech cause he satte ful stille and herd Ponciane with grete silens. Ponciane told him who he 20 & oþir thre felawis þat dwelt with þe emperouȝ went on a day

and Ponciane told how a friend had discovered the 'Life of St. Anthony' in a cave and was converted to hermit-life by it. in-to þe wodis to her disport, and happed Ponciane and his felaw to walk in þe o side of þe wode, and þe oþir too felawes in þe othir side. On of þese too with whech Poncian was not cam in-to 24 a cane where a heremyte dwelled, whech heremite was up-hap in-to þe cite for to fecch him mete, and fond þere a book with Seynt Antonies lyf; he sat down and red it, and in þe redyng was

Leaf 18, back. sodeynly compunct to forsake þe world. Thus saide he þan ‖ on-to 28 his felaw: Here in þis same place I purpose me for euyr to serue God, and þis same houȝ I wil be-gynne. If þou list not to do as I wil, I pray þe, grucch not my dede. His felaw answered a-gayn on þis maneȝ, þat he wold not part cumpany, but swech lif as he 32 hath chose he wil folow, to forsake al þis world and leue þere in solitarie lif. Ponciane and his felaw sey þe sunne draw fast to inclinacion, sout þese oþir too felawis, fonde hem and hasted hem homward, for þe day was ny at a ende, as þei saide. Tho told þei 36 her holy purpos on-to hem, what a-vow þei had mad whech þei wold not breke. Ponciane and his felaw praised heȝ entent, and þankyng God of her holy *conuercion*, went a-geyn on-to þe paleys. Thus dwelt þese men stille þere in þat caue, *perseuering* in holy lif, and to ȝong women whech schuld be weddid on-to hem, be her 4 exhortacion avowid her maydenhed to God.

[CHAPTER XV.]

¶ What sorow Augustin mad aftir þis exhortacion. **xv.**

GRETE sorow and horribil ran in Augustin mynde þanñ whan he had herd þese holy exaumples of þe seruauntis of 8 God, whech seruauntis our Lord God had brout[1] fro þe grete blaknesse of synne on-to þe fair white *vertuous* lyuyng. For all þese exaumples had Augustin gadered in-to þe bosom of his hert, whech brent him ful sore and mad him a-schamed þat he was not 12 þus disposed. And whan Ponciane had take his leue & was go, thoo Augustine with a troubled mynde be-gan ¶ to loke up-on his felaw Alipius, and with a sobir voys þus he cried : What suffir we ? What are þese þingis þat we here ? These onlerned men 16 rise and sodeynly wynne heuene, and we with all our doctryne are drenchid euene in helle. Be-cause þei went be-fore us þerfor schul we be a-schamed to folow hem ! Whil Augustin saide þese wordes Alipius besily loked up-on him, for he pronounsed not his 20 wordis as he was wone to doo. For nowt only wer þese wordes expressed with labour[2] of his tunge[2], but his forhed, chekis, his eyne and all his *membres* in *maner* laboured in pronounsyng of þese wordes. Sodeynly þanñ he stirt fro þat hous in whech he 24 had herd þese þingis, and in-to a gardeyn whech was annexid to þat hous he stert; Alipius folowid him foot be foot, merueling sor of þe sodeyn compunccion þus neuly com. Thus þei sat in þe gardeyn as fer fro þe hous as þei myth sitte, and Augustin be-gan to 28 accuse him-self sor in þe sith of our Lord of þe slauth of his returne to God, and þe grete hepes of synne whech he had vsed he gadered on-to mynde, whech mad him for to wepe plenteuously, and þat he schul haue þe mor leyser to wepe, he roos fro his felaw Alipius and 32 went on-to a figge-tre. Þere he þrew him-selue down vndyr þe tre,

Augustine was deeply moved by the tale of Ponciane's friend,

Leaf 19.

and, with a trembling voice, addressed Alypius.

Then he went into the garden; his conscience smote him and he wept.

He threw himself on the earth by a fig-tree,

---

[1] broñ *crossed through.*   [2]–[2] *written in red in margin.*

and swech lamentable voyses he þrew on-to heuene : O blissed Lord,
who longe, who longe ? Who longe wilt þou suffir, Lord, þat I go so
ferre fro þi seruyse and differre my *conuercion* fro day to day ?
To-morow, schal it be to-morow ? Why not now, Lord, whi schal 4

not þis same houre ‖ make an end of all my filth ? Whil he lay
þus with grete contricion of hert and with ful sobbyng voys

Suddenly he
heard a voice
saying 'Take
up and
read!' He
opened his
book, and
he read
'Romans'
xiii. 13.

uttirryng all þese wordes, al sodeynly he herd a voys, as þou3
it had ben at þe next hous, soundyng þese same wordes : Tak and 8
rede, take and rede ! Tho be-gan he for þink with-inne him-selue if
childyrn with ony game þat þei vse had ony swech wordes in her
playing, and he coude not þink þat he had herd ony swech. He
þout þan þat þis voys cam fro heuene, 3euyng him a warnyng þat 12
he schuld ope þe bok whech he brout with him fro þe hous on-to
þe gardeyn, and þe first letter þat his eye felle up-on he schuld
rede. Thus ded he, and þese same wordis red he : Non in
comessacioni*bus* & ebrietati*bus*, non in cubili*bus* & impudiciciis, 16
non in contencione & emulacione, *sed* induimini *dominum* ihe*sum*
chri*stum* et carnis curam ne fece*ritis* in desideriis[1]. The sentens
of þis texte may be englisched in þis wise : Not in grete festis ne
in dronknesse, not in soft couchis and in schalful dedis, not in 20
strif a[n]d[2] envye, but be clad with ou*r* Lord Ihe*su*, & fulfille not
þe bisinesse of þe flesch in his desires. He sperd the bok whan he
had red þis and leyd at þe same reson a merk be whech he myth
rydily turne þertoo, for þis same texte put in his[3] hert a lite of 24
swech a grace þat alle þe derk errouri*s* whech he had hold we*r*

passed a-wey fro him. Tho toke he þe book on-to his felaw
Alipius, and with his fynger or sum othir tokne schewid him
þe clause be-fo*r* red. Alipius red ferþe*r* whech Augustin had 28
not red, and schewid to Augustin what it was þat[4] folowid. Þus
folowith in þe texte : That man þat is feynt in þe feith, loke

3e be ‖ redy for to receyue. In-to þe hous þei go both ; *þere* þei

Then they
both went to
tell Monica
the news,
who was
glad and
grateful to
God.

fynde þe blessed woma*n* Monicha, þe modir of Augustin ; þei 32
told hir al þis processe þat sche whech had be in so mech sorow
for hir son schuld haue part of his new ioye. Sche þankid God
with ful humbil hert þat oure Lord had grauntid hir hir long
desi*r*, & mech more þat sche desired, for not only He had brout 36

---

[1] *In margin* Ad Romanos 13.   [2] MS. ad.
[3] s *inserted above.*   [4] t *inserted above.*

him[1] to purpos to be a cristen man, but He had stered his hert to despise al þis worldly plesauns.

[CHAPTER XVI.]

¶ Who he left his skole of rethorik only to haue his hert
4 fre to God. **xvj.**

NOW be-gan his hert to be sette stedfastly in ouꝛ Lord[2], for In order to be free to serve God,
þoo vanytees and þoo opinyones in whech he had be-foꝛ serve God,
ful grete ioye, now aꝛ þei falle clene fro him, and þat skole whech Augustine gave up his
8 was a peyne to him þat he schuld leue it, now for to leue it, school of rhetoric,
it is to him ioye. But Ᵹet him þout for to leue his skole sodeynly
and his skoleris desolat, þat it was not best. For þe heruest
dayes weꝛ ny whan skole is wone to cese; so longe he þout for
12 to suffir hem, þat þei schuld solemply goo fro him. Whan xx
dayes were go, for þan entred þe cessacion, whech dayes weꝛ
on-to him longe for þe grete desiꝛ þat he had to serue God with
moꝛ solitarie lif, than was he dysmittid of his grete labouꝛ whech
16 he had in teching of rethorik. And because þat al his desire
was for to prey and study solitarily, he left þe cite of Melan, and retired to a field of
and forth in-to þe cuntꝛ he went, in-to a feld þei[3] cleped Cassiate, Varecundus, where he
to a place longing to a worchipful man cleped Verecundus. This wrote
20 Verecundus graunted him to dwelle þere ‖ on-to þe tyme þat he Leaf 20, back.
schuld be baptiꝝed. So in þis same place abood he and Alipius,
and oþir frendis of his, with his modir, all in o desire to forsake
þe delectable onstabilnesse of þis world. And in þis same place mad
24 Augustin dyuers bokes, þat is to sey a book De Achademicis, whech 'De Achademicis'
soundeth in ouꝛ tonge of on-certeyn opiniones. For Achademia
was a town where Plato tawt and all þoo disciples of þat skole
held þis opinion, þat no þing is sette in certeyn. This book of
28 Augustin serueth not mech, for he was fayn aftir to make a book (afterwards annulled by 'Contra Achademicos'),
a-geyn þis secte, and þat is cleped *Contra* Achademicos. Aftir
þis he mad a-noþir book in þat same place, whech he clepith 'De Ordine,'
De Ordine, in whech book, as me semyth, he tretith be what
32 order or what forme a man schuld studie. The þird book mad

---

[1] *inserted above.*   [2] *inserted in red above.*

[3] i *added in red.*

and 'De
Beata Vita.'
he in þat same place whech he clepith De *Beata* Vita; þat is
to sey, of þe blessed lyf. The cause whi he mad þis book is þis.
Many men in þis world, specialy þe hethen men, mad a gret
feest þat day þat þei were bore. Augustin had vsed þis al his 4
lyf on-to þat tyme. So happed þat day to falle þe same tyme
þat he dwelt in þat possession of the forsaid man *Verecundus.*
And be-cause he wold chaunge þat fleschly fedyng in-to goostly
talking, þerfor with his moder and certeyn of his frendis, he mad 8
þat day þat book wheᵽ he disputeth what we schuld calle þe
blissed lyf. Alł þe cumpany saue his moder saide it is a blessed
lyf a man for to haue alł þat he desireth. His modir put moo
wordis on-to þis diffuncioñ. Sche saide ‖ he hath a blessed lif 12
whech hath al þat he desirith, and eke þat he desire no-þing but
good þing. Mech moᵽ þing is touchid in þis book, speciali of
þe knowlech of God, whech þing as now we may not declaᵽ.

Why he wrote the latter book, and what it contains.

Leaf 21.

[CHAPTER XVII.]

¶ Who bisily he red holy scriptuᵽ and speciali þe Psalmes of 16
Dauid,[1] & of his baptem [1]. **xvij.**

Augustine became a constant reader of Scripture,

NOW is þe delectacioñ of Augustyn only sette in redyng of
holy Scriptuᵽ; grete swetnesse hath he now in þoo lessones
whech kyndeled þe fyre of his hert and mad him to encrese sore 20
in þe loue of God. He mad ful grete sorow þat he had be so
bold to berke a-geyn þese holy letteris, whech be swete as hony
to þoo soules þat desiᵽ heuene, for þei weᵽ dewid fro heuene
be þe holy vesseles of þe prophetis, and most specialy be ouᵽ 24
Lord[2] Ihesu and his aposteles. Tho cam Augustin on-to þe
Psalmis of Dauid, whech he red with ful ryp deuocyoñ, and
specialy in iiij Psalme; þere mad he grete tarying, redyng euery
vers by and by with gret sobbyng of hert, with wepyng and 28
lamentable voys. And whan he cam to þat vers: In pace, in
idipsum dormiam & requiescam, þan wold he crye: A þou pes,
a Lord, þou art þe very pes in whech we schal both slepe and

and particularly of the fourth Psalm.

---

[1]-[1] *added in margin.*   [2] *added in red above.*

rest! A-mongis all þese swete consolaciones our Lord sent him _{Augustine was smitten with grievous sickness in the head and teeth,}
sum bittirnesse, þat he schuld tast þe loue of our Lord both in
bittyr & in swete. For þat same tyme in whech he was come
4 to þis grete deuocioñ, he fel in greuous seknesse of þe heed, most
special of þe teth, whech peyne encresed so þat he myth not
speke. Tho ran it in his mynde for to pray þo men whech wer _{Leaf 21, back.}
about him to make a ‖ supplicacioñ on-to our Lord, þat he
8 schuld of his mercy relese sum of þis peyne. And be-cause he
myth not speke þis for peyne, þerfor he took a peyre tables, and
wroot in þe wax al his desir, þat þei of pite schuld pray for him. _{and by the prayers of his friends was cured.}
And sodeynly, as þei alle sette hem down on knees to pray for
12 him, þe peyne went a-wey. Of whech chaunge he was gretly _{He asked Ambrose what part of Scripture he should read, and was told to read Isaiah; and did so;}
astoyned, for he had neuyr non experiens of so[1] sodeyn helth in
al his lyf. Tho sent he letteris to Seynt Ambrose, in whech
letteris he renounsid for euyr all his elde errouris, and in þe same
16 letteris he desired of Ambrose þat he schuld assigne him what
book of holy Scriptur was most neccessarie for him to rede, be
whech redyng he myth be mor able and more redy to receyue
þe cristen feith. Ambrose wrote on-to him a-geyn þat he þout
20 best he schuld rede þe book of Ysaie, þe prophete, be-cause þat
þis book tretith most openly of callyng of hethen men to þe feith.
Augustin red þis book, and þe beginnyng was passyng straunge
on-to him, for he had not mech vsed þat[2] maner stile, wherfor
24 he leyd þis book a-side as for a tyme, tyll he were mor vsed in _{but being unused to the style, laid the book aside for a time. He went to Milan for baptism and wrote there 'De Immortalitate Animae.}
study of scriptur. Sone aftir þis he went to Melan a-gay[n],
only for he cast him þere to be baptiȝed, and ȝet or he was
baptiȝed he mad þere a book whech is entituled, De Immortalitate
28 Anime. This book tretith who þat a mannes soule is not dedly
but hath lif for euer. Aftir þe makyng of þis book he was
baptiȝed of Seynt Ambrose, þe ȝer of his age xxxiij, in þe pase-tyme,
in ‖ þe baptisterie whech is halowid to þe name of Seynt Ion _{Leaf 22.}
32 Baptist, all þe cite of Melan standyng aboute, meruelyng and
praysing God. And þese too men in þe time of baptising, whan _{He was afterwards baptized by Ambrose and then these two composed 'Te Deum.'}
þe principal sacramental wordes wer said, mad þis ympne whech
þe cherch vsith now, cleped Te Deum. Ambrose be-gan þe first
36 vers, and Augustin þe secund, and þus þei said it to an ende.

---

[1] *inserted above.*   [2] *þe with at written over it.*

All this is
told in the
'Chronicle'
of Dacius. This witnesseth a seynt clepid Dacius, bischop aftir of þe same cherch of Melan, in his Cronycle whech he mad, þe x. book, þe first capitule.

[CHAPTER XVIII.]

¶ Of his son Adeodate whech was baptiȝed with hym, and of 4 othir also.   **Capi*tu*lum xviij.**

Augustine
had a son,
called
Adeodatus,
by a single
woman to
whom he was
true.
AUGUSTIN had a son be a sengil woman whech folowid up-on him wheP he went as long as he was hethen, on-to þat ¹tyme þat¹ he and his felawis weP sette in þat purpos for to 8 wedde wyues of good birth, for² aftir þat tyme þe woma*n* sewid him no moP.   These be his wordis in his Confessiones, wheP he seith eke þat he had neu*er* no woma*n* but hiP, ne sche no man but him.   O child was boP be-twix hem too, whom þei cleped 12

Adeodatus
was a child of
remarkable
intellect,
who, at the
age of
sixteen,
surprised his
father by his
subtlety.
Adeodat*us*, þat is to seye, ȝoue of God, a mal child, a child ful of witte and of vertu, but ouP Lord took him sone oute of þis world aftir he was cristened with his fadeP.   His witte was so gret and so sotiȴ, as Augustin tellit, þat it passed in conyng 16 many³ men of grete age and grete exp*er*iens.   Augustin his fader had gret m*er*ueyl of him þat a ȝong þing of xvj ȝeP age schuld so m*er*uelously asken questionis, so sotilly⁴ argew.   His fader had

Leaf 22,
back.
moP bisinesse for to ȴ take heed at his questiones þan𝐷 at þe 20 answer*is* whech schuld be ȝoue p*er*too.   This child, with ful grete bisynesse, laboured to knowe þe trewe wey of God, both in study of sotiȴ sciens and eke folowing with vertuous lyf.   But sone

Soon after his
baptism the
son died.
aftir his baptem ouP Lord took him oute of erde, & sette him⁵ 24 in swech place wheP he is sikir of euyrlasting ioye.   This same

Adeodatus
caused his
father to
write 'De
Quantitate
Animae.'
Adeodat*us* caused his fadeP to write þat book whech tretith of þe qua*n*tite of þe soule, for it is a dialoge be-twix to, wheP on makith int*er*rogaci*o*nes and⁶ þe oþir ȝeueth þe answeres.   Thus 28 aftir her baptem Augustin*us*, with his felauchip ⁷, leued in ful grete ioye þat þei had receyued so clene a lif, whech lyf was more dere on-to hem þan gold or precious stones.

---

¹⁻¹ *added in red in margin.*   ² *added in red above.*
³ *a character crossed through.*   ⁴ *ag crossed through.*
⁵ MS. hin.   ⁶ *a crossed through.*   ⁷ *ip written in margin.*

[CHAPTER XIX.]

¶ Who Augustin had grete delite in þe song and ympnis songen in þe cherch of Melan. caᵐ. **xix.**

THUS whan he was confermed in þe feith of holy kirk, al þe
4 ioye and þe hope whech he had in þis world he forsok,
and *in* þis tyme myth neuyr his soule be saciat or fulfillid of
good desires, most *special*[1] consideryng who þat ouʀ Lord of His
hie councell had refreschid ma*n*kynde with His presens. He[2]
8 be-gan at þese dayes for to vse þe cherch mech, wheʀ he herd
redyng and syngi*n*g of delectable materes and swete melodies,
whech melody was on-to him a ful grete solace. Ambrose had
þat time mad neuly many ympnys, for all þe temporal ympnys
12 ar ny of his maki*n*g, as P*ri*mo die*rum*[3] omn*ium*[4], & þoo þat
folow, and þis same bisschop Ambrose mad hem to be sunge
delectabily with consent of dyu*ers* tewnys whech ‖ had not be
used þ*ere* be-foʀ. The cause whi þat þese newe songis were
16 be-gunne þus in Ambroses tyme is þis. The empe*r*esse cleped
Iustina was infect with þe venemhous heresie of þe Arianes,
whech held þat þe Fadeʀ and þe Son and þe Holy Gost be not
of o substauns, for þe Son calle þei a creatuʀ mad of þe Fadeʀ,
20 and þe Holy Gost clepe þei a creatuʀ mad of a creatuʀ, þat is
to sey of þe Son. Thei sey ferþermoʀ, þat Crist took flesch and
blod with-outen ony soule. This woma*n*, þus infecte, at instauns
of certeyn prestis whech taute hir þat heresie, hated Ambrose,
24 for he p*re*chid mech a-geyn hem. This p*er*secucion was so gret
þat Ambrose was constreyned to kepe þe cherch both nyth and
day, and mech of his puple abod still with him in tuycioⁿ of
his p*er*son, redy for to deye with her fadeʀ. So for to make
28 hem moʀ lith in heʀ wecch, þis same bisschop ded ordeyn swete
songis and delectable, aftir þe vse of þe cherchis in þe est side
of þe world, þat þe puple þus occupied with swech swete songis
schuld forgete þe heuynesse and þe perel in whech þei stood. Eke

Marginal notes:
Augustine, thus converted, used church a great deal,
where he sang the hymns of Ambrose.
Leaf 23.
The empress Justina followed the Arian heresy,
and persecuted the church of Ambrose, forcing him and his people to remain in the church night and day.
To make their watch more light, therefore, Ambrose wrote his sweet songs

---

¹ who *crossed through.*   ² ha *crossed through.*
³ conditor *crossed through.*   ⁴ *in margin.*

whan þis *persecucion* was ended ȝet þe good custom of þese songis
abood stille. For on-to þis day þe vse of þe cherch is for to
singe his ympnis with mery notes, whech is plesauns to God
and a grete encres of mannes deuocyon, specialy whan þei be 4

songe deuoutly. For in þese songis had Augustin so grete delite
þat he herd hem with ful bisy eres, for þei mad him to þink
on þo songis whech au*ngelles* syng in heuene, and iu þis same

deuocion be alle ‖ his felawes now whech ar newly baptiȝed. Thus 8
can oure Lord make dyuers bodies lyue in on hous with o soule
and on entent in þe seruyse of God.

[CHAPTER XX.]

¶ Who Augustyn aftir þis took an habite of Sympliciane whech
his heremytes used.   **xx.**
                                                                    12

BE-cause þat Simpliciane with his holy exhortaciones had
brout Augustin on-to þe feith, þerfor had Augustin grete
recors on-to him, most *special* aftir his baptem. For of þis same
Simpliciane took he þe forme of an habite whech his heremytes 16
vsed aftirward, and he eke. And nowt only þe habite but þe
maner of holy *conuersacion* lerned he of þe same Simpliciane rith
as he sey with his eyne. The forme of þis habite is touched in his
bokes, wher is seid þat þe habite was schape lich a crosse, and girt 20
aboue with a girdil whech had no barres, and all was of blak colour
þat he schuld neuyr forgete who þat he was hethen sumtyme and
lyued in þe blaknesse of synne. Off þis informacion whech he

receyued of Sympliciane spekith him-selue in a *sermone* þat he 24
mad and it begynnyth : In om*nibus operibus vestris* &c. Thus
he wrytith þere on-to þe prestis whech were gadered be him in þe
monasterye at Ypone, he dwellyng in desert as for a tyme with his
hermytes : What is þe cause þat ȝe grucch for I abood stille with 28
myn heremites all þese estern halidayes ? It plesed me as for
þis tyme to departe fro ȝou and dwelle with hem, whom, as
I haue said often, I haue founden swech as I desire. Whi are ȝe
troubled ? Be not þei very pore men in Crist, and for his loue 32

haue for ‖ sakyn al þis world ? Be not þei very buxom on-to all
my comaundmentis ? And in þe forme of good lyf þei ar fer be-for

ȝow. For be her good exaumples was I turned on-to þe rith feith. Euyr haue I loued hem, and euyr haue I desired for to folow heꝛ holy *conuersacioñ*. Be þat goodman Simplician, whech is amongis hem as a foundour, was I broute on-to cristendam and lerned in þe feith. Wherfor be ȝe not heuy of myn absens. Do thoo þingis whech are plesaunt on-to me, and I schal be with ȝou aƚƚ dayes on-to þe worldes ende.

He has always loved them, and by one of their founders, Simplician, he was brought to the faith.

[CHAPTER XXI.]

¶ Who Augustin went on-to Simpliciane, and Simpliciane graunted him xij heremites whech went with him to Affrik. xxj.

AFTIR þis his modeꝛ Monicha desired þat he and sche schuld go hom a-geyn on-to heꝛ owne cuntre and leue Melan and aƚƚ Itale, for sche had aƚƚ hir desire whech sche desired in þis world whan sche wist þat he was a trewe cristen man. Tho went he to Simpliciane and prayed him in most special maneꝛ to graunt certeyn persones of his felauchip whech he wold lede on-to his cuntre, as he saide, and leue þere with hem in holy *conuersacioñ*. Simpliciane was ful glad of his desiꝛ and graunted him xij þe moost proued men in parfithnesse of aƚƚ þat college. So he and his moder and þese xij, with fouꝛ of his frendis, Nebridius, Euodius, Alipius & Poncianus, mad hem redy to go to þe see, wheꝛ þei schuld schippe. Off þis mateꝛ spekith þis same glorious doctouꝛ in a sermon whech he mad of iij gendres of munkys; þus begynnyth þe sermone: Vt nobis per litteras, and þus writith he þere: These be þe parfite men to whom I drow mech in tyme of myn errour, ‖ be whom eke I receyued þe lith of my feith, & for þe fame of her holinesse was I baptiȝed in Crist. For at þe comaundment of my modeꝛ and desire of my frendis I went on-to þat god fadeꝛ Simpliciane, and desired of him certeyn persones of his felauchip, þat we schuld leue to-gidyr in þe boundes of charite at hom in my cuntꝛ. And he, ful faderly, whan he sey me wepe for swem þat I had whan I schuld depart fro him, graunted me þe same men whech I desired. But whi, hope ȝe, þat he graunted on-to me þis felauchip so redyly? For he knew wel þat my desiꝛ was to edifie a monasterie in Affrik in whech we schuld dwelle, folowyng þe

Monica now wished to leave Italy.

Then Augustine went to Simplician and asked for men with whom to found a fellowship, and was given twelve of Simplician's holiest men.

These, with his four friends, went with him to Africa. Of this he tells in one of his sermons,

Leaf 24, back.

saying that Simplician granted his request so readily because he knew that he wanted to found a monastery in Africa.

steppis of þe apostoles, specialy in forsaking of worldly richesse

The names of Augustine's first monks, and in chois of wilful pouerte. Of þe men whech I led with me fro Simpliciane in-to Affrik, þese be þe names: Anastasius, Fabianus, Seuerus, Nicholaus, Dorotheus, Ysaac, Nichostratus, 4

Of Vitalis he speaks in 'De Verbis Domini et Apostoli,' Paulus, Arillus, Stephanus, Iacobus & Vitalis. Off þis Vitalis speketh he specialy in a book cleped, De Verbis Domini & Apostoli, in þe sermone lxxxiiij whech beginnyth þus: Beati apostoli epistola, where he tellith þat þis Vitalis was an huscher 8 of gramer in Melan or þat tyme whech he cam to þe skole of

how he found a bag of gold, and set up scrolls to find the owner, Simpliciane. So happed him to fynde a grete bagg of gold þat a marchaunt had lost. And a-non, as he had found it, he sette up scrowes[1] on certeyn gates in Melan, þat what man cowde telle 12 very toknes schuld haue his gold a-geyn. The man cam þat had rith þertoo and told him þe very toknes, & he delyuered him his

Leaf 25. gold with[-oute] ony delay. Tho þat ‖ man þat had lost þis mony sey þe treuth of þe fynder, profered him for his labour xx s; 16

and refused to take reward, Vitalus wold non receyue. He profered him x s, and þan v s, & euyr he refused it. He þat had lost þe mony was in partye wroth with þe fynder for he wold not take for his labour, þrew

but was forced to, and gave it to poor men. down þe bagge, saying on þis maner: I lost nowt, take þou al. 20 So was þis Vitalis compelled in partie to receyue þis v s as for his labour, and he a-non gaue it to pore men, kepand to him-selue no part. For þis good dede praiseth Seint Augustin þis man, and

Of this Augustine writes. for þis dede writith he here a comoun proposicion mech used in þe 24 decrees: Quicquid inuenisti & non reddisti rapuisti. This is to sey in our tonge: What-so-euer þou fyndist and gyuyst not a-geyn, þou stelist.

[CHAPTER XXII.]

¶ Who Augustin with all þis meny went to Rome to take þe se 28 in Hostia fast by Rome & whi he taried þer. xxij.

Monica was as a mother not only to Augustine but to all his friends, TO all þis felauchip þus gadered in fer was Monicha a very moder, as goodly and as frendly to hem all as þou3 sche had be moder to hem alle, and eke as seruyseable on-to hem as 32

---

[1] scl *crossed through.*

þou‡ sche had be doutir on-to hem. Fro Melan he went to Rome _{and served}
be Tussie, wheꝛ he fond many heremites dwellyng in wodes and in _{them as
though she}
feldis, euene sette in þe same purpos in whech he was sette. Alle _{had been
their}

4 þese men for þe moost partie he visite with swete exhortacioñ of _{daughter.}
ouꝛ Lord, with whech both he and þei weꝛ ful vertuously refreschid. _{When
Augustine}
Than cam he to Rome, and þere herd he mech noyse of þe Manichees _{reached
Rome he}
whech weꝛ in Rome at þat tyme, teching here errouris ful pryuyly, _{wrote 'De
Moribus}

8 be nyth specialy, ¶ for aspying. There at þe prayeꝛ of cristen _{Leaf 25,
back.}
men be mad too bokys. On hith De Moribus Manicheorum, the _{Manichaeo-}
oþir hith De Moribus Ecclesie Catholice. This is to sey in Englisch, _{rum'
and 'De}
of þe maneris of Manicheis, and of þe maneris of hem þat be in þe _{Moribus
Ecclesiae}

12 cristen feith. In on of þese bokes tellith he þat þe Manicheis held _{Catholicae,'
in one of}
heꝛ skoles be nyth, and þedir cam both men and women, and all _{which books
he tells how}
sodeynly aftir þe lesson, þe lith schuld be blow out and þan schuld _{the Mani-
chaeans held}
þei pley, as Wiclif disciples played, Sistir me nedith. In þis cyte _{their schools
by night}

16 eke, or he went ouyr þe se, mad he þe book of whech we spoke _{and played
'Sister me}
be-fore; it is cleped þe book of þe quantite of þe soule, whech is _{needeth,'}
mad [1] be maner of a dialoge be-twix him and his son Adeodatus, in _{like Wyclif's
disciples.}
whech book many sotil þinggis ar touchid whech long not to þis

20 maneꝛ of wryting þat is cleped narratyf. In þis same cite and _{Here also he
wrote 'De}
þis same tyme eke mad he a notable book þat is cleped De Libero _{Quantitate
Animae' and}
Arbitrio, þat is to sey, of þe fre choys þat a man hath to good or _{'De Libero
Arbitrio,' also}
to euele. This book was mad in maner a-geyn þe Manicheis, for _{against the
Mani-}

24 heꝛ he determineth a-gayn hem þat all euele spryngith of þis fre _{chaeans.}
choys, for þei seid þat euele was coeterne with God; so þei put to
þingis coeterne, on called þei good, þe oþir euele. All þis þing
witnesseth him-selue in his first book of his Retractaciones.

[CHAPTER XXIII.]

28 ¶ Who þei went all in fere fro Rome in-to Hostie. cap. xxiij.

THUS all þing sped at Rome for whech cristen men had _{Then all his
party went to}
reqwired him in defens of ouꝛ feith, with all his felauchip _{Ostia, the
port of Rome.}
¶ he went forth to Hostie. Hostie is a fayꝛ town xvj myle fro _{Leaf 26.}
32 Rome where þat Tibir rennyth in-to þe se, for Hostium in þe
Latyn tonge is a doꝛ, and þat is clepid so as a doꝛ of þe se. Theꝛ

---

[1] be mad *crossed through in red.*

One day he
and Monica,
leaning out
of a window,
lifted up their
hearts in
contempla-
tion and fell
into spiritual
communion.
þei abood þe wynd and mad hem redy for to sayle. So up-on
a day, as his moder and he stood lenyng out at a wyndown and
lokyng in a gardeyn whech longid on-to her, in fer fro pres of
puple þus a-lone, þei too talked ful sobirly of þe euyr-lestyn lif 4
whech is ordeyned for blessid soules. Thei talked so long þerof
and lyft[1] up her hertis in contemplacion of þat holy place, þat þei
had for-gete in maner þis world and all erdly þing, so wer þei
rauyschid with[2] her holy wordis. Thei stood stille both a grete 8
while and þout swech þingis as þei ooude not vttyr, and eke ageyn
in[3] her holy comunicacion þei fell. Tho saide sche on-to hir son
swech maner wordis: Son, as to my part, I telle I haue no delectacion in no maner þing þat is in þis world. What I schal do in þis 12
world, or why þat I am here so longe, I wote not veryly. Sumtyme
I desired to abyde þat I schuld se þe a trew oristen man or I deyid.
God hath graunted me þat and mech mor, for I se þe now nowt

Soon after-
wards a fever
took her,
and she lost
conscious-
ness, but
recovered
for a time,
and gave
those about
her instruc-
Leaf 26,
back.
tions as
to her burial
and their
remembrance
of her.
only a cristen man, but I se þe[4] a special seruaunt of God, for þou 16
hast despised all worldly felicite. This saide sche to hir son with
ful sobir chere, and with-inne v. dayes aftir sche fel in a feuer,
whech feuer encresed so sore up-on hir þat in maner as for a tyme
it had a-wey hir wittis. And whan sche was restored a-geyn to hir 20
wittis sche lokid on hir son, and þus sayd on-to him: Wher was I ?
Thei þat ‖ stood a-bout were al astoyned, and answered not. Than
spak sche a-gayn in þis maner: Ley þis body whan I am ded in
what place ȝe wil; haue no besynesse in no maner wher it schal be 24
byryed. O þing I pray ȝou of specialte, wher-euer ȝe be, at ony
aucter wher ȝe schal ministir þe holy sacrament, in þat place haue
of me sum special mynd. Sche had forgetyn, as Augustin tellith,
al her cuntr and þe byrying of hir husbond whech was mad ful 28
costly and a space left for hir wher sche schuld ly. For a litil
be-for her seknesse þei þat wer aboute hir, aftir grete communica-
cion of þe contempte of þe world and[5] of desire of good deth, þei

She was not
afraid to die,
inqwyrid of hir if sche was not aferd for to deye so fer fro hir 32
cuntr; sche answered to hem rith þus: No-þing is fer fro God.
I am no-þing a-ferd þat God schuld not knowe fro whens he schuld

---

[1] MS. left *with* y *written over in red.*
[2] MS. with with, *the first crossed through in red.*
[3] MS. in heli her; heli *dotted underneath.*   [4] *inserted in red above.*
[5] MS. and and; *the first crossed through in red.*

reise me. So þe ix day aftir þe seknesse took hiꝛ, þat religious and her soul was released
soule, þat meke soule, was losed fro þe body, þe ȝere of hir age ỻvj, in the fifty-sixth year of
þe ȝere of Augustyn age xxxiij. And many noble men and religious her age, as we read in the
4 women cam to hir exequies, as hir son tellith [in] þe ix book of his 'Confes-sions'. She
Confessiones. Thus was sche biried at Hostie and lay þere a mᵗ ȝeꝛ was buried at Ostia.
and moꝛ or sche was translate to Rome.

[CHAPTER XXIV.]

¶ The comendacioñ & þe orison of Augustiñ for his moder.
8 **xxiiij.**

IN þe nynth book of his Confessiones, in þe last ende, þere In his 'Confes-
touchith he þe deth of his modir and þe grete compleynt sions' he tells of the
mad for hiꝛ both be oþir men and be him. Thus aftir oþer complaint
12 þingis he seith of hir: Thi seruaunt, Lord, whom ‖ þou hast now Leaf 27.
take on-to þi mercy, as þou knowist & as I be-leue, aftir þat made at her death.
tyme þat sche had take þi feith and þi baptem, sche defouled Augustine says her
neuer hir lippis with no vnclennesse whech schuld be offense words were pure,
16 on-to þi lordchip ; no lesingis weꝛ founde in hir tonge, no slaunder,
no vice whech longith on-to þat membir. Thou saide, Lord, þat
what man with angri hert said on-to his broþir euele, or cleped
him fool, was gilty on-to þe peyne of helle. Here me, Lord, now and asks God to give
20 clepyng on-to þi grace for my moder whech stant in þi grace. her grace
Heꝛ me for þe medycyne of þoo woundis whech þi son souered
in his body for þe helth of ouꝛ soules. Forgif hir aꝉꝉ þe trespas and forgive her.
with whech sche offendid þe in þout, word, or werk. Entyr not
24 with hir in-to þi dom. Lete þi mercy flete aboue þi dom.
I hope veryly þat þou hast doo now al þat I pray þe, but ȝet
alowe my good wil whech i offer on-to þe for hir as a deute of
hir child. Sche bond hir soule on-to þe prys of thi blod whil She was pious while
28 sche lyued, for þere was no day left but sche wold be present she lived,
where þe sacrifise and þe memory of þi holy blod schuld be had
in mynde. Inspire, Lord, aꝉꝉ þe rederes of þis book þat, in presens and her son asks all
of þe sacrament of þe aucter, þei may haue of þe soules of Patrik, readers to think of her
32 my fader, and Monicha, my moder, deuoute mynde, be whos at sacra-ment.
flesch I was brout forth on-to þis wor[l]d¹: Many oþir holy
conceytes hath Augustiñ heꝛ if we had tyme to reherse hem.

---

¹ MS. word.

3

[CHAPTER XXV.]

¶ Aftir deth of his moder who he went in-to Cartage with his
felauchip. cap. **xxv.**

Whanñ his moder was ded and byried at Hostie, as we seid
be-for, with þe next wynd he and his felauchip sailed stieit 4
‖ on-to Cartage, whech was a grete cite and strong, and mech
named in þe world, specialy amongis marchaundis. I haue mynd
þat I haue red in Augustin bokes, I wot not now wheŕ, þat alĺ
marchanndise and al maneŕ makyng of schippis be-gan þeŕ. Theŕ 8
weŕ þei herborowid in a worthi mannes hous; þei cleped him
Innocent. This same Innocent, swech tyme as Augustin was
þere, had a greuous soŕ, whech soŕ myth not be hol, as þe lech
said, with-outen þat it weŕ slitte. The man was weyk and dred 12
mech þe knyf. So Augustin, meued of very compassion, prayed
deuoutly to God for helth of his hoost, and sodeynly he was hool.
Theŕ was gret merueyle of hem þat dwelt aboute, but þei alĺ

with grete deuocion þankid[1] God of his werkis. Of þis same 16
myracle don at Cartage spekith Augustin in þe xxij book of þe
Cite of God, [2]so feŕ[2] as þouȝ a-noþir man had do þe same. Fro
Cartage went þei hom to þe houses and[3] feldis þat longid on-to
Augustin of herytage. Thus leued þei alle of þo godis whech 20
weŕ left him be his frendis, not vsyng husbondry but seld, now
o part now an-oþir, for þei leued alĺ be þat possession ny iij ȝere.[4]
Augustin had take ȝet non ordres, but brout with him certeyn
prestis a-mongis þoo heremites whech he had of Simpliciane, and 24
þei alĺ folowyng þe steppes of þe apostoles, dwelt to-gidir in on

hous with o soule in prayeŕ and fasting, ‖ and he him-selue, swech
þingis as God had schewid to him, vttered it to oþir men in
writyng and teching, to her gret lernyng.   28

[CHAPTER XXVI.]

¶ What bokes he mad whil he leued þus in his owne possession
in þe town of Tagatenses. cap. **xxvj.**

Dwellyng þus in his owne possession he wrot too bokes
ageyn þe Manicheis, & þese cleped he De Genesi, for þere 32
tretith he mech of þe werkis of ouŕ Lord whech he wrout in þe

---

[1] o and a stroke crossed through.   [2-2] in margin.
[3] ad in text; and in margin.   [4] Thus crossed through.

begynnyng of þe world. Þeŕ al-so mad he an ende of vj bokes of Musik whech he be-gan at Melan. The first v. bokes ar not redyly founde, þe sexte is had wheŕ he tretith who we may ascende in owŕ
4 vndirstanding fro bodely and chaungable noumbres on-to goostly and permanent, whech permanent noumbres be in þat treuth whech is God. So he concludeth þat þoo inuisibil þingis whech be [1] in heuene ar vndirstand þe bettir for knowlech of bodely þingis whech God
8 mad in erde. He seith ferþermoŕ þat þouȝ þer be certeyn men heŕ in erde þat haue so dul wit þat þei can-not vndirstand þis mateŕ, ȝet if þei kepe treuly þe cristen feith, þei schul sumtyme se all þese þingis, & fele hem in swech sikirnesse þat þei may not
12 fayle. He seith eke þat summe men þat haue sotil wittis and vndirstand þis wel I-now, if it be so þat þei despise Crist, for al her [2] sotil kunnyng, þei schal be da[m]pned in hell. In þat same tyme eke, mad he a-noþir book þat is entitled þe [3] bok Of þe
16 Maistir. Þis bok is [4] ‖ in maner of a dialoge be-twix him and his son, for sone aftir þe bok was mad his son deyid. In þis book he seith þat þere is no very mayster to tech men þe treuth but God alone. That same tyme eke he mad a-noþir book whech
20 he nameth De Vera Religione, wheŕ he tretith þat þere is no trewe ne very religion in al þe world but in þe cristen feith.

[marginal notes:] and 'De Musica', five books of which are rare; in the sixth he treats of earthly things as symbolical of heavenly,

knowledge of which cannot save despisers of Christ.

Leaf 28, back.

He wrote also 'De Vera Religione'.

[CHAPTER XXVII.]

¶ What was þe cause whi he went first to Ypone. **xxvij.**

THUS lyued ouŕ maystir in holy study and contemplacion so þat his fame be-gan to sprede, what lyf he held and
24 what doctrine he comuned to hem þat cam on-to hym, [5] so þat þe lith of his doctrine myth not be hid but raþer spred him-selue þorw þe cuntŕ. Of him herd a certeyn rych man þat dwelt þat tyme at Ypone [6] swech meruelous tydyngis þat þe man was gretly
28 stered to se him a[n]d [7] speke with him. For whech cause he sent messageris and letteris on-to Augustin, in whech letteris he comendid gretly his cunnyng and special his deuocioñ, þat he

[marginal notes:] So he lived at Tagaste,

till a rich man who had heard of his fame desired to see him,

---

[1] *inserted above.*
[2] *r afterwards inserted.*
[3] *a letter crossed through.*
[4] *MS. is is.*
[5] *MS. hem with y written above.*
[6] *part of swech written and crossed through.*
[7] *MS. ad.*

and asked
Augustine to
go to Hippo,
for he was
ready to
follow him.
Augustine
went,

was only ʒoue to lernyng and good lyf, for whech exercise he had
despised al þis worldly felicite. This man wrote ferþermoꝛ þat
if he wold com to Ypone he was redy to forsake al þe couetyse
of worldly possession and folow his steppes in þe wey of God. 4
For þis cause Augustyn consented on-to þe man, hauyng[1] a grete
desire to wynne swech a soule to Goddis seruyse whech was
so defouled in worldly vanyte. A-noþir cause was þere eke,
for Augustyn þoutʒ he schuld lyue þere in moꝛ quiete *contemplacion* 8

Leaf 29.

þan at hom amongis his kynrod and aqueyntauns. ‖ For he is

having the
purpose also
of building
a monastery,
and met the
man, who,
however, was
not then
converted.

in very purpos to edifie a monastery and to lyue þerin with his
brether aftir þe forme and þe ordinauns of þe aposteles. Thus
is he come to Ypone, and þe man þat sent aftir him receyued 12
him ful worchipfully, but þe *principal* cause whech Augustin
supposed to spede, þat failed. For þe man herd deuoutly all
hise wordes but to þe very *contempt* of richesse coude he not
bring him as ʒet. Summe men suppose þat he cam to þat ende 16
aftirward, for, as þei sey, it myth not renne in veyn, þe labouꝛ

Of this
Augustine
speaks in
one of his
sermons,

þat ouꝛ Lord purueyid in so swete a vessel. That þese to þingis
weꝛ þe cause why þat Augustin went on-to Ypone, he witnessith
him-selue in a sermone intitled Of þe Comoñ Lif of Clerkis, wheꝛ 20
he seith þus: I, þat with þe grete *mercy* of God, ʒe se now ʒouꝛ

made after
he was a
bishop.

bischop, I cam ʒong on-to þis cite, and many of ʒow knowe.
I soute þat tyme a *conuenient* place where I schuld make a
monasterie, to lyue þere with my bretherin. I cam eke on-to 24
þis cite for to wynne my frend on-to God, þat he schuld lyue
with us eke in þe monasterie. Me-þout at þat tyme a sikir
comyng on-to þis cite, be-cause þei had a bischop. For þat
place whech had non I refused as suspecte, þat I schuld not 28
be chose.

[CHAPTER XXVIII.]

¶ Who he edified a monastery in desert for him and *certeyn*
heremites. **xxviij.**

At Hippo
he made the
acquaintance
of Bishop
Valerius,

HE had not longe dwelt at Ypone or he fel in[2] aqweyntauns 32
of Valery, bischop þan of þat cite. This Valerie was
a ful goodly man, fre-hertet and namely on-to straungeris. So

---

[1] MS. haue, e *crossed and* yng *written over in red.*   [2] q *crossed through.*

Augustin, not fer fro þe cite þorw his fauour, edified a monasterie
in desert, ‖ and sowt all þe wodes aboute, for all þe heremites
whech he myth fynde he gadered in-to o congregacion, as he
4 witnessith in a sermon writyn on-to þe prestes of Ypone and
alleggid be-fore, wher he seith þus: As ȝe know, I cam on-to
þis cyte with my welbeloued frendis Euodio, Simplicio, Alipio,
Nebridio & Anastasio. I cam hidir with a maner of a sikirnesse,
8 for I wist wel þat þe good fader Valerius was bischop her. I cam
hidyr, not for to haue powere ouyr ȝou in dignite, but for to
dwelle as an outcast in þe hous of our Lord all þe dayes of my lyf.
I cam hidir, not for to receyue seruyse of oþer men, but for to
12 lyve¹ pesibily in desert with my breþerin. I brout no richesse
with me, but fauoured with þe grace of our Lord and with þe
good help of þe old man Valerie, I mad a monasterie here in
desert with grete labour and bisinesse, whech monasterie stant
16 alone fer fro þe puple, and with grete þout I haue gadered þere
seruauntes of God whech dwelt alone, disparplied be þe wodes,
and þere begunne we for to lyue after þe maner and þe forme
of þe aposteles lif, þat all our godis schul go in comon and no
20 man haue no maner þing propir to him-selue. Thus lyue þei²
in prayer, and wecch, and fasting, & many oþer vertues mor þan
we may now expresse. That þis good old bischop gaue fauour
and god on-to edifiyng³ of þis first monasterie witnessith Augustin
24 eke in þe forsaid sermone, Vt nobis per litteras, wher he seith
þus on-to þo same heremites: ȝe be my vyne, chosen of me, sette
in þe myddis of þe cherch, as þouȝ it ‖ were in þe myddis of
paradys. This vyne haue I, in þe vertu of God, gadered to-gydyr,
28 and werkmen haue I sette⁴ þere þat þei schuld trauayle and
bryng forth frute in her tyme. To þis vyne I haue chose ȝou,
to þis heritage I haue gadered ȝou, with þe fauour of þe holy
man Valery, whech of þe cherch godis ȝaue me grete plente to
32 þe edificacion of my monastery, for my patrimonie myth not
suffise to þe⁵ grete expense and he had not holpe me.

Marginal notes:
Leaf 29, back. through whose favour he edified a monastery in the desert and near the city, as he tells in a sermon. He went to Hippo for humility and not for dignity,

and in his monastery were gathered the hermits from the woods,

who passed their time in watching and fasting.

In his sermon he speaks of the help of Valerius, Leaf 30.

who gave him goods of the church.

---

¹ *word wrongly written and altered in red.*
² *in margin in red,*   ³ *MS.* edifieng *with* y *written over.*
⁴ þidir *crossed through.*   ⁵ *added in red in margin.*

[Chapter XXIX.]

¶ Of þe noumbyr of þo heremytes whech he gadered, and of her holy conuersacion. cap*itulum* **xxix.**

IN þis same monastery Augustin, or he were prest, gadered a grete noumbyr of heremites whech lyued, as we sayde 4 be-for, aftir þe forme and þe ordinauns of þe apostoles, and he her[1] began þat ordr whech we clepe at þis day, and þe cherch of Rome clepith hem þe same in all þe bullis of her preuylegis, þe ordre of þe heremites of Seynt Augustyn. First dwelt þei 8 in dyu*er*s wodes, her on and þere anoþer, and euerych of hem lyued as hym lyked tyl þat our auctour gadered hem to-gidyr & mad of anachorites cenobites. He spekith him-selue[2] of hem[2] in þe *sermone* often rehersid, þus: I cam in-to Affrik, my good 12 modyr ded, & edified, as 3e se, a monastery in desert ferr fro dwell-yng of men. And blessed be God, I haue gadered þere a noumbir of breþerin whos hertis are so inspired with gostly lith þat not only þei be folower*is* of holy faderis whech lyued in solitarie 16 lif, but now þei folow þe noble s'teppes of þe aposteles, for al þing is comon on-to hem. Many faderis wer be-for me whom for to folow is ful profitable, but non of hem went nyher þe apostoles lif þan I. Therfor ‖ may I sey þat I am fader and hed 20 of 3ou all. The habite of þis ordr was a blak cope girt with a girdil of ledir with-outen ony barr, as he witnessith in þe forsaid *sermone*, hauy*ng* þese wordes on-to þe prestis þat dwelt in þe monasterie: Go to myn heremites and lerne of hem to be 24 meke of hert, pore of spirit, and childyrn of obediens. Loke if 3e be swech as þei be. Wold God 3e were swech as I fynde hem. 3e be renneres a-boute þe cyte; and þei fle þe sith of men. 3e be arayed with dyu*er*s colour*is* and dyuers furris; þei 28 are content with a blak cloth. 3e haue girdilis lich knytys; and þei with þongis of chamel skynnys, as Hely and Ion, go[3] girt in her lendes. To þese same heremites mad he a book of certeyn reules, who þei schuld lyue, whech reules he cleped þe Margarites of 32 Paradise, and þei be comprehendid in þe first *sermone* þat he

---

[1] *in red in margin.*

[2-2] *added above in red.*

[3] *l crossed through.*

mad to hem [1] whech sermone beginnyth, Fra*tres* mei & leticia cordis mei.   Many of þo same put he aftirward in his reule whech he called a Mero*ur* *as* [2] a man may sone p*er*seyue.

compre-
hended in
his first
sermon to
them.

[Chapter XXX.]

4   ¶ Who Augustin was chose prest of þe monaster*ie* vndir Valery þe bischop, to haue þe reule of þe cherch.   **xxx.**

IN þis same tyme þe prest of þe cherch at Ypone was ded, and þis Valer*ius* gadered þe puple and þe clergie to ordeyn a 8 new successo*ur* whech schuld be*r* al þe charge of þe cherch, for þe bischop was old and myth not labou*r*; he was alsoo a Grek of birth [3] and coude not p*ar*fithly þe langage of þat cu*n*tre.   A-mongis all oþir Valery sent for Augusti*n*, and before all þe puple sayde it 12 was þe custom ∥ þat þei schuld haue þe chois, but neu*er*-þe-lasse [4], þe puple knew wel be certeyn toknes þat he wold preferre Augusti*n* to þis dignite.   Augusti*n* be-cause he had take ȝet non ordres stood a-mong*is* þe puple in a man*er* of a sikyrnesse, as he þout þat no 16 man schuld chese him be-cause he was not in ord*r*.   Thus as he stood, sodeynly all þe puple chase him with o voys, leyd handis up-on hym, and as þe man*er* was, p*re*sented him on-to þe bischop.   He wepte, and with-drow him meruey*ling* sore þat þei we*r* þus set on 20 him, allegg*ing* þe *per*el of þat dignite to haue gouernau*n*s of so grete a puple; but þe mo*r* he refused it þe mo*r* þei desired him, and cryed fo*r* þat Augusti*n* schuld be her prest.   Thus was he brout on-to þe bischop, and he, with ful grete reu*er*ens and deuo-24 cio*n*, gaf him his ordres.   Afftir he was þ*us* mad prest of þe cherch he dwelled stille with his h*er*emites whos felauchip he had eu*er* desired, but þe bischop say wel þat it was ouyr fer*r* fro þe cite euyr for to go to and fro, ånd þe occupacio*n* of þe cherch was 28 grete, þe desi*r* eke of Augustin eu*er* for to be with his h*er*emites, of grete discrecio*n* ordeyned þis mene whech fulfillid [5] both þing*is*, þat is to seye, þat [6] þe cherch schuld be wel s*er*uyd with þe presens of

The priest of
the church
at Hippo
being dead,

Valerius
asked the
Leaf 31.
people to
choose a
successor,

and they all
cried out for,
Augustine.

He wept and
refused,

but they
insisted, and
he was
invested by
Valerius.
Yet when he
was priest he
dwelt still
with his
hermits.

---

[1] MS. to hem to hem, *the first crossed through in red.*

[2] and *crossed through and as written over in red.*   [3] h *added in red.*

[4] þe-lasse *added above in red.*   [5] fulfill *in text,* llid *in red in margin.*

[6] t *added in red.*

Augustin, and eke he schuld not be fer fro his welbeloued heremites.
The mene was þis, þat a fayr̃ place schuld be mad fast be þe
monasterie and certeyn[1] heremites schuld be chose fro þe first
place and dwell in þe secund with whech our̃ Augustin myth 4
speke whan he list.   This was fulfillid in-dede, and summe of þe
best of þis first[2] monasterie[3] wer̃ drawe to þis secund, and Augustin
gadered to her̃ noumbir mo owt of ‖ þe world, not lewid men but
clerkys and lerned men, and þere sette he hem in þe same reule 8
þat þe first monastery had, þat þei schuld lyue in comoñ, and no
man to haue noþing propir to him-self.   This same processe
writith þis doctour ful pleynly in a sermone De Communi Vita
Clericorum, allegged be-fore, and in a-noþir sermoñ to þe prestis of 12
Ypone begynnyng, In omnibus operibus uestris.

[CHAPTER XXXI.]

¶ Who Augustin lerned þese men of þe secund monasterie, &
who he prechid eke in presens of his bischop.   Capitulum xxxj.

THESE men þus chosen to þe secund monasterye studied in 16
dyuy[ni-]te[4] and in morall bokes at þe comaundment of her
maystir, for he lerned hem so þat þei schuld come to þe cite to
preche þe puple & edifye hem with Goddis word.   The bischop
Valery, seyng þe grete cunnyng of Augustin, and eke þe grete 20
desir̃ þat he had to preche þe word of God, þankid God often sithe
þat he had sent him in his age so good a viker̃.   For, as he seid to
þe puple, his prayer was herd whech he had long prayed, þat God
schuld send him swech a man þat myth edifie his puple both with 24
exaumple and doctryne.   For he him-self was not rith redy to
swech þingis, for he was not gretly letteryd, and eke born he was
of þe Grek tonge and coude not mech skil on Latyn bokes whech
wer̃ vsed most in þe prouynce of Cartage.   Wherfor̃ he graunted 28
Augustin leue a-geyn þe custom of þe cherchis of Affrik to prech in
þe cherch in his presens.   For whech þing many oþir bischoppis
grucchid a-geyn þis new custom, be he rowt not, ne sette no pryse

---

[1] MS. her *crossed through.*   [2] *added in red at margin.*
[3] *wat crossed through.*
[4] MS. dyuyte *with contraction mark over first y.*

be swech grucching *tongis* þe whilis þat Augusti*n* supplied[1] swech
good ‖ werkis whech he coude not do him-selue. For be þe prechyng Leaf 32.
of Augusti*n* many soules were gote*n* to God.   He ferd lich a gret and by this means many
4 lith sette all on hy, þat all men in þe grete hous of our Lord[2] had were brought to God.
direccion in her werkys be his schyny*n*g.   This ensau*m*ple ran oute Throughout Africa this
þorw þe lond of Affrik, þat þo *prestis* whech weꝛ wel-lerned men example was followed.
had leue to *preche* in *presens* of her bischoppis.   And as we saide
8 be-fore, Augustin gat leue of Valery þat[3] þese *heremites* whech
dwelt in þe secund monastery were admitted to preche and
schryue, not alle, but þoo whech were lerned in diuinite and
custu*m*ablely vsed in good lyf.   This witnessith he in þat *sermone* Augustine speaks of
12 often alleggid, Vt *bene* nostis, where he seith þus: Tho bretherin the preaching of the
sette in þe monasterie whech ouꝛ good fader Valery endewid, þou3 brethren in the mona-
it be so þat þei dwelle not in þe cite, be-cause heꝛ fame was[4] mech stery en-dowed by
boꝛ a-mong*is* þe puple, þ*er*for haue I ordeyned þat þei[5] schul preche Valerius, in
16 þe word of lif on-to þe puple, and bry*n*g trew soules be heꝛ gode one of his sermons.
ensau*m*ples to Him þat mad al of nowt.   Behold who þai deme þe
erde and by*n*de it & lose swech as þei wil eu*er* with þe fauouꝛ
of God.

[CHAPTER XXXII.]

20   ¶ Who he disputed with a grete *heretik* clepid Fortunat*us* and
conuicte hi*m* of heresie.   **xxxij.**

I*N* þat same tyme þe heresie of þe Manicheis encresid i*n* þe At that time the Mani-
cite of Ypone, þorw labouꝛ and doct*rine* of a grete capteyn chaean heresy was advanced
24 of hem cleped Fortunate, whech had *peruerted* many soules fro þe in Hippo
trewe feith.   For whech cause þe best citeceynes requyred heꝛ by Fortuna-tus, and the
prest, Augustin, to speke with þis Fortunat, & refelle, if he myth, people asked Augustine to
þe heresie with whech he had deseyued many soules.   Augusty*n*, contest him.
28 whech was redy ‖ to answere eu*er*y man and for to talk of þe feith, Leaf 32,
hope and[4] charite whech weꝛ plenteuously with-inne him, forsok back.
not þis conflicte, but obeied rydily heꝛ peticioꞃ, inqwyri*n*g of hem
if Fortunate wold consente to þis dede.   Tho went þei to Fortunate,
32 and reqwyrid him with swech instau*n*s þat he myth not denye heꝛ

---

[1] *a character crossed through.*   [2] *in red in margin.*
[3] *þ and a stroke crossed through.*   [4] *w crossed through.*
[5] *added above in red.*   [4] *w crossed through.*

desi?. Thus is þe day come of þis comunicacioñ; grete puple is

Augustine
met him and
had notaries
to record his
words.

gadered and notaries sette on both sides whech schuld repoit treuly
þe wordis þat we? saide. For þis was euyr þe practik of Augustin
whan he schuld dispute with ony heretik, to write he? wordes, þat 4
þei schuld not denye o tyme whech þei graunted anoþer tyme.

The contro-
versy lasted
two days, and
was on the
origin of evil.

Too dayes lestid þis disceptacioñ. The question disputed amongis
hem was þis, Fro whens þat euel comth. Augustin held þis
opinion, þat euel be-gynnyth in a man rith of his fre choys, for 8
þere schuld no euel be in him but he wold. Fortunate held þat
euel was a natu? coeterne with God, þat is to sey, euene as God
hath be, euyr so hath þat natu? euele[1] euyr be. In þis disputacioñ

Fortunatus
was van-
quished by
Augustine
and fled.
This is all
recorded in a
book.

þis Fortunat coude not hurt Augustin with[2] non argument, ne his 12
owne opinione coude he not defende, so faylyng in his answeres
& foule aschamed, he fled oute of þe cuntre, and þat heresie whech
[3]he held[3] fel fro euery mannes hert. This act sette Seynt Augustin
in a book, þat men aftirward schuld knowe þe conflict be-twix hem. 16

At this time,
too, he made
a book on

In þis same tyme mad he anoþir book whech he clepith Of þe[4]
Sermoñ of Crist saide in þe hiħ, where he hath a notable exposicion

Leaf 33.

up-on þe Pater-Noster, ‖ for þat same is a grete part of þat sermon
whech Crist sayde in þe hiħ. Thus prechid þat nobil prest, Augustin, 20

the Sermon
on the
Mount.

with grete auctorite distroyed heresie and planted new religioñ, so
þat his name[5] was spred þorw þe lond.

[Chapter XXXIII.]

¶ Who Augustyn was chose bischop Vale[r]y lyuyng in þat see.
cap. **xxxiij.**

24

All this time
Valerius
feared that
Augustine
might be
appointed
bishop in
another city,
and there-
fore wrote to
the bishop of
Cartage.

Amongis aħ þe ioye þat þis bischop Valery had for ou? Lord
had sent him swech a preest, he caute with þat a gret fe?,
and in partye a gelosie, þat Augustyn schuld not go fro hym, and
be chose a bischop in a-noþer cyte. For þat same had he do or 28
þis tyme had not Valery sent him owt of þe weye, wenyng to
many men þat he schuld not sone come a-geyn. For þis cause he
sent priuy letterys to þe bischop of Cartage, primate of þat lond,

---

[1] u crossed through.   [3] o crossed lhrough. .
[3-3] in margin in red.   [4] cr crossed through.
[5] added above in red.

þat Augustyn schuld be promoted to þis dignite, in whech let*t*res <small>asking for his appointment in Hippo.</small>
he alleggid his age, his febilnesse, and eke who he was not redy in
langage to erudicioῆ of þe puple and destrucciou of heresie as
4 Augustin was. The bischop of Cartage þat knew Augusti*n* wel
sent down let*t*eris of confirmacion þat aḥ þat Valery had reqwyrid
him he held ferme and stable. This bischop of Cartage was <small>He gathered the primates of Africa at Hippo,</small>
primate þorw aḥ Affrik, þan was þere anoþir bischop primate of
8 al Numidie, and for him sent Valery, and eke for a-noþir worthi
man, þei clepid him Megasie, bischop of a cite clepid Orilamense;
mo bischoppis sent he foῆ and clerkys to Ypone, and whan þei were
gadered to-gidyr, be-fore þe puple sodeynly he vttir his desire þat <small>and there asked that Augustine</small>
12 Augustin schuld be bischop and þei both schuld lyue to-gidyr in <small>Augustine</small>
comoῆ of þe ‖ ¹cherchis good. The puple, whaῆ þei herd þis, þei <small>Leaf 33, back.</small>
þankid God heyly and with o uoys þei cryed þat Augustyn schuld <small>should be appointed bishop, while he lived. Augustine demurred, for the appointment was against the statutes of the church,</small>
be bischop. He mad grete allegaunce ageyn þis elecciou and seide
16 it was not con*n*enient þat þei schuld chese a-new, þe old lyuyng, but
for aḥ þat he coῧde say, Valerie is desiῆ was fulfillid, and Augustyn
consecrate, and þe cure leyd only in him. And a-geyn þis maneῆ
of eleccion wrot Seynt Augustyn aftirward to þe court of Rome, þat
20 he schuld be excused of his errouῆ, for þere was mad a statute of
holy cherch in þe counceḥ at Antioche, þat þere schuld no bischop
make a-noþer whil he lyued, as it is pleynly con*t*eyned in þe decres²,
cap*it*ulum viij, qu*aestione* 1., episcopo non licet. So Seynt Augustin <small>but the appointment was made.</small>
24 wold not þat þing do, in him not rithfully schuld not be drawe to
oþir men in³ ensaumple. Thus whan he was bischop with gretteῆ
auctorite and more feruent loue, he prechid þe word of God, nowt
only in his owne diosise, but wheῆ-euyr he was reqwyred, most
28 specialy wheῆ heresie regned, þidir went he to defende þe feith.

[Chapter XXXIV.]

¶ Off þe þird monasterie whech he gadered of chanones with-inne þe paleys. cap. xxxiiij.

Whanῆ he was mad bischop he say weel þat for þe grete <small>Augustine saw that, as a bishop, he must keep a household,</small>
32 multitude of causes & þe grete prees of straungeris þat
daily cam on-to him, he must hold a houshold, and he myth not go

---

¹ cherchis *wrongly written and crossed through.*
² þe secunde *crossed through.* ³ *written small above.*

and therefore
he chose
certain good
to his refecoion eu*er*y day to neþir of þese to monasteries of whech
we spoke, þerfor he chase certeyn prestis of good lyf and gret
Leaf 34.
lettiruꝛ to leue with him in þat college, and ǁ þo same men bonde
priests to
dwell with
him aus-
terely in a
'college',
whence come
the Canons
called now
Augustinian,
to leue vndir obediens, chastite and fro p*ro*pirte of temp*or*al richesse, 4
as þo heremites lyued in þe to monasteries saide be-fore. And owt
of þis colege cam þese chanones þat ar called at þis day of ordꝛ of
Seint Augustin, þouȝ it be so þat þei be distincte in oþer habite
þan¹ þei þat weꝛ with Seint Augustin, for þei went in dyu*er*s 8
colouri*s* a[n]d² furri*s*, as chanones do now in cathedral cherchis.
But be-cause þat þese chanones in blak habite kepe moꝛ streytly
þe reule of Seynt Augustin, as touch*i*ng þat poynt to lyue in
comoꝛñ, þerfor, I suppose, þat þei be nyher Seynt Augustin þan þe 12
othir.³ And þerfor is þere meued a question in þe lawe wheþir
and concern-
ing whom
there is
moved a
question as to
the rule.
þe chanones of cathedral cherchis be bounde þorw-oute þe world
for to kepe þe reule of þis doctour whech he⁴ mad on-to hem, & it
is cleped De Vita Clericor*um*, or nowt, and þei sey nay þerto, for 16
be-cau*s*e he myth bynde⁵ no cherch but his owne. Wherfor me
semeth þat þo chanon*is* whech be clepid reguleꝛ ar moꝛ ny Seint
This third
monastery is
mentioned in
Augustine's
sermon, and
also the
reason for its
establish-
ment.
Augustin þan þoo þat be clepid seculeꝛ. This same glori*ous*
doctouꝛ in a famous sermone whech he mad of þe comoꝛñ lif of 20
clerkys, and it beginnyth Propter q*uo*d nolui & rogaui, makyth
mynde of þis þirde monas*te*rie in swech maneꝛ wordes: It
plesid God for to sey on-to me þat I schuld ascende to hier degre,
for aftir þe tyme þat my fame was bore in þe puple, I be-gan to 24
drawe me fro eu*er*y place whech wanted a bischop. But a seruaunt
may not sey nay to his lord. Wherfor, whan I was mad bischop,
I aspied wel þat I must chere men þat ca*m* on-to me with mete
Leaf 34,
back.
and drynk, for if I ded not, I schuld ǁ be hald on-gentil, and if I led 28
my gestis on-to þo monasteries whech I haue mad, þe custom
schuld not be good, for þe most p*ar*t of þo *h*eremites desire not
mech to haue grete conuersacioñ with þe puple. This was þe
cause whi þat I gadered þese clerkis in o colege with-inne þe hous 32
or þe place whech longith principaly to the bischoprich. These
same wordes hath he in a sermone to þe same pr*e*stis of Ypone
whech be-gynnyth: In omn*ibus* op*eribus* vestris. Many þingis

---

¹ *written wrongly and n written above.*   ² MS. ad.
² *þer crossed through.*   ⁴ *written small above.*
                  ³ *written small above.*

myth we plant in here, who þat he loued bettyr þe felauchip of
þe heremites þan of þe prestis in þe cathedral cherch, and [1] what The priests
grucching þe same prestis made a-geyn þis affeccioñ, but alł þis were jealous of the
4 I ley be-side and wil procede to þe oþir part of his lif. hermits.

[CHAPTER XXXV.]

¶ Who þese heremites weŕ founde be þe possession of þe cherch
and what worthy men grew of his college. **xxxv.**

NOWT only þe prestis of þe colege were founde and fedde with
8 þe possession of þe cherch, but eke þe heremites had part,
þouȝ heŕ part weŕ not so [2] plenteuous as was þe oþir. In a In one of his
sermone þat he mad on-to þe same heremites, entitled, Of prayer, sermons, 'Of prayer,' he
he makith mynde of þis mateŕ, and þus he seith : Be not wery of speaks of the blessedness of
12 ȝouŕ prayer, for ȝe haue bettir leyseŕ to pray þan summe oþir hermit-life, and how he
haue. ȝe be not ordeyned for to gouerne oþir men, but [3] for to cared for the hermits.
leue in solitary lyf and deuoute prayeŕ to God. And þat ȝe
schuld pray þe more hertly, and not be lettyd with no cold whech
16 schuld withdrawe ȝouŕ deuocioñ, for þis cause, of swech godes as
longe to þe cherch of Ypone, I haue ▯ do mad ȝou clothis & hosyn Leaf 35.
and schon þerto an hundred and xł, whech I wil þat þei be kept in
a comoñ vestiary, þat euery man may haue part as him nedith.
20 Thus norchid þis noble man þese pore creatures, and on þe othir Others who
side þoo persones þat dwelt with him in þe cherch he lerned hem dwelt with him he
dyuynyte, for at euery mel [4] had þei notable communicacioñ of holy taught divinity.
scriptuŕ, and euer alle þe answeres must fynaly come fro Augustiñ.
24 Owt of his hous, as we rede, him lyuyng, were chose x bischoppes [5], Out of his house ten
men of gret lettiruŕ and of parfith lyf. For many famous men at bishops were chosen, and
þoo dayes, seing þe grete perfeccioñ and holy conuersacioñ of þat many famous men
felauchip whech Augustyn had drawe on-to him, forsok all þe joined him,
28 pomp of þe world, com and lyued with him in ful gret perfeccioñ,
summe a-mongis þe heremites, summe a-mongis þe prestis, euery
man aftir þat he sauored. And many of hem, whañ þei had be
with him ȝeres and were roted in religioñ, with his leue went fro

---

[1] *of crossed through in red.*   [2] *written in red above.*
[3] *written in red above.*   [4] *written in red in margin.*
[5] *s added in red.*

and some of
his men
founded
monasteries
in other
lands. him in-to oþir cuntres, mad monasteries, gadered felauchip and so
encresid his ordre, not only in Ypone, but þorw þe lond, him
lyuyng.

[CHAPTER XXXVI.]

¶ Of þe maneres and þe habite of Seynt Augustin aftir he was 4
bischop. **xxxvj.**

In all things
Augustine
was sober
and serious,
exhorting
religious
people, and
cheerful to
seculars.
Leaf 35,
back. THIS same glorious doctouȝ, fader and norcher of clerkys, in
his habite, in goyng, in sittyng, in his wordes, contenauns
and maneres, was of swech sadnesse þat euery man whech cam to 8
his presens was edified be him.   To religious men and women he
was in his exhortaciones sad and sobir, ȝeuyng hem grete ensaumple
who þei schuld do.   To othir ‖ seculeȝ men þat were occupied in
þe world he was familiaȝ, and in his talkyng had on-to hem in 12
maneȝ of mery langage with stedfast cheȝ of sadnesse.   The o puple
coumforted he with sad talking to conferme hem in heȝ holinesse.
The oþir puple gadered he on-to a perfeccioñ with goostly myrth
He corrected
wrong-doers
gently. and deuoute iocundnesse.   Transgressiones a-geyn Cristis law or 16
his holy preceptis he correctid not boystously, but fadirly and in
fayre maneȝ, þat many euele men, seing his swete correccioñ, weȝ
His clothes
were neither
costly nor
wretched, þe rather turned fro synne.   His cloþis whech he wered dayly,
& his cloþis þat serued to his bed, þei weȝ not ouyr costful, ne 20
ouyr wrecched [1], but in þe most mesurable maneȝ, he ordeyned þei
schuld be.   In summe men we lakkyn þe grete cost of aray, and
but made in
the mid-way. with summe ar we wroth with heȝ sluttynesse.   Þerfor went þis
man þe myd weye, þat he schuld ȝeue ensaumple in cloþing to hem 24
þat weȝ [2] his foloweris, and oþir men whech weȝ not of his skole
schuld haue no mateȝ of detraccioñ.   Thus spekith he in a famous
He desired
no man to
give him
costly clothes,
which would
distinguish
him from his
brethren. sermon þat begynnyth: Caritati vestre.   I wil þat no man ȝyue
to me so precious cloþis whech þat I, as of a specialte a-boue oþir, 28
schuld weȝ.   Ensaumple he puttith.   I sette case þat sum man
gyue me an amyse moȝ precious þan I am wone to were, þat
I schuld haue swech a singuler þing passyng all my breþerin.
Vphap it semeth a bischop for to were swech on, þouȝ it semeth 32
not Augustyn a pore man, born of mene men.   For if I receyued

---

[1] d *added above.*   [2] her *crossed through.*

swech a þing and wered it, ‖ men schuld sey þat I haue founde[1] Leaf 36.
moꝛ precious garmentis in þe cherch þan I myth haue had in my
faderes hous. Lete men gyue me swech cloþis þat in nede my He required only clothing
4 breþerin, be þei prestis, dekenes or subdeknes, may were þe same. such as any
I am a-knowe be-for God and ȝou þat of a *precious* cloth I am of his brethren
a-schamed, for it is non *pertinent* to ouꝛ profession, ne *conuenient* might wear.
to my white herȝs.

[CHAPTER XXXVII.]

8   ¶ Of his diete and seruyse at his table. cap. **xxxvij**.

L YTIL mete for þe most partye vsed he at his table, for he He ate little
   had more delectacioñ in þe herying of holy lessones and at table, and lived
talkyng aftir up-on þe same þañ in bodely mete. Flesch ete he mostly on roots and
12 but seldom, and þat was whañ he had gestis; wortes and letuse lettuce.
and swech herbis ete he most. I trowe þat he had þe vse of Itaile
whilles he studied þere, and coude not litly out of þe same vse, for
þei ete not mech at onys. Wyn drank he euyr ful mesurablely, He drank little wine,
16 and þat medeled with watyr, for þe wyn of þat cuntꝛ is hoot. and that diluted. All
Swech mete and drynk[2] as he had in vse was not warned to no were free to
man þat wold ask it, weꝛ þei dwelleris of þe cite, weꝛ þei his table.
strauñgeris. A-mongis all oþir vices he hatyd gretly detraccion, He hated detraction,
20 specialy at mel, for a-geyn þat vis had he writyn at his table þese and had two lines against
too vers: Quisquis amat dictis absentem rodere vitam, Hanc mensam it engraved
vetitam nouerit esse sibi. Þis is to sey in Englisch: What man on the common
with wordis absent bitith his broþeris name, This bord fro him board.
24 forbodyn it is with blame. Sumtyme þei þat sat þeꝛ wold speke
largely of hem þat weꝛ absent, & þanñ ‖ wold Augustyn say on-to Leaf 36,
hem þat, but þei wold leue her detraccioñ, he must rase oute þo back.
vers. Eke sumtyme whan þei wold not leue lithly, he wold rise
28 and go fro hem fastyng. Grete wast was not in his hous of sotil No great delicacies
metes. For on a tyme certeyn gestis schuld dyne with him, and were to be had in his
a licorous felaw a-mongis hem stert in-to þe kechyn to loke what house.
mete was þere in araying, and fond þe hous cold. Tho cam he
32 on-to þe bischop and inqwyrid of him what mete he had ordeyned
for his gestis, and Augustiṅ answered him þat he knew no moꝛ
þan he. Deuoute puple cam moꝛ to him for goostly *communica-*

---

[1] *p crossed through.*   [2] *written above in red.*

Upon the poor he had compassion and gave them of the church's goods.

cioñ þan bodely mete. Vp-on pore men had he grete compassion, and gaf hem largely of þe cherchis good. For sumtyme made þe vesseles of syluyr whech longed on-to þe cherch to be molten, and þe weggis þerof be sold and departed to poꝛ men. And whañ he 4 was in grete nede þat he myth not[1] gyue hem whech weꝛ in myschef, þañ wold he openly denouns þis to þe puple, and þei[2]

He gave little to his kindred,

wold brynge him sufficiens to his entent. To his kynrod also he wold gyue part of þat same cherchis good, but in no grete plente, 8 for he wold help hem with þat good, but not make hem rich. Thus spekith he in þis mateꝛ in þat same sermon þat beginnith,

saying that the goods of the church were for the poor,

Vt nobis per *litt*eras: We bischoppis may not haue þese tempo*ral* godes of þe cherch as ouꝛ possessioñ, ne I þat am a bischop haue 12

Leaf 37.

not þese godes to non oþir entent but for to dispense & departe hem on-to pore men, for þe godes of þe cherch ‖ þei be þe patri- monie of poꝛ men. And þerfor I must be ful war þat I take not þe godes of my cherch fro poꝛ men and gyue it rich men, and God 16 be þankid, I haue in þis mateꝛ do wel on-to þis tyme. For I haue mech folk of my kynrod, and summe of hem rich and wel at ese, and summetyme come þai to me with þretis, sumtyme with fayꝛ

and there- fore he had never en- riched his own people. Poor men were nearer his heart than rich men.

wordis, and þus þei sey: Fader, we be þi flesch & þi blood; gyue 20 us sum of þat good þat þou hast in dispensacioñ. And for aꝛ heꝛ crying, þankid be God and ȝouꝛ gode prayeres, I haue no mynde þat euyr I mad with þe cherchis godes ony of my kynrod rych. Pore men be moꝛ ny myn hert þan rych men, for we[3] þat be 24 cleped in-to þe paꝛfite lif in þe cherch, if we haue cloth and mete, we schuld be *content* with-al, and in tokne þerof be ouꝛ hedes schaue al baꝛ, þat euene as þe her is baꝛ þeꝛ, so schuld ouꝛ hertis be voyd fro couetise.   23

[Chapter XXXVIII.]

¶ Off his *conuer*sacion and oþir blessid condiciones whech he had and vsed. Capi*tul*um xxxviij.

He was kind to orphans, widows, and sick men.

FADERLES childyrn and widowes[4] whañ þei weꝛ in ony tribulacioñ he wold visite, and seke men eke with his owne 32 handis wold he lefte and coumfort, and sumtyme þo whech he

---

[1] *written in red above.*   [2] *written in red above.*
[3] *written above.*   [4] *þ crossed through.*

visite weᵽ made hool and sound. Theᵽ weᵽ certeyn men whech He cast out
weᵽ vexid with wikkid spiritis and he prayed for hem, and þei spirits;
were hool. In þe xxij book of þe Cyte of God he tellith too
4 myracules of him-selue in swech maner as þow a-noþir man had
do hem. I knew, he seith, a virgine at Ypone whech virgine he healed a
receyued¹ oyle of a prest, and whech tyme² sche had anoynted Hippo
hir with þe same oyle and þe prest with bittir teris prayed ‖ for Leaf 37,
8 hir, sche was hol. A-noþir tale he tellith þere; he seyth he knew back.
a bischop þat prayed for a ჳong man in whom þe deuele had prayers;
entered, and a-non, aftir his prayeᵽ, þe ჳong man was hool. out a devil.

To elde men was þis fader a very noryce and supported hem He cared for
12 with ful grete reuerens, as men may rede in a sermon whech he in a sermon
mad a-geyn ydilnesse, and it beginnyth: Apostolus Petrus, wheᵽ young monks
he seith þus: If it be so þat þere be a-mongis ჳou in ჳouᵽ the aged and
monasterie eld men þat passe iiij score ჳere, whech haue lyued in them,
16 clennesse of body and soule many ჳeres, and endewred in holy
exercise, þat is to seyn, fastyng, wakyng, and oþir bodyly penauns,
These men fro þat age forward schul beᵽ non office ne no charge of
þe monastery, for þei ded whil þei myth. Grucch ჳe not þat be
20 ჳonger, þouჳ þei do not now as þei ded sumtyme, for þei³ may not.
If þei rest whan ჳe labouᵽ, merueyle not. If þei be worchippid of me
as elde faderes schuld be, lete no heuynesse take ჳou, for þei be wel
worthi to receyue swech worchip. Therfor we wil, and in þe name
24 of Crist here we ordeyn, þat þei þat drawe to þe age of a hundred and ordains
ჳere, þei schal sitte stille in her beddis and sey her Pater-noster, nearing the
and ჳe with-outen grucching schul serue hem. This seruyse schul should be
ჳe do with þe bettir wil, for I wil þat ჳe knowe who þe conuersa- rest.
28 cioñ of hem is now in heuene, and ჳe schal þe sonneᵽ com þidir
be-cause of heᵽ prayer. A-noþir condicioñ had þis glorious Seynt Augustine
þat he wold neuyr occupie him-selue with non ⁋ worldly occupacioñ, Leaf 38.
for hous ne feld wold he neuyr bye, and many heritages þat men himself never
32 wold leue on-to him he forsook hem; he seid it was moᵽ conuenient affairs, but
þat her childyrn schuld haue hem þan þe cherch. The charge of yearly
his houshold, both in receyuyng and in paying, he committed stewards,
on-to þe best a-vised clerkis whech dwellid with him; on had þe
36 gouernauns o ჳere, a-noþer a-noþer ჳere, and at þe ჳeris ende he

---

¹ d *inserted above in red.*
² *word not distinct in text and rewritten above in red.*   ³ i *added in red.*

who handed
in accounts.

þat went fro þe office ʒaue clere acountis both of þe receytis and eke of þe expenses. He him-selue wold neuer beꝛ[1] keye of non office, ne no tresoꝛ, but euyr was he ʒoue to study and goostly occupacioñ. To þese swete occupaciones inclined he his entent, 4

He com-
missioned
others to do
new works.

labourand in þe law of God day and nyth. Newe werkis, whan þei schuld be mad, he comitted to oþir men, for he wold not haue his soule implicat with swech bysynesse, but kept it fre to holy meditacioñ and deuoute lesson. He despised not hem þat wold 8 haue þis occupacion, ne seid not a-geyn hem, lesse þan þe werkis

He allowed
no woman
within his
house, not
even his own
relatives;

were ouyr costful, þañ wold he grucch. Theꝛ dwelt no woman with-inne his hous, nout his owne sistir ne þe douteres of his broþir, and ʒet weꝛ þei weddid to God in holy religioñ. He wold 12 sey þus: With my sistir or my necys is þere no suspecioñ, but þere schuld cqme many women to hem, and eke þouʒ I be of her kyn, al myn houshold is not so. He wold neuer speke with no woman

he was never
alone with
a woman,
which is an
example to
Leaf 38,
back.
all, for he
knew the
power of
temptation.

alone, þouʒ it were rith grete councell. If he schuld speke with 16 hem, clerkys and seruauntis schuld stande aboute, and þouʒ þei herd not what was sayd, þei myth se what was doo. This cautele of so wyis ‖ a man schuld be to[2] us all a grete lernyng. We rede þat he wold sey sumtyme to hem þat were aboute him: Leue me, 20 in þat I wil sey as a man þat hath in þis materꝛ gret experiens. Be-foꝛ God, þat I sey, I lye not. The grete cedꝛ trees of Lyban, þe grete lederes of þe cristen flok, haue I-knowe þat þei haue falle be þe pestilens of lecherye, of whos fal I had no moꝛ suspecioñ 24 þan I had of Ambrose or Ierom.

[CHAPTER XXXIX.]

Of oþir meruelous condicionis of þis man.   **xxxix.**

He entered
no convent
of nuns
except upon
great
necessity,
and he learnt
three wise
principles
from
St. Ambrose.

THE monasteries wheꝛ nunnes dwelled wold he neuyr entyr with-oute a grete and a notable cause. Thre þinggis he 28 seyde he lerned of Seynt Ambrose. The first þat he schuld neuyr procuꝛ no wyf to no man; þe secund þat he schuld neuer councell man to go to werre; þe þird þat he schuld go to no feest. The cause of þe first is þat if þe husbond and þe wyf acorde not weel, 32

---

[1] be *in text with* r *added in red and* ber *in margin.*

[2] a man *crossed through and* us all *written above.*

þei schuld curs hym þat mad þe mariage. And also it is not semly ^{The reasons} *The reasons for these* þat he whech is a religious man and boundyn to chastite schuld *three wise principles.* excite oþir folk to fleschly lykyng. The cause of þe secund is, if it 4 be soo þat he whech schal fytyn make ony fals chalange, þan schul men wite it on him þat ʒaue him councell. The cause of þe þird is, if a man go often to festis he schal ete or drynk sum-tyme oute of mesuꝛ and speke sumtyme þat myth be left.

8 Othis hated he gretly and most special in religous men, for at *He hated* his bord was mad þis statute, þat what man rehersid ony oth þere, *oaths, and his monks* he schuld lese o disch of his seruyse ; ¶ for it was assigned of grete *Leaf 39.* discrecioñ who mech mete a man schuld haue at his bord, and eke *were punished for them.* 12 who mech drynk, and all were þei serued equaly vndir o propor-cioñ. He praised mech þoo men þat haue desire to deye, and to *He praised men who desired death,* þis conclusion he wold often reherse exaumples of thre bischoppis. *and often rehearsed the examples of* Seynt Ambrose, whan he lay at his last ende and schuld deye, his *three bishops* 16 disciples þere prayed him þat he schuld ask of ouꝛ Lord lenger lyf, and he answered þus to hem: I haue not lyued so a-mongis ʒou þat I am a-schamed for to lyue lenger, ne eke I am non aferd to deye, for we haue a good Lord. This answere of Ambrose, Augustin 20 praised mech.

Anoþir bischop, he seid, lay on deying, and þei þat weꝛ aboute *The words of a bishop on* him desired gretly his lyf, for he was, as þei said, ful nececarie to *dying,* þe cherch. He answered þus a-geyn in schort sentens : Neuyꝛ wel, 24 but if euyꝛ schal it be wel, why not now ? He ment as long as a man lyueth he is neuyr in parfith goodnesse, and if euyr schuld he com to rest and parfith pes it schal be at his deth, specialy if he deye weel. Of þe þird bischop seith he þat Seynt Cypriane *and what happened to* 28 told þat[1] whan þis bischop cam to his last ende and schuld deye, *another bishop.* at instauns of hem þat were aboute him, he prayed God to make him hool agayn. And þan, as he tellith, a fayꝛ ʒong man stood be his bed-side and loked angryly vpon him for þat desire, and rith 32 þus he saide on-to him : To suffir tribulacioñ and miseries of þis[2] world, ʒe be euyr aferd, and for to go oute of þese tribulaciones whan messageris com for ʒou, ʒe haue no will. What schal I ¶ do *Leaf 39,* on-to ʒou ? Seldom wold he write for ony causes to lordes or *back.* 36 astates with-outen grete informacion of treuth, and whan he wrote *When he wrote to lords* he tempered so his wordes þat he schuld haue þe grete part of his *he was careful to be right.*

---

[1] t *added in red.*　　　[2] world *commenced wrongly and crossed through.*

He was
readier to
make peace
between
strangers
than friends;
his reason. peticioñ. He was moȓ redy to make acord be-twix hem þat weȓ
not gretly of his aqweyntauns þañ be-twix his frendis, for he wold
sey if he mad acord be-twix to þat weȓ not of his knowlech, he
myth peṛauentuȓ fauouȓ þe o partye whech had moȓ treuth, and 4
þanne schuld he wynne on of hem to his frenchip. And be-twyx
his frendis it myth falle þe reuers, for þat man þat had not his
desiȓ wold þe rather falle fro his frenchip.

[CHAPTER XL.]

¶ Who he hatid heretikes and pursewed hem. **Cap*itul*um xl.** 8

He hated
heretics HERETIKES, hated þis man with an holy angir, as þe Psalme
seith: Beth angry and synne not. He was an hard hambyr,
euyr knokkyng up-on hem, and þei were so aferd of his argumentes
and they
desired his
death, þat þei desired his deth, in so mech þat þei prechid a-mongis hem 12
to hem þat weȓ of heȓ secte, þat for to kylle Augustyn it was no
synne but an holy dede and a meritory, and what man þat durst
do þis dede, þei durst vndirtake all his synnes schuld be forȝoue of
and
attempted
to kill him, God for þat dede doyng. Thei layde grete wayte up-on him oftin- 16
tyme, but ouȓ Lord euyr defended his knyth whech was ful nececarie
on-to þe cherch. For whan he was oute in þe cuntȓ sumtyme to
preche þe word of God and to lerne cristen soules þe trewe byleue,
þei leyd men of armes pryuyly in þe weye to kille him homward. 20
Leaf 40.
but God
saved him. But I by þe grace of God he was stered to take a-nothir weye, and
so was he saf fro his enmyes. And whan he knew what perel he
was in and who meruelously God had delyuered him, him on-wetyng,
For all this
he ever
attacked
heretics,
especially the
Donatists and
Manichaeans. þañ þankid he God with ful deuoute hert. But for all þese perelles 24
he cesed neuyr fro edificacion of þe puple and destruccioñ of þoo
enmyes whech berk a-geyn þe feith. Many heresies were in his
cuntȓ at þat tyme, both of þe Donatistes and eke of þe Manicheis,
and both, with þe myty grace of God whech was plenteuously 28
The Donatists
were
apparently
chaste, with-inne him, he conuicte and ny distroyed. The Donatistes
were þei þat be cleped Rebaptiȝatores, for þei wold admitte no
man to heȓ secte but if he weȓ baptiȝed newly with heȓ baptem.
Thei lyued in *continent* lif, þat is to seyn in chastite as ferȓ as 32
myth [1] be aspied [1]. Þei had eke a secte with-inne hem whech þei

[1]-[1] *in margin.*

clepid Circu*m*celliones; þis meny ru*n*ne a-boute on nytes with *but some of them, armed, attacked men.*
wepu*n* and armuꝛ and compelled[1] men with strokis to her heresie.

The Mancheis had many oþer fals opiniones, for þei said þat *The false opinions of the Manichaeans.*
4 Crist was no very man, but lich a man, and þat he took no flesch
ne blood of þe mayde as we beleue, but he took, I wot not veryly
what þei mene, a body, þei sey, of þe eyr, in whech he ded aꝲ þoo
myracles and in whech he suffered passioꝪ. These folk with sly
8 termes deceyued mauy men.

There were also in his tyme oþir heretikes cleped Pelagianes, *The Pelagian heresy.*
and þei held þis opynyoꝪ, þat a child be-goten of a cristen man and
a cristen woma*n* schuld[2] not be baptiȝed, ne nedith nowt, and aꝲ
12 þis secte ouꝛ Augusti*n* distroyed. These be þe names of heretikes *The heretics with whom he disputed.*
whech wrote a-geyn hym, and to whom he gaf answeꝛ ful sub-
stancial: Felix, Maximin*us*, Felician*us*, Faustus, Pascenou*s*, Secu*n*-
‖din*us*, Petilia*nus*, P*er*menian*us*, Fortunat*us*, Orestoni*us*, Gauden- *Leaf 40, back.*
16 cius, Julianus, and many oþir. A-geyn aꝲ þese þis sou*er*eyn maystir
of þe cherch stood as a strong geau*n*t, wrestli*n*g with argume*n*tis
for þe clennesse of þe feith, and enforsyng of þe cherch and confirma-
cioꝪ of p*ar*fite soules. Many a man eke þat was in errouꝛ, þorw *He brought many men from error to truth.*
20 his preching and disputy*n*g, was brout to þe trew wey of ouꝛ Lord
and on-to cristen feith. Sumtyme in his prechyng wold he make *Sometimes he made digressions in his preaching,*
a grete digression fro þe mateꝛ þat he spak of on-to an-oþir
desp*er*at mateꝛ, and þaꝪ wold he sey þat þis was þe dispensacio*n*
24 of ouꝛ Lord, for þeꝛ was sum ma*n* in þe audiens þat had nede to
heꝛ þat mateꝛ. On a tyme he happid in a *ser*mone to go fro his *and thus he converted*
mateꝛ and speke a-geyn þe errour of þese Manicheis, and a rich *a rich man from*
marchau*n*t þat was of þat heresie was sodeynly co*n*uerted þer-by. *Manichaeism.*
28 WhanꝪ he was cleped to ony councelle*s* of bischoppis or of *pr*inces
he wold gladly[3] go to hem and euyr in þoo cou*n*celle*s* peysed he moꝛ
þe causes þat long on-to God þan þoo þat long on-to men.

[CHAPTER XLI.]

¶ Of many bokes þat he mad aftir he was bischop. cap. xlj.

32 Aꝲ þat tyme whil he was bischop he was gretly occupied in *He wrote many books*
studying and wryting and makyng of bokis. On of þe *when a bishop, and*
first booke he mad is entitled to Symplian. This Simplician, aftir *one to Simplician,*

---

[1] MS. compleled, *first* l *dotted beneath.*   [2] be *crossed through.*
[3] gadly *in text,* gladly *in margin.*

who was
chosen
Archbishop
of Milan,

Seynt Ambrose was ded, was 'chose archbischop of Melan. For whan Ambrose lay in deying, þe clerkis of þe cherch comound a-mongis hem who schuld be bischop aftir, and he assigned hem þat þei schuld chese Simpliane. This same was þe man, as we 4

Leaf 41.
and who
brought
Augustine to
the faith.

∥ saide befor, þat with holy lif and deuoute exhortaciones brout Augustin to þe feith. And whanne he herd sey þat Augustin was bischop at Ypone and famed þorw þe world as for þe grettest labourer in study and þe grettest enmye to heretikes, eke þe grettest 8

Simplician
sent
Augustine
questions

dissoluer of qwestiones þat was leuand,—heryng al þis he sent to him certeyn questiones, praying him to dissolue hem and declare on-to him þe doutis þat þei conteyned. And Augustyn wrote on-to

and was
answered
in two books.

him a-geyn with ful grete reuerens to notable bokes in whech 12 he declareth his questiones with swech wordes þat þei be ful delectable to studious men. ²This book beginnyth Gratissimam³

At this time
Augustine
wrote his
'Confessions'

plane. In þis same tyme wrote he xiij bokes of his Confessiones, in whech bokes he schryuyth him ful deuoutly of his euel dedis 16 and of his good dedis; he praysith our Lord both mercyful and rithful. Be þese bokes he his-selue was excited to ful holy lif & þe makyng of hem inflawmed his hert to gret loue of our Lord. I dar

—books
which will
move the
hardest
hearts.

sauely sey þere is not so hard-hertid man in þe world þat redith 20 þese bokes and vndirstand hem, but þei wil ster his hert to swech deuocion þat, perauentur, he hath not had experiens of swech deuocion be-for. For all þe processe of þese bokes and all þe wordes are steryng on-to þe loue of God, and þo ar spoken with so swete 24

He wrote also
'De Opere
Mona-
chorum'.

langage þat þei ⁴ sounde no-þing but deuocion. He mad þat tyme eke a book whech he clepith Of þe Werkis of Munkis, for in his cuntr at þoo dayes were encresed many monasteries of munkis and mech noumbir of religious men, for all þoo heremites whech lyued 28 in desert, to whom he was first fader and norcher, wer cleped at þat tyme munkis, for monnos in þe oþir tonge is as mech to sey as

Leaf 41,
back.
The institu-
tion of
St. Benet.

solitari, ∥ and so monachus, þat is⁵ to sey,⁶ a munk, is swech a man þat lyueth in solitary lyf. But whan Seint Benet cam, þan mad be 32 þe ordr of þo men whech be clepid now munkys propirly, for⁷ oþer orderes ar now distincte in her propir names, and at þat tyme þat

---

¹ chop *crossed through.* ² In þis same tyme *crossed through.*
³ sane *crossed through.* ⁴ i *added in red.*
⁵ MS. it. ⁵ y *added afterwards.*
⁷ a character *crossed through.*

Augustin was, þis *monachus* was a comoun name to all religious.
For not only Seint Benet mad þese Cenobites, whech is as mech to
sey as many men lyuyng to-gidir in on hous and vndir o reule, but
4 Seynt Augustin mad swech eke, for his principall labour, as we
rede, was þis whann he cam first to Affrik, to gadere [1] swech solitari
men and bryng hem to o lyf and o reule. For Augustyn was be-
for Benet, as ferforth as I haue red, vp-on a hundred ȝer and fifty.
8 So þis book, De Opere Monachorum, of munkys werkys, mad he to
þis entent. Summe of þese religious men saide þat it was not
nedful [2] on-to hem [3] to praye [3], but þei wer bounde [4] to labour with
her handes. Thei wer menyd to þis opynyon be a texte of Seint
12 Poule, whech seith þat he whech wil not labour schal not ete. And
in a-noþir place he seith þus: Be nyth and eke be day haue we
laboured þat we schuld greue non of ȝou all. Summe held þe
reuers opynyon and enforsed hem with þe gospell wher he seith:
16 Take hed at þe birdis of þe eyr, þei sowe neythir ne repe, and ȝet
ȝour Fader of heuene fedith hem. And in þat same place he seith:
Take hed at þe lylyis of þe feld, þei spynne not ne carde, and ȝet
Salamon was not clad so freschly in al his ioye. This contencion
20 roos on-to so grete partye þat all þe cherch was set o rore with þis
mater, so ferforth þat þe bischop of Cartage, whech hith Aurelius
at þat tyme, wrote down on-to þ Augustyn letteris in whech he
prayed him and reqwyrid him, in Cristis name, þat he schuld
24 ordeyn sum remedye in þis mater. And for þis cause our fader
Augustin wrot þis book in whech he schewith þat certeyn houres
it is [5] most conuenient to religious men to synge, rede or pray.
And whan þo orisoues ar do whech ar ordeyned be constituciones
28 of þe cherch, þan is it ful nececarie to do sum labour with hand,
þat ydilnesse, whech is [6] step-modir of all vertu, schul non entr
haue in hem.

'De Opere Monacho-rum' was written to settle the question of the labour of monks, who were at dissension over two texts.

Through Aurelius,

Leaf 42.

bishop of Carthage,

Augustine wrote this book.

---

[1] MS. gadered, *final d dotted.*
[2] MS. not only leful; only le- *crossed through and* ned *written above.*
[3-3] *written in margin twice and once crossed through.*
[4] þerto *crossed through.*   [5] *written above in red.*
[6] stp. *crossed through.*

[CHAPTER XLII.]

¶ Of oþir bokes whech he wrote at þat same tyme. cap. xlij.

IN þo same dayes he wrote eke þe bokys Of þe Trynyte, xv, of grete and hy sentens, oute of whech bokes aff þe dyuynes þat haue writyn sithe, specialy in skole mateɼ, haue þe reulys 4 of aff dyuynyte. For Hugo de Sacramentis, and þe maister of sentens, Seynt Thomas Alqwyn, and aff oþir, haue heɼ special groundes þeɼ.

He made eke a-noþir solempne werk clepid Of þe Cyte, and þe 8 cause why he mad þis book is þis: Whech tyme þat Rome was take of hethen men, þe same hethen men scorned cristen men and blasphemed Crist in þis maner: Thei saide as long as Rome seruyd his goddis Iubiter, Iuno, Appollo, Minerue and swech othir, so long 12 was it kept be permision of þoo immortal goddis, þat þere myth non of her enmyes ouer-com hem. But aftyr þat tyme þat Petir and Paule had brout in þe feith of Crist, a-non aff her enmyes
had þe bettyr of hem, of whech ymaginacioñ[1] þei added to her 16 blaspheme þat Crist had neuyr so mech poweɼ to defende his puple as had Iubiter whech stood in heɼ capitoff. A-geyn þese grete blasphemes Seynt Augustin answered in þese xxij bokes.
In þe first v. bokes he repreuyth þe errour of hem ‖ þat seyde alle 20 þe richesse of þis world and aff þe prosperite is ȝouen on-to men be
þoo immortaff goddis, for he schewith heɼ pleynly þat þoo ydoles whech þei clepe goddis ar dampned spirites, and þoo[2] men þat ded worchip on-to hem regned in as gret myschef as euyr ded ony 24 men. In þe oþir v. bokes he laboureth a-geyn þe errouɼ of hem þat seide good and euel in þis world haue her variauns aftir place & tyme and persones, þat sum place & sum tyme and sum persone schal haue ioye euer and sum noñ. In þe oþir xij bokes he spekith 28
of too citees, Ierusalem and Babilome; Ierusalem, as he seith, longith to God, Babilome to the deuele. These too citees spryngin of too loues. The loue of ouɼ-selve, þat causeth þe cite of þe deuel, whech growith in heith tyl he comth on þat abusion þat he despiseth God. 32 The loue of God, he makith þe oþir cite, and he may growe so hy to

---

[1] þai *crossed through.*
[2] þat *crossed through and* þoo *written over in red.*

Goddis plesauns þat he schal, for Goddis loue, despise aff worldly
felicite.   Be-side þese werkys he mad many a book, tretys, epistoles, He also wrote many other
sermones, omelies, þat a man schal not fynde a clerk at þese dayes works, all of which no man
4 þat may sey he haue red aff, for þe noumbir of hem ar gessid on-to has read.
a þousand.   Of his werkis spekith a gret clerk in a vers rith þus.
Mentitur quem se[1] te totum legisse fatetur.   Thus it meneth in
Englisch: He lyeth þat seith he hath red al þi bokes.

[CHAPTER XLIII.]

8   ¶ Who Augustyn red ouyr aff his bokes a litil be-for his deth
& corrected hem. ‖ Cap. xliij.   Leaf 43.

A FTIR tyme he had mad aff þese bokes he ouyr-lokid hem After he had written all
a-geyn, þat þer schul no-þing be þerin but trewe. This these books, he re-read
12 þing ded he for many causes, on was for he mad many bokes or þe them,
tyme þat he was gretly vsed or exercised in holy scriptur. A-noþir
cause was for certeyn materis whech[2] he had wrytin, þei wer dirkly
seid, wherfor he declared þoo materes in þis secund writyng. The and having
16 þird cause was þat he was not a-schamed[3] to be a-knowe þat he reasons for changes,
had wrytyn mech þing whech myth a be bettir, and for þis cause
he mad þat book whech he clepith his Retractaciones. And þat he wrote his 'Retracta-
he schuld haue þe mor leyser to study and write, specialy for in tions'.
20 too councellis aff þe bischoppis of þe lond had reqwyrid him þat
he schuld entend on-to exposicion of holy scriptur, for þis cause
certeyn 3eres be-for his deth he prayed ful mekely þe clergy and þe
puple þat fyue dayes in þe weke he myth haue pesibily to his He gave five days a week
24 study in scriptur, and þe oþir too dayes wold he 3eue attendauns to study and two days to
on-to her causes, to sette rest and pes be-twix hem[4]. But for al his people, but his
þis graunt oft-tyme was his studie interrupt for her causes, to his work was interrupted;
grete vexacion, but special coumfort of his puple. For þis skil[5]
28 he ordeyned a-noþir remedye: he say wel þat he fell fast in age,
and deth, þat no man may escape, was ful ny, be-cause he felt him- and therefore, feeling also
selue so febil; he dred eke þat aftir his deth sum ambicious man that he was getting
schuld be mad bischop, whech schuld distroye al þat euyr he had feebler,

---

[1] *in margin.*   [2] ch *added in red above.*
[3] d *added above in red.*   [4] I *crossed through.*
                [5] cause *crossed through and* skil *written over in red.*

he asked the
Leaf 43,
back.
people to
choose some
man to attend
to them and
afterwards
take his see.

Thus he and
they chose
Heraclius one
of his clerks.

After his
'Retracta-
tions' he
wrote other
books.

edified: þerfor laboured he on-to þe puple þat þei schuld chese sum good man and iuste þat ‖ myth occupie þat se aftir his deth, whech man schuld determyn þe causes of þe puple, lest þat þei were grete causes, þo wold he kepe to him-self. To his desir 4 þei consented all and mad compromisse on-to his persone þat whom he wold name þei schul consent on-to him. Vp-on þis Augustin named on of his clerkis, þei clepid him Eraclius, a man wel-named in þe puple whom Augustin had enformed in þe weye 8 of Crist in þe best maner. And to þis man comitted Augustin all þe charge of þat diosise, lest þan þere com ony grete causes, þat he schuld haue þe mor leisir to study and wrytyng. Thus er he deyid he ouer-say all his bokes and mad þese Retractaciones. But aftir 12 making of þat werk he mad many oþir bokes whech be not touchid þerin, as a man may se in þe redyng.

[CHAPTER XLIV.]

¶ Who his cyte was be-segid of dyuers naciones. xliiij.   16

At this time
Hippo was
beseged by
the Alans,
Goths, and
Vandals.
The home of
the Alans.

The home of
the Goths.

The home of
the Vandals.

After scourg-
ing Europe,
these people
invaded

Leaf 44.
Africa and
beseged
Hippo.

They spared
nobody,

IN þis same tyme iij sundry naciones beseged þe cite of Ypone; þei ar[1] cleped[2] þus, Alani, Gothi and Wandali. These Alani dwelle in a gret cuntr her in þis part of þe world cleped Europe, whech cuntr þei calle Sithia; it is hens northest 20 toward Constantinople.

Gothi dwelled[2] fast by hem, for þese cuntres occupied ny fro þe grete flod cleped Danubius[3] un-to þat cuntr whech we clepe Denmark, for of þese Gothis cam þese Danes.   24

Wandaly dwelled sumtyme in þe same place wher Lumbardes dwelle now a-boute Melan and Pauye. All þese puple þus gadered to-gidyr ded mech harm her in Europe a-boute Rome and in Ytale, and þan went þei ouer þe se in-to Affrik, and þere distroyed þe 28 cuntr, and ‖ at þe last ende of Augustin lyf, þei beseged þe cite of Ypone. Vnder þis tribulacion Augustin had ful heuy dayes and wept both day & nyth for þe myschef þat he say whech þese men ded, for þei spared no cherchis, ne prestis, ne nunnes, ne non ordr. 32 And whan Augustin say sum deye in captiuite, sum in prison,

---

[1] *inserted above.*   [2] *d written above.*
[3] *us crossed through.*

su*m*me of þe swerd, and þat þe *ser*uyse, þe messis, þe ympnis of þe and the
cherch cesed, and many cherchis weꝛ brent in þe cuntꝛ, and þe services of
clerkis fled, so þat sacramentis weꝛ not ȝoue*n*, and þouȝ a ma*n* ceased.
4 wold haue hem, þ*ere* was no ma*n* to gyue hem, he seing [1] al þis,
had ful grete sorow, so þat he fełł in-to greuo*us* seknesse. But
ȝet, among*is* al þis sorow he had þat consolacio*n* of þe wise ·man
whech saide þus : He hath no grete wisdam þat sorowith whan
8 stones falle, and whan þei deye þat must nedis deye. In þis Augustine
tribulacio*n* he cleped his breþ*er*in to-gidyr and þus he saide on-to prayed to
hem : Behold now, in what mischef we stand in, and I se no God
remedye ; God wil pu*n*isch us in þis wyse for ouꝛ synnes. Wherfor,
12 I haue prayed my Lord þat he schuld delyueꝛ us of þese p*er*elles, for one of
or elles send us paciens þat we may suffyr hem mekely, or elles, if three things,
he se þat we be worþi for to haue hem leng*er*, I haue prayed God
þat he schal take me oute of þis lyf. This same prayeꝛ þat he
16 prayed, þei prayed ałł, and so on of þese iij peticiones was grau*n*ted and in the
him, for in þe þird month aftir þei had be-segid þe cyte, þe feu*er*ys of the siege
took him so soꝛ þat [2] he was fayn to kepe his bed. he fell ill.

[CHAPTER XLV.]

¶ In what man*er* ∥ Augustyn deyid, and what occupacio*n* he Leaf 44,
20 had in his last sekenesse. Capit*u*lum xlv. back.

IN þis same seknesse of whech he deyid þ*ere* cam on-to hym Before he
a *cer*teyn man, praying hi*m* in þe name of ouꝛ Lord þat he died a man
came asking
wold touche him with his hand, for he seide if he wold ley hand to be made
24 up-on him, he schuld make him hool of þat seknesse whech he had whole;
longe boꝛ. Augustyn answered to hym a-geyn and seide he was Augustine
not wys in his desire, for if he had swech poweꝛ to make men hool demurred,
he wold rather exercise it on him-self þa*n* on oþir men. The ma*n*
28 replied on-to Augustyn in þis man*er* : He saide þat he had in but the man
man*er* of a goostly consolacio*n*, in whech he was warned þat he insisted, and
schuld go to Augusty*n* þe bischop, and with touching of his hand
he schuld be mad hool. Augustyn, seing þe grete feith of þis man,
32 leyd his hand up-on him & blessed him i*n* þe name of God, and Augustine
þus was he mad hool. Thus encresid þe seknesse up-on him þat cured him.

---

[1] seying *crossed through* ; seing *in margin.*   [2] *part of* w *crossed through.*

Augustine knew he was dying, he vndirstood wel he schuld sone deye, and be-cause he had prechid ofte sithe þat þere schuld no cristen man passe owt of þe world with-outen mornyng and compleint for defautes in whech he hath

and made his notary write the seven Psalms of the Litany for him to read. falle, þerfor he mad his notari for to write him þe vij Psalmes, þoo 4 same whech we rede with þe Letanye, in a fayr parchemyn skyn, and þis was sette on þe wal a-geyn his beddis hed. Þese red he with ful gret deuocion and grete wepyng be-for his deth. And þat þere schuld no man interrupte him of þis deuocion, ten dayes 8 be-for his deth he ordeyned þat þer schuld no man com with[1]-inne

Leaf 45. þe chaumbyr wher he ‖ lay but his leche and þei þat brout him mete and drynk, and all þis tyme with ful grete deuocicn and

On the fifth kalend of September, he passed away, mech wepyng he comended his soule to God. And þus þe v. kalende 12 of September, with hool mynde and all þe membris of his body not hurt but hool, standyng his breþerin a-boute him, and comendyng hys soule to God, he ȝald þe goost on-to þe Fader of heuene. Thus hath he left in erde his holy foot-steppis, many men & women 16 of his religion taute be his doctrine. He hath left eke grete

leaving the church the treasure of his books, in which he is immortal. instruccion to þe cherch in tresour of his bokes, þat þouȝ his body be drawe from vs, ȝet his spirit abideth with us, as þe poete wrot ful wel of all hem whech leue emolliment of wrytyng be-hinde hem ; 20 rith þus he wrot in Latin: Viuere post obitum vatem vis nosce viator, Quod legis ecce loquor vox tua nempe mea est. Thus mene þei in Englisch: Thou man þat passist by, if þou wilt knowe þat a clerk lyueth after his deth, That þou redist I speke, þi voys eke 24

He lived seventy-six years. is myn. Augustyn lyued clerk and bischop ny xl. ȝere, alle þe dayes of his lyf, or seuenety and sex. Thus endith þe lyf of þis glorious doctour whom all cristen men ar bounde to do worchip, most specialy clerkys and lerned men þat haue grete stuf oute of 28

The Author hopes the gentle woman for whom he wrote will do the Saint honour. his bokes to her lernyng. And as I hope, ȝe gentyl woman, ȝe schuld plese wel þis Seint if ȝe wold se his place onys in a ȝer, and þouȝ ȝe left a day in heruest of ȝour labour, he coude make retribucion in oþer party. Thus I comende ȝou to God aud me to 32 ȝour prayeris, þat we both may com sumtyme wher our Fader is, we schal prey both   Amen.

---

[1] inne *wrongly written and crossed through.*

LIFE OF ST. GILBERT

[CAPGRAVE'S PROLOG.]

TO my wel-beloued in ouᵽ Lord God maystir[1] of þe ordeᵽ Leaf 46.
of Sempyngham[2], whech ordre is entytled on-to þe name For the master of Sempring-ham,
of Seynt Gilbert, I, ffreᵽ I. C.[3], amongis doctouris lest, send
4 reuerens as to swech dignyte, desiring clennesse to ʒouᵽ soule and
helth to ʒouᵽ body. Now with-inne fewe dayes was notyfied who had seen and liked his
on-to me þat þe lyf of ouᵽ fader Seynt Augustyn, whech þat 'Life of St. Augus-tine'.
I translat[4] in-to ouᵽ tunge at instauns of a certeyn woman,
8 was browt to ʒouᵽ presens, whech lykyd ʒow wel, as it is told, Capgrave writes this work.
saue ʒe wold I schul adde þerto alle þoo relygyous þat lyue vndyr
his reule. But to þis I answeᵽ þat it was not my charge, but if men
like for to knowe þis mateᵽ diffusely þei may lerne it in a sermon His sermon preached at Cambridge.
12 þat I[5] seid at Cambrig þe ʒeᵽ be-foᵽ myn opposicion, whech
sermon vnphap I wil sette in Englisch in þe last ende of þis
werk. Than aftir ʒe had red þis lyf of Seynt Augustyn ʒe sayde
to on of my frendes þat ʒe desired gretly þe lyf of Seynt Gilbert
16 schuld be translat in þe same forme. Thus mad he instaunce
to me, and I graunted both ʒour petycion, this[6] for I wold not
frustrate him of his mediacion. To þe honouᵽ of God and of
all seyntis þan, wil we begynne þis tretys, namelych for the This book is for the
20 solitarye women of ʒour religion whech vnǁneth can vndyrstande Leaf 46, back.
Latyn, þat þei may at vacaunt tymes red in þis book þe grete maidens who know little Latin.
vertues of heᵽ maystyr. For heᵽ may þei loke as in a glasse, who
þei schal transfigure heᵽ soules lych on-to þat exemplary in whech
24 þei schul loke. Of þe interpretacion of his name, what it schuld The meaning of the name 'Gilbertus'
mene in Englisch, for we haue it not redily in ouᵽ bokes of

---

[1] *In the margin,* M. Nicholas Reysby.
[2] simpyngham *with* e *written ouer.*
[3] *In margin, in a later hand,* John Capgrave.
[4] MS. transalat, a *dotted underneath.*   [5] *inserted above.*
[6] *in margin.*

'Gilbertus' contains two Hebrew words and a Latin word; interpretaciones, we wil speke in swech maner as auctouris whech dyuyde names in partes. Gyla, þei sey, is a word of Hebrew, as mech to sey as he þat passeth fro o cuntř to a-nothir. And ber is a welle, or a pitte, eke deruyed fro þe Ebrewe tunge. Tus [1] 4 is a Lateyn word, in Englisch a swete gumme, whech we þrowe in ouř encenseris whan we schal doo a special honouř to God. Thann soundith his name þus on-to ouř heryng: This holy man was a walkeř heř in erde þat passed fro þe welle on-to [2] þe swete 8

and is descrip-tive of the Saint's life. sauour. The welle clepe I þe holy baptem in whech he was wasch fro Adam his synne. The swete sauour name I þe holy opynyon of this man whech sauoured so swetely in þis land þat it mad many men to selle al þat þei [3] had and folow þe steppes 12 of pouerte. Of this sauour spak þe blissed apostel [4] whan he saide: We be þe good odour of ouř Lord Crist in euery place,

Leaf 47. both to hem þat schul be saued ‖ and eke to hem þat schul perisch. To summe be we sauouř of lyf and to summe sauouř 16 of deth. So semyth it þat þe clene lyf of Seynt Poule, and þe deuoute preching of hym, was on-to hem whech weř chose to be saued a sauouř of euyr-lasting lyf, & to hem þat weř reprobat a sauour of euerlastyng peyne. Añ þis is seid to acording of 20 Seynt Gilbertis name þat al his lyf from his baptem on-to his deth ran in swech a swete sauouř þat ʒet at þese dayes þe deuoute virgines of his ordre beren witnesse þat of þe rote of his doctrine

This 'Life' is translated from the Latin, and contains besides matter which the author has learnt from his fellows. sprange añ þese fayre flouris of virginite. This is þe preamble 24 or elles þe prologe of Seynt Gilbertis lif, whech lyf I haue take on hand to translate out of Latyn rith as I fynde be-fore me, saue sum addicionis wil I put þertoo whech men of þat ordre haue told me, and eke othir þingis þat schul falle to my mynde in þe 28 writyng whech be pertinent to þe mateř.

[CHAPTER I.]

capitulum p[m].

Gilbert's birth-place.

His parents. THIS man was bore in þat same place cleped Sempingham. His fader was bore in Normandye, his modyr lady of þis 32 place be-foř seide. His fadeř, as þei sey, was a knyte of Normannye

---

[1] Thus *in text;* tus *in red in margin.*   [2] *added above in red.*
[3] i *added above.*   [4] *In margin in red,* 2 Cor. 2.

whech cam in-to þis lond with Kyng William at ‖ þe Conqwest and
weddyd þe lady of þis place, so þat be heritage Seint Gilbert
was very eyer of þis possession & of many othir.   That þis is
4 likly to be soth, I a-legge a testimonie whech I haue be informacion
of my Lord Beamound, Ion, þat now lyuyth.   He seide þat his
kynrod cam first out of Frauns with þis same Kyng William,
and on of hem, a notable knyte, weddid þe lady of Folkingham
8 at þat tyme, and so of heʀ issewe cam all þe Beamoundis þat haue
be sithe.   Swech many othir myth we reherse & make þe boke
ouer longe and tedious to þe redeʀ.   Than was þis man medeled
with too blodis, Norman of þe fader side, Englisch of þe moderis
12 side.   What auctoris write of þese too naciones & what comendacion
þei reherse of hem is pertinent to sette heʀ in magnyfying of þis
man.   The Normannes, þei sey, þei cam fro Norweye &[1] conqwered
þe lond wheʀ þei dwelle, a puple gentyl of condicion, wise and
16 redy in batayle & grete tilleres of corn.   The descripcioñ eke of
þis nacioñ must mech a-corde her-to, be-cause þei conqwered us
and at þis day heʀ succession dwellith with us.   So semeth it
þat þis man was not bore of[2] no wrecchid nacioñ, ne of no seruage,
20 but of puple gentil & fremanly & large, both on þe fadir side
and ‖ þe moder.   He was in his ʒong age, and in his simpilnesse
ful gracious lich on-to Iacob, whom for his clennesse & innocens
þe modir Rebecca, þorw inspiracioñ of God, preferred to be lord
24 of all his breþerin, lich as þis man is preferred to be maystir
of al þis religioñ.   And also, as it is seid in þe bok of Iob[3]:
The lampe whech was despised in þe þoutes of rich men was
arayed agayn a-noþir tyme ; in whech ʒe schal vndirstond þat
28 þoo vertues whech grew with þis child in ʒong age, þañ despised
of þe world, were ordeyned for to be hald in moʀ reuerens in
tyme comand.   He was at þat age set to skole and lerned groundly
in þoo scienses whech þei clepe liberal, as gramer, retorik, logik
32 and swech oþir.   But his corage at þat tyme was moʀ enclyned
to lerne good maneris þan sotil conclusiones, eke be-cause aftirward
þat he was ordeyned to be a techer of vertuous lyuyng, it was
conuenient þat he schuld first be a disciple in þat in scole of

---

[1] *written above.*   [2] *part of* w *crossed through.*
[3] *In the margin in red,* Iob 12.

honestie. In al his ȝong age was he clene fro swech vices as
childyrn vse, as lying, wauntown ragyn, and oþir stynkyng
condiciones. Euene þann be-gan he to be lich a religious man,
to whech lyf he was applied be God. For in all his lyf, as þei 4
bere witnesse þat sey his *conuersacion*, touched he neuer woman.

Touchyng ‖ clepe I vicious handelyng in þe selue or ellis swech
maner circumstauns of bodely aproximacion be whech ony man
myth deme euele.   8

[CHAPTER II.]

cap. ij.

IN þat same seculer lyf and in þat tendyr age, he folowyd,
as he coude and myth, þe reules of religious lyf, and to
hem all of whech he had ony power he ful benyngly gaf exaumple 12
þe same reules to folow. For first was he a maystir of lernyng
to þe smale petites, swech as lerne to rede, spelle and synge.
Tho childyrn þat were vndyr his disciplyne he taute not only
her lessones on þe book, but be-side þis, he tawt for to pley[1] 16
in dew tyme, and here playes taute he þat þei schuld be honest
and mery with-outen clamour or grete noyse. For þouȝ he had
not at þat tyme experiens of þe good customes whech be vsed
a-mongis religious men in monasteriis, ȝet had our Lord God 20
at þat age put in his brest þese holy exercises, for he taute[2] þoo
disciples þat he had to kepe silens in þe cherch[3]; all an on our to
go to bedde & eke to ryse[4] to her[5] lessones; all wente þei to-gidyr
to her pley or ony oþir þing. His moost labour and grettest 24
desir[6] was to wynne soules to God with word and eke ensaumple,
for þe best sacrifise on-to God is þe gelous loue of soules. Lich
on-to þis man was þe holy Athanas in his ȝong dayes,[7] ‖ þat same
Athanas whech mad *Quicunque* Vult. We rede of him þat in his 28
childhod he wold gader to-gydyr many childyr of his aqweyntauns,
and lede hem to þe watirside, and þis was at grete Alisaundr.
Than wolde he enqwyre of hem wheythir þei were cristen or
nowt, and if þei wer not cristen, he made his felawis, as in game, 32
to make þe child naked & so dippe him þries in þe cold watyr,

---

[1] C. 29 play.   [2] C. tawht.   [3] C. chirch.   [4] C. rysse.
  [5] C. there.   [6] C. desyere.   [7] *þat crossed through.*

he standing sadly and saying þe very sacramental wordis of baptem. This noyse cam to þe bischoppis ere, whech at þat tyme hite Petyr; he sent aftir þe childyrn and enqwyred of hem what
4 Athanas saide on-to hem, what þei answered, vnder what forme he wasched hem, and [1] whan he sei þat [1] all þing was doo rith as þe cherch vseth, he determyned þat þo childyrn weʀ baptiȝed, notwithstandyng þat it was doo in pley, comaundyng his prestes
8 to take þe childyrn and sey ouyr hem [2] þe oþir orisones whech þe cherch vseth. Al þis is seid for ouʀ Gilberd, þat in so ȝong age had so sad condiciones and so grete ȝel to lede soules to heuene. Whan he was promoted to þe ordre of presthod and had

<small>When he became priest,</small>

12 soules in gouernauns [3] and eke had receyued poweʀ to make ministracion of þe goostly giftis whech be vertue of oure Lordes ‖ blod ar left in þe cherch, þan, as a trewe steward of his Lordes tresouʀ, he departed his Lordes whete to hem þat dwelle in þe

<small>Leaf 49, back.</small>
<small>he was a true steward of his Lord's wealth.</small>

16 houshold of ouʀ feith, to ech of hem as it neded. Þat is to seyn, þe word of good exhortacion was not hid in him, but he delt it oute frely to hem þat wold lerne. For his auditorye was so endewyd with lernyng þat it sempt in all heʀ gouernauns þei had
20 be norchid in monasterye amongis þe seruauntis of God. Thei vsed non insolent drynkyngis [4], ne no longe sitting þere, ne [5] vsed not to renne to wrastillingis, beʀ-baytingis and swech oþir onthrifty occupaciones, whech summe men now on dayes preferʀ be-for dyuyne

<small>His people went to no vain wrest-lings and bear-bating,</small>

24 seruyse; this used þei nout, but þei used to pray deuoutly in þe cherch, to pay treuly heʀ tythes, to walk a-boute and visite pore men, to spend heʀ good in swech weye as is plesauns of God and coumfort to pore. Who-so had seyn hem [6] with-inne þe cherch

<small>but paid their tithes,</small>

28 he myth sone discerne wheþir þei weʀ Gilberd parischones or nowt, he had tawt hem so wel to bowe heʀ bakkes and heʀ knes to God and so deuoutly to bid heʀ bedes.

<small>and behaved devoutly.</small>

[CHAPTER III.]

cap. tercium.

<small>Gilbert was first in the household of the Bishop of Lincoln,</small>

32 IN his first promocioñ he was in houshold of þe bischop of Lincolñ, cleped Robert Bloet. Thidir was he ‖ drawe first

<small>Leaf 50.</small>

1-1 C. 29 b. what he sayde þat þus: *in our MS. a d has been erased after sei.*
2 *added above in red.* ⁣ 3 C. governans.
4 MS. drynkyns, *with* gis *written over last syllable.* ⁣ 5 *inserted above.*
6 C. 30. them.

5

& mad a chapeleyn half ageyn his wil, for he was special with þe
lord, & to him was comitted to ransake all þe greuous crimes or
synnes þorw-oute þe diosise, he to correcte aftir his discrecioñ.

where he was
a judge of
crime. For he was a *general* iuge, as it semeth, to make his remissiones 4
and *comminaciones* rith as he list. In all þis astate he was not
prowd of beryng, ne founde in no costly aray, but þe heyeꝛ he was
in dignite þe loweꝛ was his soule[1], for in all his mevyngis no-þing
seculeꝛ, but lych a chanoñ reguleꝛ or a cloystireꝛ, semed he euyr. 8

Here he led
an austere
life, In so mech þat whil he was in þis seruyse in court he fastid gretly,
he wook[2] as to oþir mennys wakyng *importably*, prayed euyr, and
eke oþir goostly[3] *exercises* weꝛ neuyr left behynde. He was so
wel occupied in þat admin*istracion* þat he wold *compleyne* of him- 12
selue aftirward[4] whan he had begun*ne* þis religioñ, þat he was
even more so
than after his
conversion. moꝛ parfit in lyf be-foꝛ þat *conuer*cion to religioñ þañ he was aftyr,
notwithstanding þat aftir tyme he had take þis holy habite he was
enmye grete I-now on-to his owne body. But þat he dyde lesse 16
penauns to his body aftyr he had take þe religioñ, it is not to
This was due
to his charity. aretten to slauth and necligense, but rather on-to charyte, whech
Leaf 50,
back. entendith moꝛ to oþir mennys profith þan his owne. ¶ So rede
we þat Seynt Martyn had lesse vertue ȝoue on-to him after his 20
as with
St. Martin. promocioñ to þe bischoprych þañ he had be-fore. This man whech
we talk of now, be-foꝛ all vertues loued pouerte, for a grete and
Gilbert
refused an
archdeaconry, a good archideconry profered to hym be þe same bischop Robert,
he fully refused. For he wold sey sum-tyme þat þese benefices of 24
grete expense be often-tyme a redy wey to losse of a mannes-soule.
For whech cause all þe goodes whech left of his benefises be-side
his neccessarie lyuyng, he gaue it frely on-to þe profite of pore men.
Whañ he was oute of his owne possessioñ he receyued euyr Crist 28
and helped
the afflicted. as his gest in faderles childyrn, *in* widowis, in elde folk, in seke
and feble, whom he susteyned with his *propir* goodis, and eke with
þe cherchis *prouentis*, clad hem & fed hem. And þat he schuld
go[5] on-to þe grettest sum*me* of *perfeccioñ*, all þat he had he gaf 32
to pore men swech as he, þorw þe inspiracioñ of ouꝛ Lord, had
chose and made to lyue in wilful pouerte, whech[6] heꝛ-aftir for his
temporal goodys þat he spent in worchip of ouꝛ Lord, schuld

---

[1] sole *in text;* soule *in margin.*   [2] C. 30 *b.* woke.
[3] exercise, *dotted beneath.*   [4] he *crossed through.*
[5] *added above in red.*   [6] schuld *crossed through in red.*

receyue him[1] in-to euyr-lastyng tabernacles, as þe gospel berith
witnesse. Thus, of trewe dispensyng of worldly goodes and grete
loue whech he had to soules, he was worthi ‖ of ouℛ Lord to receyue   Leaf 51.
4 a dobyl reward.

[CHAPTER IV.]

cap. quartum.

THO he þoutȝ a-mong oþir þingis þat virginite was a grete
   astate, on of þe grettest vertu þat may plese God,
8 whech frute boℛ be hem is most alowed in heuene, for þis cause
he ordeyned first seuene maydenes whech, be his teching, weℛ   He took seven
inflaumed[2] with þe loue of God, þat þei schuld be sperd up fro   maidens and
þe vanytes of þe world and serue ouℛ Lord in qwyete contem-   shut them up from the world,
12 placyoñ. So vndyr þe wal of þe cherch of Seynt Andrew he mad   giving them
hem celles wheℛ þei myte prey and haue parte eke of all dyuyne   cells by St. Andrew's
seruyse, both in seying and in eryng. Aftir þat he ioyned on-to   church, and appointing
heℛ seruyse oþir certeyn women þat weℛ not letteryd, and men   women and religious men
16 eke þat weℛ conuerted to religioñ, but no clerkys; þese alle weℛ   to tender them.
ordeyned to þe seruyse of þe forsaid virgines. Aftir þis don he   Then he appointed
ordeyned certeyn clerkis, letterid men and boundyn to streyt   clerks to govern them.
reules, þat þei schuld haue þe gouernaunce of all þis puple forseyd.
20 On-to þese alle ordeynẹd he mete, drynk, cloth, and oþir neccessaries
of his rentys and of oþir good lefully goten. To heℛ soules eke
ordeyned he goostly mete, on-to þe nunnes þe reule of Seynt   The nuns were under
Benedict, on-to þe clerkys þe reule of Seynt Augustyn, be-side   St. Benedict's
24 þese certeyn instituciones he ordeyned, as þe holy a‖noyntyng   Leaf 51, back.
taut him, whech be þe Holy Gost is sent fro heuene. Thus he   rule; the
sette hem lawes medeled with swech attemperauns þat a-mongis   monks under
dyuers kyndes, dyuers habites, dyuers degrees, he exorted hem in   St. Augus- tine's.
28 ouℛ Lord þei all schuld haue but o soule and on hert fixid in God.
What schial we sey moℛ of his congregaciones ? Be-side þo elmesse-   He made alms-houses;
houses whech he mad for pore men, for seke men and women in
languoℛ, for misellia, for wydowes, for faderles & modirles, whech
32 houses he sette in dyuers degres and in dyuers disposicioñ, be-side
all þese, he edyfied in his lyue þirtene conuentual cherchis with all   and built thirteen
oþir houses pertinent, fouℛ of chanons dwellyng be hem-selfe, nyne   conventual churches.
of nunnes with heℛ breþerin and clerkys, & persones þat weℛ

---

[1] *added above in red.*   [2] MS. infalaumed; a *dotted beneath.*

onlerned ordeyned to seruyse of þe nunnes, as we seid be-foꝛ.

And verily, as we suppose, he left at his deth swech persones dedicate to God vp-on too þousand too hundred, be-side hem þat· weꝛ dede er þat tyme he passed from vs.   And many moo monas- 4 teries myth he a mad, ne had be þe streyt consciens whech he had in receyuyng of worldly good, for with ful gret dreed and mech heuynesse receyued he worldly rychesse whech was profered him ;

sum-tyme was he compelled ‖ for to take þo ꝣiftis ; summe-tyme he 8 refused hem, so was honest pouert roted in his hert and so wel beloued. Thus semeth it þat he was sette in þe mene weye, as was Salamon þat sayd on-to God[1]: Gyue me, Lord, neythir rychesse ne pouerte, but graunt me swech þing whech is nedful on-to me.   So 12 þis man had desire to þe mene, neþir to be rich, ne for to want, but to haue swech þing as was neccessarie to þe[2] grete noumbyr newly gadered be him, þat þei schuld not fayle of heꝛ dayly prouysion.

His purpos was euyr to dwelle a-mongis hem þat weꝛ meke, þerfor 16 it plesed ouꝛ Lord for to heyne him þat him-self so lowed.

[CHAPTER V.]

cap. v.

WHO þat he be-had in his prelacye and who faderly he was at al tymes on-to his subiectis, I suppose, veryly, þat it is 20 now not onknowe on-to al þe kyngdom of Ynglond, in so mech þat his childyrn be so encresed and growen to swech a noumbyr as we may se at[3] eye, þat rithfully we may applie þoo wordis of scriptuꝛ

to him whech weꝛ said to Iob[4]: Thi seed, he said, schal be 24 multiplied and þi kynred encresed as herbes on þe erde.   This multiplying of his religion, þe wise men þat lyue now suppose

veryly it be[5] þe myracle of his good lyf. ‖ The man stood in a maneꝛ of merveile to all þat knew hym for þe grete prerogatif 28 of good dedys with whech he was endewed, eke for þe new plantes of mercy and charite whech he had griffid in þe gardeyn of Cristis

---

[1] *In margin in red, Prouer.* 30.   [2] *inserted above.*
[3] *þe crossed through.*   [4] *In margin in red, Iob 5.*
[5] *be veryly crossed through in red.*
[6] *The embellishment of capitals in red is omitted from this and the following page.*

cherch, more-ouyr for þe grete multiplying and wise gouernauns
of þe same. For He þat pored wisdam in his breest for to þinke
and to begynne swech þingis, He gaf him vertue in þe administra-
4 cion & conseruacion of þe same. It is open at þis day what His holiness
cunnyng Seynt Gilbert hadde & what holynesse, for and þese openly;
giftes had not com fro God, þer schuld neuyr a risen on-to so
parfite an ende, for þe man tawt no-þing but þat he ded, for in al he did all
8 his lyf his doctrine was accordyng to his werkys; his holy doctrine taught.
expressid his clene lyf and his holy lyf brout his doctrine on-to
effecte, þat is to se, a parfiþth ende. Aftir tyme þat he was
preferred to haue gouernauns in dispensyng of Goddis giftes, he
12 ded þe part þat longed on-to his office, he left rith nowt þat
longid on-to his goostly helth or elles to þe charge þat longed
to gouernauns of his breþerin. The man was plesaunt and mery, He was a
wys in wordis and of vsed eloquens fulfillid, hauyng no-þing in his pleasant man,
16 wordes þat was likly to be lakkid, wherfor I with grete reuerens Leaf 53.
was he be-loued both of his owne familiar puple and eke of
straungeres. In all his behauyng owtward he was conformed
on-to his breþerin; he was, if I schuld not lye, þe forme & þe
20 exaumple in whech þei myth loke for to transfigur her lyf to þat the perfect
example for
exemplarye. Meke he was a-mongis hem as on of hem, as it is his followers,
seyd in Salamon : A prince haue þei mad þe be with hem as on of
hem; [1] for al þat euer he comaunded his subiectis to do he fulfillid
24 him-self; his cloþis wer not whiter þan oþir of his felawes; his not different
from them in
mete was not dite mor deliciously þan [2] it was for couent; he had clothes or
food.
no special chambir for to slepe in, but in þe dormytori he took his
rest; his bord was not owt of þe refectory, lest þat gestis caused
28 it. In his riding had he no costful hors, no wastful aray, not
many hors, ne many seruantis, but on of þe on-lerned of his ordre
and too of þe clerkis whech schuld be pryuy and se al his conuersacion, at all tyme þei went with him. In his rydyng he spent When he
rode he told
32 not [3] þe tyme with veyn tales or flying tydyngis, but with Psalmis no vain tales
by the way.
and orisones sewe he al þe weye, euyr hauyng a purs redy to gyue
elmes to pore men whech þat he mette. His In to whech he
schuld come was stuffid with I habundauns of vitaile ful discretly [4], Leaf 53,
back.

---

[1] a crossed through.   [2] MS. þat.   [3] inserted abore.
[4] 1 written abore.

'His inn was
free to all. nowt only for him-selue but for hem þat wold ask it and had nede
þerof. At mete was he myri; he talked moꝛ þan ete, and with
solacious countenauns wold he glade his gestis.

[CHAPTER VI.]

Cap. vj.   4

He accused
himself of
over-eating,
when he had
eaten little. HE wold compleyne sumtyme whan he roos fro þe bord þat he
had synned in vnmesurable etyng or drinkkyng, whan þei
þat weꝛ *conuersaunt* with him ¹ had *meruiel*¹ who þat a man myth
lyue with soo litil mete or drink; whaꞔ he schuld sitte to ete 8·
often-tyme he wold wepe for be-cause, he seyde, þat oure nature
euery day is compelled of very nede to receyue mete and drynk þat
He abstained
from meat,
but ate fish,
except in
Lent and
Advent. he fayle not. Fro flesch and all þat longith to flesch abstined he
euyr, lest þat he weꝛ sek, þanꞔ þorw councell of his frendis he 12
wold ete sum. Fysch ete he þorw þe ȝere, saue in Lentoꞔ and in
Aduent, þan wold he non ete; his mete was paꞔ wortys, letuse
and oþer herbes, whech he ete as þei had be delicasises; whan he
was febil þei weꝛ fayn to dite him fisch in swech maner þat he 16
knew it nowt. This did his *seruauntis* for pite of his febilnesse
He gave the
first part of
his food to
the poor. and whan his mete cam be-fore him þe first part wold he gyue to
God, whech was boꝛ to sum poꝛ man; ny al þe oþir del departed
he on-to hem whech soten a-boute him. In his refeccioꞔ he took 20
Leaf 54. moꝛ ¶ heed þat his soule schuld be fed with holy scriptuꝛ þaꞔ his
He worked
after eating,
and read. body with delicat metis. Aftir mel wold he haue sum bodely labouꝛ,
and þaꞔ rede and pray, and so occupie his tyme. Thorw-oute þe
He wore the
same clothes,
Winter and
Summer. ȝere was he clad equally; he wered no mo clothis in Wyntir þanꞔ 24
in Somyr; with o cote ²he went² and no more, for furres wered he
It was
wonderful
how his old
body lived. neuyr. Thou schuld had merueyle if þou had seyn þe membres of
þat eld body, who þe bones and þe skyn myth vnneth hange to-gidir,
his schulderis croked, his teth oute of þe mouth, who þat swech aꞔ 28
eld body myth lyue whan alle hete was drawe fro him, both natural
and accidental, þat for discoumfort sumtyme his body was ny
contract. Be-twix þe lynand and þe hayir he chase þe mydwey,
and al for he wold haue a conformite be-twix his subiectis and him, 32
and eke for he wold fle þe veynglorie of þe world whech make men

¹⁻¹ *in margin.* ·   ²⁻² *written above in red.*

ofte to lose heꝑ mede. This myd wey clepe we, þat he vsed, wollen He wore woollen cloth next his body.
cloth next his body, for hayir wered he non, ne lynand wold he
non were.   Whan he was compelled [1] be þe prouocacioñ of natuꝑ
4 to go to bed and [2] to rest he wold sey first certeyn Psalmes whech He said Psalms before resting.
he knew of [3] vse, first for him-self and for his breþerin, þañ for
kyngis and bischoppis, and all [4] cristen folk.   This was his ‖ vsage, Leaf 54, back.
at seuene of clok he wold go to rest; seldom wold he ly on his bed,
8 but he sat [5] þeron comounly.   His cloþis whech he wered on day He wore his day-clothes at night, and had no pillow.
he put hem not fro hym at eue, but lay with hem al nyth; ne
vndir his hed wold he no pilow haue, so þat whan he slept his hed
hing down with-outen sustentacle and touchid sumtyme his brest.
12 We rede in þe elde faderes lynes of Egipt þat þei cleped slep heꝑ
enmy be-cause at þat tyme, as þei þoute, þei sesed fro þe seruyse
of God.   So ded ouꝑ Gilbert, as I suppose; he wold not ly soft
þat he schuld not slepe longe, for þei þat haue mech mete must
16 haue mech slep.   And þerfor þat on-mesurable diete & þat diuturne
slepe was forbodyn be Crist whan he saide to his aposteles [6]: Be-waꝑ, Christ forbade much sleep.
he said, þat ȝouꝑ hertes be not greued with ouer mech mete, or
drynk, or slep.   On his bed had ouꝑ maystir Gilbert no cloþis but
20 of wolle and no bolstering but strawe.   Whan he was sette þere
onys schuld [7] no man heꝑ him speke a word tyl in þe morownyng.

[CHAPTER VII.]

cap. vij.

AFTYR þat laudes weꝑ said in the cherch þan wold he reherse After Lauds Gilbert rehearsed saints' lives, and made his confession.
24 certeyn seyntis lynes; þan wold he sey certeyn orisones [8]
for hem þat aꝑ ded and assoyle hem; after þis wold he mak a
meke and ‖ a long confessioñ, not only for him-self but for all his, Leaf 55.
asking of his breþerin of all his defautes forgyuenesse, and he
28 assoiling hem all and gyuyng hem all his blessing lich as Seynt Iob
ded þat euery day offered on-to God for helth of his childyrn. [9]

---

[1] d *written above.*   [2] *not clear in text and re-written above.*
[3] *a character crossed through.*   [4] *his breþerin crossed through.*
[5] *sad in text; sat in red in margin.*   [6] *In margin in red, Luc 21.*
[7] d *added in red.*   [8] s *added in red.*
[9] *In margin in red,* Iob i.

He was never
idle. This maystir Gilbert was neuyr ydil, but al þe day occupied, eythir
in redyng, or in orison, or in lesson, or in contemplacioñ, or in oþir
holy werkys, now and now chaungyng fro on to a-noþir, aftir tyme
and leyser þat he had.   And þouȝ he had mech to do ȝet went he 4
fro no mateꝝ til it hadde a parfith ende, ne he letted neuyr no
circumstauns of his perfeccioñ for ony straunge mateꝝ, þat is to
sey, for no temporal profith he putte not Goddis seruyse behinde[1],
ne þe holy obseruaunces whech longed to þe cloyster weꝝ not lettid 8
with besinesse whech was oute-ward.   In compassioñ he was[2] a
fadyr to all men, in contemplacioñ moꝝ suspense þan oþir men.

He wept in
the singing
of Psalms. Offten wold he wepe in ympnis & Psalmys redyng, and in þe swete
songis of þe cherch whan he herd þe melodye, so was his soule 12
repleschid with swetnesse, but ȝet had he moꝝ delectacioñ in þe
wordis þañ in þe notes.   And a-geyn þese veyn þoutes þat come
sodeynly on us, avoyding þe swete deuocion þat we wold' haue,

Leaf 55,
back. a ‖ meruelous vsage had he.   For in-as-mech he knew wel þeꝝ 16
myth no man want hem, he sette certeyn merkys of his fingeris and
his ioyntis in what place of þe Psalme he was, þat sone aftyr þe
temptacion was voyded he myth retorne a-geyn on-to þe same place

He chose one
of his people
to succeed
him. of his orison.   And ȝet moꝝ-ouyr, þat he schuld fulfill al rith- 20
wysnesse, he chase on[3] of his subiectis whom he knewe be þe
Holy Goost þat he schuld succede in his office aftir his deth.
This man chase he specialy, and to him he mad his profession and
permitted his stabilnesse on-to þe hous of Sempingham, and so 24
of[4] þis same mannes handes took Gilbert þe habite of professioñ.
What constans and manhod was in þis mannes hert is ful manifest
in too maneꝝ þingis.   On is þat þe grete causes he went a-boute he
sped hem wyth-outen ony vexacioñ or perturbyng of soule.   A-noþir 28

He forgave
all wrongs. is þat alle þe wrongis whech were[5] do to him or his at þat tyme,
he bare hem so paciently þat he was neuyr mevid for hem.   Be-side
all þis vexacion þat he had owtward, þere was a-noþer þing whech
stood nyher his hert, þe grete besinesse in spirith, for þo houses 32
whech he had rered, for þe soules whech he had gadered, for þe

Leaf 56. grete fere þat he hadde þat he schuld heꝝ ‖ no euel tytandis of
hem.   And whan it happed þat ony euel report was mad he wold

---

[1] *written above.*   [2] MS. a a fadyr; *perhaps* as a fadyr.
[3] MS. of bis of bis, *the first two words crossed through in red.*
[4] MS. þis þis, *the first crossed through.*   [5] *written above.*

blisse God, and speke sum mery wordis and turne all in-to solace. He brushed aside evil report,
He loued treuth and rithwisnesse so wel þat whan he was vexed
with ony materis, eythir with-oute þe religion or with-Inne, he
4 wold sey sumtyme he had leuer chese to be exiled, or elles his
þrote to be cutte, þan he schuld suffir in his tyme þe lawes of þe And insisted ever on the laws of the Church.
cherch & þe good customes of religion schuld fayle.

[CHAPTER VIII.]

cap. viij.

8 IN þe last ende of his age, not-with-stande þat he was blynd, Though he was blind in his old age,
ȝet þe grete strength of his soule was not apeyred, for as
grete ȝel and as grete bysynesse had he at þis age to encrese of
religioñ and snybbyng of vices as euyr had he in his ȝong dayes.
12 His witte as fresch, his vndirstandyng as redy, his mynde as tow, yet he possessed all his other faculties.
his reson as clene were at þat ouɍ, and all oþir þingis þat longe to
þe soule as euyr þei were, whech was merueyle to se[1], specially in
a man þat hadde a hundred wyntyr in age[2]. He myth heɍ with þe
16 best. His tonge fayled not of his office. His hand qwaked not
with no palesye. His feet weɍ stabil to beɍ his body, and his[3] oþir
membris. Non of hem denyed his seruyse ¶ to þe body; lych Leaf 56, back.
he was on-to Caleph or Moyses, whech too at grete age had þe vse
20 of all heɍ membris, saue þis differens is þere, þat þis man had lost
his sith. It is worthi[4], as summe men þink, þat þei whech serue
God with dew obediens schuld haue heɍ membres obedient to hem[5].
For in þe mynde of þis man of whech we speke now was ful grete
24 hete[6] of charite, both on-to God and to all men, for in his hert Crist
wanted neuyr, men myth know be his mouth whech was euyr
spekyng of Crist. Eke his tonge and his handis weɍ euer redy to He was ever ready to help his neighbours.
help of his neybouris. This was þe cours of his lyf; þis was þe
28 maner of his lyuyng; þese be þe experiment of his vertues; þese
be þe good aray of his tecches with whech he was magnified with
grete men; for in vertu he was gretter þan þei, and nowt only was
he foloweɍ of þe blissed lyf of religious men, but he had a lif in He was a paradigm to his followers.
32 him-self whech religious men may folow: let se what man at þoo
dayes was so commendable of good[7] werkis þat he myth be set as

---

[1] C. 32. for to se.   [2] C. wynteyr of age.
[3] C. for to bere his body and all his.   [4] C. wordy.   [5] C. them.
[6] C. hete *omitted, and grete appears* greme.   [7] we *crossed through.*

equal to þis man; what man coude now gader so grete richesse with
swech[1] pouerte, ʒet[2] most merueyl of all, a seculer man, dwellyng
in court, seruyng in court, and newly drawe oute of þe world, whech

¶ lerned neuyr of no man þe reules swech as[3] longe to þe monasterie, 4
þat he schuld[4] be parfite so sone and so sone knowe þoo reules[5].
Mor-ouyr þat he schuld[6] make reules in whech so many persones[7]
schuld[8] rise to parfitnesse, of þis had men wondyr. Wherfor þis
man for his holynesse was beloued[9], and for his magnificens stood 8

in merueyl[10] to men, but both to God and man he stood in grete
worchip. Kyngis and princes þei honoured him, bischoppes and
prelates þei receyued him ful deuoutly.

þei þat wer ny him and eke þat dwelt fer fro him, þei loued 12
him, and schortly to sey, al þe puple held him in grete reuerens.
Eke þe vertu of our Lord whech gaue him al þis grace added
þertoo ful grete ioye, for he þat sette all þese good werkis in him
mad þe same werkys to schyne with vertues.   16

[CHAPTER IX.]

cap. ix.

AND þouʒ[11] it be so þat þese dayes be not vsed with myracles as
þe former dayes were, in[12] whech wer doo many myracles,
for as þe[13] Psalme saith, we se now no toknes, now is þere no 20
profete for to telle us what schal befall; and þouʒ it be so þat
Seynt Gilbert be mor worthi to be in worchep for his merytory[14]
dedes þan for doyng of myracles, ʒet on-to þe wytnesse of his good

¶ werkys, be-side þe grete bysynesse he had in wynnyng of soules, 24
whech is of mor vertu þan curyng of bodies, ʒet were þere, þorw þe

grete merit of his holy lyf, doo many toknes þorw whech his doctrine
was commended and his holynesse confermed. And euene as þorw
his wordis and his dedes þe rudenesse of many a soule was reformed, 28

rith soo be þe touchyng of his cloþis, his hosen, or his girdyl, or
swech oþir[15] þingis whech[16] he touched his lyue, many a body was

---

¹ C 32 b. such.   ² C. ʒet þe.   ³ C. as *omitted*.   ⁴ C. chulte.
⁵ C. reules þer-of.   ⁶ C. chulte.   ⁷ *final* s *added above*.   ⁸ C. schulde.
⁹ C. beloved.   ¹⁰ C. grett [mer]uell.
¹¹ MS. þow *dotted under and* þouʒ *written above*.   ¹² *inserted above*.
¹³ spl *crossed through in red*.   ¹⁴ *first* y *inserted above*.
¹⁵ MS. oþis, s *crossed through and* r *written over in red*.   ¹⁶ *in margin*.

restored to helth aftir þe feith whech þei put in him. Theꝛ Some of his bread was kept sixteen years, and many were healed by it.
was bred kept sextene ȝere aftir his deth, on-corupte, on-mouled,
whech he blessed and sent to a[1] deuoute woman whech asked þat
4 in Goddis name, of whech bred many men haue ete and be holed
of dyueris seknesse. Thus aftir he had fulfillid þe grete merites
of his perfeccioñ and[2] sette in a parfite stabilnesse all his congregaciones, eke whañ ouꝛ Lord had disposed to rewarde his laboures
8 with euerlastyng ioye and þe tyme of his clepyng was ny, he
be-gan to wax more feble þanñ he was wone to be and sayde on-to
his bretherin he schuld not long lyue with hem, for þat þe membris
of his body be-gan to fayle, and nature, whech is propicius to helth,
12 had withdrawe sum-what[3] ‖ hir fauouꝛ. Thus, seknes growyng, and Leaf 58.
age of an hundred ȝere touching, he was in party compelled for to Finding himself growing feeble,
passe fro þis lif in whech he was gretly broken for penauns whech
he had þolyd in Goddis seruyse, but ȝet were all his[4] membres
16 hool as we saide be-fore, saue his sith. Tho sent he letteris on-to he sent letters to the Churches of his order,
all þe cherchis of his order, in whech he notyfied on-to hem þat his
day was come in whech he schul leue his body here and goo to saying that he was near death,
Goddis mercy, praying hem deuoutly in þoo same letteris þat þei
20 schuld recomende his soule[5] with heꝛ prayeris to God, most specialy
at þat tyme whan it schuld forsake þe body. Eke in þoo same letteris
he gaue Goddis blessing and his[6] to alle[6] þat aftir his decese[7] schuld
loue þe ordre and kepe þoo congregacionis in parfith loue and
24 charite, and defende þe same ordre fro heꝛ enmyes. More-ouyr to
alle þat þis[8] comaundment fulfillid he sent pleneꝛ absolucioñ of all and giving absolution.
þoo defautes in whech þei had trespased eythir a-geyn þe reule or
his instituciones. And in þoo same letteris he wrot on-to all þoo
28 þat in þe order schuld make ony discord or ony scisme þat þis
present absolucioñ schul neuyr fauouꝛ hem, but þat þei schuld
knowe hem-self, but if þei ded penauns þat þei weꝛ reprobat of
God. ‖

---

[1] *written above in red.*   [2] *St sent crossed through.*   [3] *what in margin.*
[4] *þoo crossed through in red and his written above.*
[5] *inserted above in red.*   [6] *inserted above in red.*
[7] *MS. dicese, e written over in red.*   [8] *inserted above in red.*

[CHAPTER X.]

cap. x.

Leaf 58,
back.

When near
death he was
at Cadney,

and was
removed
secretly to
Sempring-
ham, lest his
body were
arrested.

All the
leaders of his
order went
to him,

Leaf 59.

and were
blessed.

His successor
was with him.

What he said.

THUS whan þe tyme was come in whech þat holy soule schuld leue þe In of his body[1]; in þe nyth in whech our Lord[2] Ihesu was born, it happed him to be at a hous of his in a ylde, whech 4 hous þei clepe Cadney, for in þat same hous at þe beginning of his seknesse he receyued þe sacramentis of penauns and of hosiħ, and þus many dayes aftir þat abode þe tyme assigned be ouꝛ Lord in whech his soule schuld passe fro his body with gre[te] auysement 8 and ful ryp deuocioñ. Thoo þei þat weꝛ with him, his chapeleynes and breþerin, þoutȝ þei wold remeve him fro þat place, for if it so happed þat he had dyed þeꝛ, þei weꝛ a-ferd þat sum man of gret myth wold a-reste þe body be þe weye in his caryage and take here 12 tresouꝛ from hem. Therfor þei caried him whil he was on lyue be othir weyes þan þe comown weye, and browt him to Sempyngham, for it was conuenient, as hem þoutȝ, þat his body schuld ly þeꝛ whech he had sette a place, hed of aħ his monasteries. And in 16 þis space fro Cristmasse tyl þat day whech he dyed[3] ouꝛ Lord graunted him swech a space þat aħ þe souereynis of his ordꝛ and aħ þe prouostis of his cherchis myth come and visite him, for so þei dede come on-to him and eke many a ‖ disciple of his, for þere 20 had þei his blessing and noble exhortaciones of pes & vnite of þe rigouꝛ eke and þe hardnesse of þe ordir, who it schuld be kept aftir his daies, and þus instruct þei went hom fro him. The last day of his temporal lyf, whan aħ were owt of þe hous, he sat be his 24 beddes side, he þat was successouꝛ in his office, takyng heed at him what he wold comaunde. And aftyr he had long be stille in silens as man þat schuld sone passe, he, no man seand, no man herand, but with þe Holy Gost replet, þus spak in þe goost. For 28 þouȝ his bodyly[4] sith were rest fro him, ȝet vndirstood he in his soule þat his successouꝛ was ny him, wherfoꝛ þese wordes of þe[5] Psalme, distinctly, openly, and wyth sad auysement he sayde in þis wise: He departed, he gaf to pore men. And þanne he rehersed: 32 He departed to many men. He gaf, and not seld, to pore men, not

---

[1] MS. soule, *with body written over in red.*   [2] *inserted above in red.*
[3] h *crossed through.*   [4] ly *in margin.*   [5] s *crossed through.*

to rich men.   And þan last he seid þus: To þe schal þis longe
heꝛ-aftirward.   Thoo spak he oþer þingis to þat same man whech
we can-not reherse.   These wordes, as I suppose, weꝛ ful *conuenient*   His words were
4 on-to ouꝛ maystir, whech departed all his goodis to many folk whech   appropriate
he had called to þe seruyse of ouꝛ Lord, & gaf all þese goodes
for pure charite, for he seld hem nowt, hopyng to haue of hem ony   in him who gave his goods
worldly profith. ❡ To pore men gaf he þese goodys, non to rych, for   Leaf 59,
8 þoo giftis ȝoue to pore men,[1] þei þat lyue in wilfull pouert for þe   back.
loue of God, schuld receyue him in-to euyrlastyng tabernacles.   to the poor.
To rich men he gaf it nowt, for þei nede not, and eke for it is ful
hard on-to hem to enter in-to þe kyngdam of heuene.   For þese   For his deeds he is in
12 þingis þat he ded heꝛ, now is he in ioye and þis þat schuld be his   heaven.
successour, he lerned for to do lich as he saide.

[CHAPTER XI.]

Cap. xj.

THE last day of Seynt Gilbert lif was a Sattirday; we schuld   He died on Saturday, the
16 clepe it a Sabat-day be þe moꝛ congrue name.   Sabat is as   Sabbath-day,
mech to sey þat day whan men rest of heꝛ werkys.   This day was
conuenient to his deth, for þann rested he of all his labouꝛ whech
he had in þis mortal body.   He myth sey at his deth: Nite is
20 I-goo and day schal come; þe dirknes schal not take me ne trede
me.   The ouꝛ of his deth was whil þe couent was [2] at laudes[2], at   when Lauds were being
mateyns, for at þat tyme as Iob sayth: Praisen God, ye morow   said, on the 4th of Feb-
sterres.   That same Sabatday, þat is to say, þe fourt day of   ruary, 1189,
24 Februarij, þe ȝere of þe Incarnacion of ouꝛ Lord, a þousand,
a hundred, eyty and nyne, swech tyme as nyte chaunged in-to
day, whilys þat þe laudes were sayde in þe couent, þis man passid
fro þe þirknesse of þis lyf, fro þe ❡ laboures of þis world, ful of age   Leaf 60.
28 moꝛ þan a hundred ȝere.   Whidir þat he went ȝe schal here, for to   over 100 years old.
dwelle in þe hous of God, for to prayse God þere for euer, wheꝛ he
is sette in his ordre, þat is to say, a-mongis þe sercle and þe dauns
of virgines, as we hope, and as[3] reuelacion was mad to sum folk   He is now with the
32 afterward, þer hath ouꝛ Lord graunted him his sete.   Aftir his   virgins of heaven.

---

[1] MS. to pore men or ell; or ell *crossed through and* pore men *again written over it.*
[2-2] *inserted above.*   [3] *in margin.*

Distant
people knew
of his death
by visions,
and knew he
had joined
the heavenly
virgins,
deth weᵽ certeyn visiones & reuelaciones mad to persones of grete
credens, þorw whech visiones þei þat weᵽ dwelling fer fro him had
very knowlech of þat oure and very certificacioñ þat he was ioyned
on-to þe felauchip of aungelles in heuene. For þouȝ it be so, as we 4
beleue, þat euery man receyueth mede aftir his werkys, and as
treuth sayth, þoo frendis þat be þe god of richesse, receyue þe
makeris in-to euyr-lastyng tabernacles, of grete rith-wisnesse þis
man is for to beleued þat he is ioyned to virgynes, for as mech as 8
he mayde both body & soule & mayde in feith perseuered euyr, and
eke all his erdly goodes ȝaue on-to virgines, and for þe virginite of
many folk laboured al his lyf. For euene as he þat receyueth a

In that he
had his
reward.
rith-ful[1] man in þe name of a rithful man schal take þe mede of 12

Leaf 60,
back.
a rithful man, euene so he þat[3] receyueth many virgines in þe
name ‖ of virgines schal receyue þe mede of virgines. Eke for as
mech as þis man was prelate and begynner of mech noumbyr, both
of men and women whech schuld avowe chastite, and be-cause þe 16

He has a
centenary.
noumbir centenarie is applied as for a special reward both to
prelates and to maydenes, þerfor hath þis man for þoo too þis
special reward.

[CHAPTER XII.]

capitulum xij.   20

His body was
kept four
days, and all
his priors
came to the
burying.
THUS was þe soule of this blessed man translate on-to heuene
and þe ded body kept up-on þe grounnd fouᵽ dayes with
exequiis and missis after þe good customes of þe cherch. In þat
same tyme all þe priouris and souereynes of þe ordre weᵽ sent 24
aftir to be at þe byrying of her maystir. Whan þei weᵽ gadered

His progeny
numbered
2,200.
to-gidir and anoumbered, þe summe of his progenie cam on-to[3]
too þousand and too hundred. The fourt day aftir his deth, þat

On Tuesday
is to sey on þe Tewysday, were gadered to-gidir many prelatis, 28
both of his ordre and eke of oþir religious, with mech folk of

they washed
the body,
þe cuntᵽ[4] þat came þedir for reuerens of þe man, and aftir tyme
þe masse was sayde, þei wasched þe body with watir, whech watir

Leaf 61.
was kept, for þei þat drank þerof weᵽ restored to bodely ‖ helth. 32

arrayed it,
and buried it,
Aftir his wasching þei arayed him lych a prest, and þoo þei byried
him betwix too auteres, on of ouᵽ Lady, Seyn Mary, þe oþir of

---

[1] C. 31 ryghtfull.   [2] h crossed through.
[3] MS. on-to a þou, with þou crossed through.   [4] C. contre.

Seynt Andrew þe apostel.   He was so layd at þat tyme þat þe between two altars,
women myth com to þe graue on þe o side and men on þe oþir
side.   The ston a-boue was not layd on-to þe tyme þat all men where, as it lay, all might
4 whech weʔ present, as for heʔ last leue, myth come an touche touch it.
þe body with what þing þei wold, and kisse it for reuerens of his
holynesse.   Childyrn, maydenes, ne no degre, had no feʔ, no horrouʔ
in cyssyng of þat ded body, for feith gaf hem boldnesse to touch
8 it and loue sent hem boldnes to kisse it.   What mornyng þeʔ was There was great mourning.
of all folk, what lamentation of clerkis, what wepyng of maydenes,
for as meeh as þei haue lost[1] heʔ hed and heʔ principal, heʔ fader
and her schippard, and for þei schuld no moʔ haue him to her
12 consolacion, weʔ long to telle.   But ouʔ Lord God þat wrout all
þese werkys in his seruaunt, be whom þis same seruaunt Gilbert
had grete prosperite in all his werkis, this same Lord wold neythir
defraude his werkman of his mede ne þe good werkys of heʔ
16 parfith ende, as it schal be schewid in þis next declaracioñ.
Be-side þoo myracles whech weʔ do þe day of his byryng, and Many miracles
be-side þe myracle ɪ do in substitucioñ of his successouʔ, þer fell Leaf 61, back.
many oþir grete, of blynde men, def men, bedred, dropesie, ffevyrues, were done through him.
20 wodnesse, and oþir grete seknesse, whech weʔ cured, summe be þe
watyr in whech he was waschid, summe be oþir relikes of him,
sum be dremes and visiones, summe in þe same place of his
byryng, summe in oþir places.   It is no doute þat his werkes weʔ
24 ful plesaunt on-to ouʔ Lord, wherfor þat he schuld stand in þe
moʔ worchip a-mongis men, ouʔ Lord mad his werkis to be
magnified aftyr his deces, in so mech þat, be þe comaundment of
Innocent Pope þe þird, Hubert bischop of Cauntirbyry and[2] Hubert of Canterbury,
28 a-noþer bischop of Hely, eke þe abbot of Borow, with many oþir, the bishop of Ely, and the abbot of Borrow
mad diligent inquisioñ and redact all þis in a forme and sent it inquired into these miracles,
vp to þe court.

[CHAPTER XIII.]

cap. xiij.

32 AND whan ouʔ holy fader þe Pope had receyued þis infor- Pope Innocent III canonized Gilbert,
mmacioñ with[2] councel of his breþerin, þe cardinales, he
mad þis man, þis Seynt Gilbert, to be a-noumbred and ascribed

---

¹ he *crossed through.*
² bi *crossed through.*   ³ his *dotted underneath.*

in þe cathaloge of seyntes. A cathaloge is a schort writyng of
seyntes, in whech wrytyng is conteyned of what cuntᵽ þe seynt

and com-
maunded his
feest to be·
held

was & eke his holy lif. The Pope comaun̄ded eke þat same tyme
his feest to be solempnyȝed in þe cherch and made collectes to 4

Leaf 62.

be seyd in his commemoracion. He collmaun̄ded eke his body

and his body
to be trans-
lated.

to be translat, as it was fulfillid aftirward. For þese causes
·þis faderis day schuld be solempniȝed with þe moᵽ deuocion̄ and
with more besinesse, because his lyf was holyer, his doctrine 8
moᵽ holsom, his labouᵽ moᵽ feruent, his frute moᵽ plentenous,
his deth moᵽ prouable, his myracles moᵽ euydent þan̄ summe
oþir, and þerfor he, be liklynesse, hath be-for God moᵽ ioye and

Let the
Church joy in
the joy of her
son !

be-foᵽ men moᵽ worchip. Ioye be mad be ouᵽ moder þe cherch 12
of þe ioye to whech hir son is now newly browt, and to hir worchip
and profith of hir childyrn synge sche¹ þe praysyng of God and
hir owne, þat þorw þe prayeᵽ of hir meritis sche mytħ make pes
with vices, put awey aduersities, brynge in þe strength of vertues, 16
þe profite and encres of very religion̄, owre londes and cuntres,
God ouᵽ makeᵽ grauntyng, dispose in euyrlastyng pes, confermyng
þat ouᵽ Lord Ihesu Crist, to whom with þe Fadeᵽ and Holy Gost
euer be worchip and ioye &c. Amen.   20

[Chapter XIV.]

Heᵽ is þe secund part of Seint Gilbert lyf, þe capitule 14.

BE-cause þat a gret part of iustise is for to do non euel and
þe profite of þe same iustise is for to do good, and eke 24
for it is not i-now to ouᵽ helth þat we take not oþer mennes

Leaf 62,
back.

good wrong‖fully or desire it wrongfully, but we be boun̄de
for to ȝeue owne goodes for þe loue of God frely. For þis cause

Gilbert
worked for
the increasing
of religion.

þis very prest Gilbert stodied euery day to bere schidis to þe 28
holy fyᵽ whech brent in þe tabernacle, both nyth and day, for
þe fire of charite þat was in the tabernacle of his breest brent
him-selue, a ful delectable offering to ouᵽ Lord. And þat he
schuld not renne in blynd presumpcion̄, ne vse maneres with-oute 32
consideracion, but þat he schuld renne and take þe summe of his

---

¹ l crossed through.

merites, the best man*er* of p*er*feccio*n* and þe trewest way to
p*er*feccio*n* with grete bysynesse, he both soute and took. The
first grou*nd* of his werk he sette in heith of mekenesse, whech
4 vertu dispisith in eu*er*y man his owne excellens, for þe veri place
of meknesse is in heuene. Therfor he put a-wey þe mater of He despised worldly worth,
al erdly goodes fro him-self, for þoo same goodis sette a ma*n*
in fals excellens and þrowe a man al vndir-fote. He þrew fro
8 him all pride whech schuld ryse[1] of vertues þat we*r* with-inne
him. He took ful gret heed to þe voys of ou*r* Lord þat seith : If
þou wilt be parfith, go selle all þat euyr þou hast and folow me.
This man ded þus. He gaf his goodes to pore men, not for and gave all to the poor,
12 vanyte but for charite, and for þat gift þe mynde of his rith-
wisnesse schal dwelle with-oute*n* ende. Wha*n* ‖ he had det*er*myned Leaf 63.
in his hert þat all his goodes schuld be departed on-to po*r* men,
þa*n* chase he swech pore whos pouerte was honest, knyt[2] with who w*r*e honest.
16 þe dred and eke þe loue of God, for his desire was to sowe his
sedes in þe blessing*is* of God, þat he myth repe in þoo same
blessing*is*. In þat same tyme, þat is to seye, in þe regne of In the reign
King Herry þe secunde, as he writith in þe book mad of the of Henry II, as is said in his book on
20 construccio*n* of monasteriis, in þat same time[3] were in þe town monasteries,
of Sempyngham certeyn maydenes seculer, whos soules þe seed
of Goddis word, sowyn be þis same Gilbert, had so touchid þat
þei were rype on-to religio*n* lich as corn is white to heruest.
24 These same maydenes, desyring to be victouris of he*r* kynde & eke certain maidens at
of þe world, eu*er*y day entendyd to no[4] oþir þing but to plese and Sempringham had been led
to be kynt to þat[5] spouse whech is in heuene. This, aspied be by him to forsake the
Seynt Gilbert, spe*ci*aly wha*n* he had in his avow mad a p*ro*misse world.
28 þat his possession of Sempyngha*m* and of Tyrington schuld be He gave his possessions
ȝoue to God, ferþermo*r* þat he wold ȝeue þis to pore, and eke to God.
he fonde no men at þat tyme wold lyue so strey[t]ly as þese
women were disposed, for þis cause, he det*er*myned to gyue þese
32 goodes to swech pore whech were po*r* in spirit & myth ‖ chalange Leaf 63,
þe kyngdam of Heuene[6] for hem & for oþir. This ma*n* Gilbert back.
mad him frendes with swech rychesse as he had, whech frendis
schuld receyue him in-to euerlasting tabernacles. The first frendes

---

[1] *rise crossed through in red.*   [2] *þe crossed through.*
[3] *inserted above in red.*   [4] *MS. no no, the first crossed through in red.*
[5] *MS. þat þat.*   [6] *w crossed through.*

6

þat he made weᷤ not of men but of wommen. Wommen chase
he first for þe similitude whech ouᷤ Lord rehersed in þe gospeli [1]
of a womman þat had lost a dramme and found it, who sche
cleped hir frendes to ioye with hir [2] for hir dramme þat was [4]
found. So þese maydenes first chosen were cause þat many oþer
schuld be cleped aftirward. A dramme is a certeyn mony of
gold weying þe viij part of an vnce. Oure Gilbert be-gan his

for it is noble
to benefit the
feebler kind.
perfeccioᷠ at þe febiller kende, for to þe febiller kynde nature [8]
techeth þat we schuld do ouᷤ benefetes. þe councel of God is
swech also [3] to help þat þing whech is moost febil, eke þe mede
for þis help is þe gretteᷤ, ferþermoᷤ [4] oure Lord in þe gospel to
þe febelest kynde applied þe grettest reward, þe hundredfold frute [12]

to virginite. Gilbert norchid þis astate, and þerfor hath he part
of her reward. Be-side al þis, ouᷤ Gilbert, aftir þe rith ordre
in elmesse-ȝeuyng, gaf his goodes to hem þat were rithful, aftir
þe councel of Salamon wheᷤ he saith: Gyue þi goodes on-to good [13]

men and receyue not ‖ þese synneres to þin elmesse.

[CHAPTER XV.]

Capitulum xv.

Seven
maidens
were the
beginning of
the Gilbertine
order.
SEUENE maydenes, as we saide be-fore, fulfillid with heuenely
desires in worchip of þat noumbir of seuene giftis longing [20]
on-to þe Holy Goost, þese were beginneres of þis holy religioᷠ
vnder ouᷤ fadir Gilbert. These seuene bodily virgines, offered to þe
noumbyr of þese seuene giftis, mad heᷤ virginite the moᷤ merytorye
be-cause þei weᷤ arayed with vertues. [5] What profitith a laumpe [24]
þat hath non oyle? What profitith clene flesch whan þe soule is
corrupt? What profitith a body clene and a hert defouled? Be
þis weye schuld þese hethen men be vertuous whos lyf is al synne.

They were
clean in body
and in mind.
Therefor, þat þese maydenes schuld be clene in soule & body, to heᷤ [28]
soules he ordeyned clene instrumentis, heᷤ bodies with whech þei
schuld werk heᷤ owne helth [6]. And be-cause þat no man whech
seruyth God may serue wel God and be occupied with temporal

---

[1] *In margin in red, Luc. xv.*   [2] *inserted above in red.*
[3] *inserted above in red.*   [4] *in black and red in margin.*
[5] *O crossed through.*   [6] *E crossed through.*

besinesse,[1] eke be-cause virginite is a tendir þing & may sone be
tempted of þe sotil deceytes of þe serpent, þe Deuele, whech is ful
eld of tyme and ful sotil of kynde & sone deceyueth virginite,
4 namely, whaṅ it is sette so open þat it is schewid to þe world,—
for tresouꝛ openly bore is put in gret perel, ¶—for þis cause he sperd ^{Leaf 64,}
þese virgines fro þe noyse of þe world, fro þe sith of men, þat þei
whech schuld[2] entyr in-to þe priuy chaumbyr of þe spouse þei
8 schuld only entende on-to þe swete halsyng of þe same spouse.
He wold not þat þei schuld walk to se vanytes, as ded Dina, but
þat þei schuld hide hem in heꝛ tabernacle, as dede Sarra, or in
heꝛ conclaue, as ded Ouꝛ Lady.   And for it is not I-now for to[3]
12 absteyne fro euel but if we doo good, þerfor he mad to hem a lawe
of holynesse & tawte hem þat same with whech þei schuld plese to
þe heuenely spouse & cleue euyr to his chast halsyngis in all maner
clennesse.   Thus gaf he hem a lawe of lyf and of loue,[4] of chastite,
16 of meknesse, of obediens, a[n]d charite, and all oþir vertues whech
lede to euyrlastyng lif, he comaunded hem to kepe.   Thei, as good
disciples, ioyfully receyued hem & deuoutly fulfillid hem.   Theꝛ
schone, or ellis schyned, in þe soule of þese women, a fayꝛ beute of
20 precious perles, of swech goostly richesse as ouꝛ Lord tellith in þe
gospell, þat a man schuld selle all þat he hath for to welde þis.
And þou3 þei lyued in fleech and not aftyr þe fleech, 3et wost he wel
as longe as þei were in flesch, be-side swech neccessaries as longe to
24 þe flesch, þei myth not lyue, ¶ þerfor al þing þat is nedful to ouꝛ ^{Leaf 65.}
fleschly febilnesse, as mete, or drynk, or cloþing, or houses, all þese
ordeyned he to þese maydenes and heꝛ seruauntis in best maneꝛ,
in mesuꝛ and discrecioṅ, þat is to seyn, swech houses as long to
28 religioṅ, with a cloystir, or a clauseꝛ, wallid abowte, and in þoo
houses he sperd þe handmaydenes of ouꝛ Lord, euyr for to dwelle
þeꝛ in solitarie lyf; and þis werk was undyr þe wal of þe cherch
of Seynt Andrew, in þe strete or town of Sempyngham, on þe north
32 side, first axid and had þe counsel and þe help of Alexaunder, þan
bischop of Lincolṅ.   Dore was þere non mad in þe wal[5] but on, &
þat was not open but swech tyme as schal be touchid afterward;

Marginal notes:
Leaf 64, back.
They were shut in from the world,
[3] and they lived according to the law which Gilbert made for them.
They were supplied with all things
necessary to life,
and dwelt in a cloister by the church, built with the help of Alexander, bishop of Lincoln.

---

[1] *In margin in red,* 2 Thi 2.   [2] *et crossed through.*
[3] *do good crossed through.*   [4] MS. lore.
[5]-[5] *added in margin; the added passage continues on the next page.*

In the wall
was a window
through
which they
received
necessaries;
þere mad he[5] [1]a wyndowiñ þorw whech þei myth receyue swech neccessaries as longe to her lif, for þouȝ þei weꝛ in the world he wold put hem oute of þe world, fro her lond, from heꝛ kynrod, from heꝛ fadir hous, þat þus exiled fro alł þese, lich a cherch, and

for the rest,
they were cut
off from the
world.
þei a cherch, þat is to seye, a congregacioñ in o feith and o charite, forgeting heꝛ puple and heꝛ fader hous, fro alł curiosite and alł couetyse, or concupiscence, fro alł pride, þus clene I-schake to þe hy kyng, schuld make a complacens in desiryng of her beute.[2] 8 Thus bonde he heꝛ bodies with-inne þoo walles at þat same place

Leaf 65,
back.
Sempingham. ∥

[CHAPTER XVI.]

ca^m. xvj.[3]

BVT he wold not, þouȝ he prisoned heꝛ bodyes, bynde heꝛ soules 12 fro God, but þis was his entent to close hem, be-cause þat conuersacion in þe world is wone to[4] departe many men fro þat familiarite whech þei schuld haue with God.   Eke be-cause þat

-Gilbert
appointed
maids to wait
upon them.
þei myth no-where go oute, þerfor he ordeyned on-to heꝛ seruyse 16 certeyn maydenes not lerned, in a pore seculeꝛ habite, whech schuld brynge on-to þat wyndowne mad in þe wal alł þing þat was neccessary for hem, and receyue of hem at þat same hole swech

The hole in
the wall, or
window, was
not always
open;
þingis as was conuenient to bere out.   That same hole left he ope, 20 but not euyr ope, for it was opened but at certeyn tymes whech weꝛ assigned, for he wold a sperd it for euyr if it had be so þat men or wommen myth a leued with-oute mete or drynk or oþer neccessaries.   For a dore was mad beside, but neuyr open 24

and the door
was only for
Gilbert to
enter by.
with-oute[5] his special comaundment, not for þe maydenes to go owt, but for him to entyr on-to hem for goostly coumfort, or techyng of religioñ,[6] or visiting of þe seke, or swech oþir

He alone kept
the key of it.
neccessarie causes; eke of þat dore was he gayleꝛ him-self; no 28 man bare þat keye but he.   Whidir þat he went, wher-euyr he dwelt, þe key of þat dore was with hym, so was he gelous loueꝛ

Leaf 66.
of here clennesse.   Aftir þis he stodyed soꝛ þat þere schuld ∥ no þing owtward breke þat pes whech þese solitarye folk had in heꝛ 32

---

[1] but *crossed through*.   [2] *In margin in red*, Ps. 4 4 (Psalm 4 v. 4 ?)
[3] *In margin*, 16.   [4] þ *crossed through*.
[5] oute *in red above*.   [6] o *and a stroke crossed through*.

clauseꝛ.   He lerned eke of religiouſ men and wise men þat it was
not conuenient, ne sykir, þat seculeꝛ maydenes rennyng a-boute þe
world schuld serue swech solitarye persones, for euel speche often
4 tyme appeyreth ful good maneres, and eke þei þat runne so a-boute
schuld bryng clatering tydingiſ, whech myth apeyre þe soules of
þe nunnes, for þis cause þoo same seculeꝛ maydenes, with þe good
counsel of heꝛ fadeꝛ Gilbert and party with heꝛ owne deuocioꝛ,
8 desired [1] to haue a religiouſ habite and so dwell with þe nunnes;
and, as þei desired, so had þei.   For þeꝛ, whaꝛ þei weꝛ clad in a ful
pore lyf, þei serued þe nunnes and lyued in ful honest conuerſacioꝛ.
Thus of o kyrnel whech ouꝛ foundouꝛ [2] þrew in þe erde grewe now
12 a-noþer ere be-side þe first spryng whech was þe nunnes.   Þan
whan Seint Gilbert say þe good ʒel of þese seculeꝛ maydenes þus
chaunged on-to God, he was ful mery for deuocion of heꝛ feith, but
be-cause þei weꝛ inexpert, not vsed in swech, and simpil and lewed
16 as touching lettirure, for swech ydiotes al day be-hest moꝛ þing
þaꝛ þei may fulfill, þerfor wold not he, ouꝛ fadir Gilbert, gyue hem
no hard preceptis ne ley no greuouſ birden on heꝛ schulderis whech
þei schuld þrowe awey aftirwardl and repent, ǀ to grete schame of
20 hem-self and grete vylony to religioꝛ.   Therfor þese neophites ar
for to proue, þat Sathanas transfiguꝛ not him-self in-to an aungell
of lith ; þat þe wolf do not on his bak a schepis wolle ; þat þe ostrich
tak not þe wengiſ of an hauke ; þat þe asse haue not þe leones
24 membris.   All þis is seid be þe auctouꝛ of þis lif whech is of þis
Seynt, þat he calleth hem neophites þat he newly conuerted to
religioꝛ ; for neophites weꝛ cleped in eld tyme folk newly conuerted
to þe feith, and all þese transumpciones folowing rehersith ouꝛ
28 auctour to þis entent, þat men of religioꝛ schuld not haue faiꝛ
condiciones owtward and euel inward, as malys in soule lich a wolf
and innocens in wordis lich schepis wolle, and soo may men
expounne all þe othir transumpciones.   For þis same cause þat
32 þese folk schuld [3] vndirstand what þei ded, and eke þat þei schuld
proue, as heꝛ age grew, what þei schuld answeꝛ, þis noble maysteꝛ
told hem be-foꝛ all þese perelleſ and lerned hem all þe scharpnesse
of religioꝛ, all þat euer þei had lerned be experiens or be tellyng of

It was not safe that secular maids should wait upon the nuns,

so these, too, took a habit;

but being simple and unused to hard life, they were just as incapable of fulfilling the difficult precepts of religion

Leaf 66, back.

as Satan is of transfiguring himself into an angel, &c.

Examples for men of religious life.

---

[1] *final d above is red.*

[2] MS. *founder, with* er *crossed through and* ouꝛ *in red in margin.*

[3] vnd *crossed through.*

Gilbert
taught his
sisters to
follow the
ascetic life.
oþer men.   To his sisteres he prechid þat þei schuld despise þe
world & cast fro her hertis all maner of propirte, þat is to seyne,
þei schuld þink no-þing was her, but al comoun, as religious folk
must doo : he taute hem þe maner who þai schuld chastise [1] her [2] 4

Leaf 67.
flesch to trauayle ‖ and to occupye hem fro ydilnesse, and neuyr to
sitte qwiete fro labour in prayer or occupacion.   He taute hem for
to wake & not to slepe mech, to fast longe & not to vse metes oute

Their living
was harsh
and they were
enclosed as in
a prison.
of tyme.   Wrecchid mete, scharp cloth, þis wold he [3] þei schuld 8
haue ; no gay aray, but sperd in cloystir as in prison, þat þei schuld
do no euele ; to kepe silens, þat þei schuld no euele speke, but
be occupied with orisones and meditaciones to avoyde euel þoutes.
Thei answered on-to him at þat tyme þat all þese preceptis plesed 12
hem weel, to take hardnesse for softnesse, labour for ese, heuynesse
for swetnesse, all þese þingis wold þei gladly suffer, so þei myth

Their poverty
drove them
to holiness ;
come wher þei desired.   The nede of pouerte constreyned hem, and
labour in begging, for to desire to ber hy þingis, to þat entent þat 16
þei myth be sykir of euyrlastyng reward.   The loue of God, eke,
þat drowe hem to þis same entent, and helth of her soules þorw

and making
a virtue of
necessity,
they came to
good.
whech þei myth deserue euyrlastyng rest.   So of nede þei mad
vertue, and þouȝ in summe of hem wer not þe very entent of 20
perfeccion, ȝet it lettid not but it gat hem þe ende of good werk.
But þis holy man wold not bynde hem sodeynly to þis perfeccion,

Gilbert gave
all one year's
consideration.
but lete hem haue a ȝere of a-visement, þat of þat grete dilacion
schuld growe þe desire of religion.   24

[Chapter XVII.]

Leaf 67,
back.
                                                             cap. xvij. ‖

But seeing
that woman's
business
profits little
without men,
Gilbert chose
certain men
to govern his
women.
THAN say our fader in his inwardly consideracion þat, with-
outen mennys solace and puruyaunce, womennes besinesse
profitith but lytyl ; þerfor chase he certeyn men whech schuld 28
ouyr-se her possessiones and haue gouernauns of all þo grete
materes whech longed on-to hem.   Summe of þese chase he of
his plowmen and of his seruauntes, summe of pore mennes childyrn
and beggeres whech he had norched fro her childhod.   He was lich 32

---

[1] MS. chastite, *with* se *over in red*.   [2] flech *crossed through*.
[3] MS. hei, i *dotted beneath*.

þe seruaunt of whech þe gospel[1] spekitb, þat at þe comaundment
of ouꝛ Lord went in-to þe lanes & stretes of þe cite, & swech as he
fonde pore or febil, brout &[2] compelled hem to enteꝛ þat his lordis
4 hous schuld be ful. To þese men, þus newly gadered, whech he To these men he ordained
say weꝛ inflawmed with þe [loue][3] of euerlastyng lyf, to þese same, a habit which taught them
at heꝛ peticioꝺ, he ordeyned a tokne of meknesse, an habite whech to despise the world,
signified to hem þat þei schuld despise þis world and for-gete þe
8 vanite þat longith perto. And þoo same preceptis, ful hard and
not esy, of whech we spoke be-fore, he wrote on-to hem, aud taute
hem þat þei schuld not faꝛ fro mynde. He taute hem ferþermoꝛ and he taught them virtue and hard exercises.
oþir vertues þat longe propirly to þe soule, as meknesse, obediens,
12 paciens, and swech oþer, whos exercise is hard and mede gret, Leaf 68.
& þei, as denoute disciples, took þese preceptis gladꝺly and mad
her avow to fulfiꝛ hem for euyr. Thus is þe tresouꝛ, or elles þe
talent, doblid, þat ouꝛ Lord took him[4], for ouꝛ Lord put first in
16 his mynde to make a congregacion of women, and now newly he
hath dobiled þis ʒift whaꝺ he gadered þese men. Thus is þe So is his treasure doubled,
iunctuꝛ of women and men ioyned as broches for þe crowne of
þe spouse, þus mad be þe handis of þe hye werkman. Now is
20 þe tyme come þat þe welbeloued masculyne with þe welbeloued for unto the women of his order are joined men.
feminine schuld go oute in-to þe feld of þis world, for to dwelle in
þe villages and in þe cytees of puple. Now was þe day come þat
þe vyne whech ouꝛ Lord planted[5] schuld fulfiꝛ þe erde with his
24 rotes, and sprede his palmes to þe se, and his braunches to þe oþir
flodes; þat is to say, þat þe membris of þis ordre schuld sprede þe
braunchis of good exaumple, þat it schuld be know wyde. Thus Many noblemen of England,
be processe of tyme, be þe wil of ouꝛ Lord God, þe seed whech he seeing his
28 had sowen be þe first faderes of þis weye, many rich men, noble- good work, helped him,
men of Ynglond, þat is to seye, Erles, Barones, and oþir, seyng and founded monasteries
and approuyng þis werk whech God had be-gunne, and seyng under his rule.
be-foꝛ what goodnesse was disposed aftir[6], þei offered many
32 possessiones to ouꝛ fadeꝛ Gilbert, & monasteries, in many prouynces, Leaf 68, back.
vndyr his reule and gouernauns, þei be-gunne ꞁ to edifie, of whech
helpes Alisaundꝛ bischop of Lincolꝺ was first, and Kyng Herry

---

[1] *In margin in red,* Luc 14. [2] *added in red.*
[3] MS. with þe *of* everlastyng, *etc.*, *of commencing a new line.*
[4] *In margin in red,* Mᵗ 25. (*Matthew xxv.*)
[5] with his rotes *crossed through in red.* [6] *added in margin.*

þe secunde, he confermed all. Our fadir Gilbert receyued þese possessiones with ful gret dred; and summe was he in maner coact to receyue; summe refused he and wold not haue hem, be-cause his desir̄ was fro þe begynnyng of his ordre þat his progenie schuld 4 lyue in honest pouerte. Honest pouerte clepe we þat a man is not in myschef for his dayly nede, ne he hath neythir no gret superfluite of good. This was þe cause þat he wold not haue ouyr mech whan it was ʒoue him, for often-tyme it is seyn þat a-mong gret multitude 8 of puple and gret plente of richesse rise ful gret spottis of pride, as it is said be þe wise man[1]: In þe multitude of þe puple[2] ioye of þe

kyng. For his first purpos at his beginnyng was for to a kept no moo but þoo seuene whech he had sperd up, þat as long as þei 12 lyued þere schuld be no moo. But he sey be þe wil of our̄ Lord þat rich men had multiplied many monasteries to encres of þis ordre; he wold not be contrarie to Goddis wil, ne lette þe deuocion of þe ʒeueres, ne be rekles of þe sustentacioñ to þe seruauntis of 16 God, knowing wel þat þis was Goddis uertu, and not his; wherfor,

he comitted al þis disposicioñ ǁ to þe profund councell of our̄ Lord whech vsetʒ þe seruyse both of good & euel after his plesauns.

[CHAPTER XVIII.]

20

WHAN our̄ maystir Gilbert say þus þe childyrn of God grow soo vndir his tuycioñ and say hem profiten day be day in þe weye of God on-to þe tyme in whech þei were gretly magnified, he demed of him-self, as it longith to good soules to haue hem-self in 24 litil reputacioñ, so demeth he him-self on-worþi for to be in swech heith þat he schuld haue gouernauns ouyr so many parfit persones.

He þoutʒ, þerfor, þat he wold put þis byrden and þis honour̄ fro him, and comitte his flok to on or elles many whech wer̄ abiler and 28 mytier þan he, þat þei schuld haue it in gouernauns. He was in þis cas a folower̄ of Moyses whech seid on-to our̄ Lord: I pray þe Lord sende him þat þou schal sende[4], menyng herby that he was not able to be sent. And in a-noþir place Moyses saide to God: 32

---

[1] *In margin in red, Prouer* 14.   [2] *added in margin.*
[3] *In margin,* 18.   [4] *In margin in red and black,* Exo. 3.

Whom schal þou gyue, Lord, for to be Gouernouꝛ and principal
ouyr þis multitude, whech multitude þou hast mad growe in-to Gilbert said
a grete puple? Thou knowist þat fro þat tyme þat þou spak to he was of lower life
4 me, þi seruaunt, þat I schuld take up-on me to be president ouyr since he became
þis puple, sith þat tyme I am a man of lower lyf, þat is to seye governor of his people.
a man of seculeꝛ ‖ conuersacioñ, whech schuld be holier þan othir, Leaf 69,
and am not. I knowe ful[1] wel þat þe dom schal be ful greuous to back.
8 hem whech ar prelates, for þei must answeꝛ for hem-self and eke
for heꝛ subiectis, and I am ful euel aferd þat if I be not bettir þan
my flok, I schal be turned fro þe first to þe last. Swech maneꝛ
wordes had he often and swech desires to leue his prelacye. In al
12 þis besinesse he herd telle þat þere schuld be a gret congregacioñ He heard of a Cistercian congress,
of þe ordre of Cystewys, whech was neuly be-gunne þat tyme be which the
Seynt Bernard. Wheꝛ it was hold, i rede not, but þe Pope Eugenie Pope
was þere, whech was sumtyme disciple to Seynt Bernard. To þis attended;
16 congregacioñ went ouꝛ Gilbert,[2] purposing for to comitte þe cure and to this he went, proposing to give
of his childyrn to þe kepyng of þese monkis. For þese mennes these monks
conuersacion knewe he best be grete familiarite whech he had with charge of his people.
hem, for often þei come and weꝛ loggid with him, and to þese only
20 told he his counsell, for þei weꝛ newer and of harder reule þañ þe
blake munkis be. Wherfor he[3] supposid þat his ordꝛ schul be in
most sikirnesse if it weꝛ committed to hem, for heꝛ new fundacioñ
and heꝛ streytnesse was moꝛ accordyng to his conceyt. His answeꝛ The Pope and the
24 had he of þe Pope and of þe abbotis whech weꝛ present: ‖ þei Leaf 70.
saide it was not conuenient þat prelatis of her order schuld be abbots, however, would
preferred to þe gouernauns of an-oþir ordre, specialy wheꝛ wommen not agree.
were. Thus frustrat of his purpos, he took his leue, and, be þe
28 comaundment of þe Pope and counsel of þe prelates þere present,
he was mad maystir and principall ouyr þat congregacioñ whech and made him principal
he had begunne. Ouꝛ Lord wold not þat þe congregacioñ at of his order.
Sempingham schuld wante heꝛ owne kepeꝛ whech was bettyr on-to
32 hem þan ten oþir, as Helchana sayd to Anna.[4] For ouꝛ Lord had
disposed þat same congregacioñ to rise to þe moost parfith noumbyr
whech was at þat tyme of an-othir condicion. This religion, whech
we clepe ouꝛ sistir, was but ȝong at þis tyme, for sche had no tetes which was
36 as ȝet, of prelates and souereynes, to gyue soke on-to þe tendyr age young then.

---

[1] þa *crossed through.*   [2] pp. *crossed through.*
[3] *s and a stroke crossed through.*   [4] *In margin in red,* I Reg. 1.

of heᵽ subiectis,. ne for to gyue mete of substauns to hem whech
were growe in-to more perfeccioꞥ, whech eke schuld dispose aꞥ þe
flok with¹ proteccioꞥ owtward and inwardly² conferment.

[Chapter XIX.]

caᵐ. **xix.**   4

*Gilbert was
given
authority
because there
was none*

THUS, be ouᵽ holy fader Eugeny was comitted aꞥ auctorite to
our maystir Gilbert in³ þe kepyng of þis holy flok, for þere
was not founde a bettir ne more sewireᵽ kepeᵽ þaꞥ þat same man

*Leaf 70,
back.*

*more fit to
have it.*

whech was gaderer of þat puple, & eke ‖ so gelous a loueᵽ of hem 8
and þe first laboureᵽ in þat holy vyne. Neuyrþelasse, he held
him-self onworþi to þe birden of swech a wyte; he alegged þe
importunyte of his age, þe onworthþinesse of him-self to swech
dignyte, þe simpilnesse to þat maystirhod, his lownesse eke to so 12
hye a prelacye. Aꞥ þis drede⁴ had he in his soule þat he was not

*He thought
himself
unworthy,*

worþi to be preferred to swech dignite; he dred eke to lese þe
solitarie rest of his contemplacioꞥ, for weel he wist þat þoo secret
councellis whech he was used too, and þe bysy swetenesse of contem- 16

*and knew his
contempla-
tion would be
interrupted;*

placioꞥ, schuld often be interrupt with worldly occupacion and bysy
oure whech longeth on-to prelates. Alle þese excusaciones of
meknesse were not amitted of þe Pope, but þe ȝok of aꞥ þis birden

*but the Pope
gave him the
charge.*

was leid in his nek, for þe Pope comitted aꞥ þis cure on-to him, 20
be-cause he say þat he had no grete appetite ne desiᵽ þertoo. The
purpos of ouᵽ fader Gilbert was euyr to dwelle a-mongis hem þat
be meke, and þe wil of ouᵽ Lord God is euyr of custom to exalte

*When Gilbert
knew God's
will he no*

hem þat moost meke hem-self. Thus, whan þis Goddis owne man 24
knew wel þat þe dome of God had erdeyned he schuld take þis

Leaf 71.

*longer
resisted,*

charge, he was no moᵽ hardy to ma‖ke ony resistens a-geyn þe
disposicion of God whech had chosen him to þat werk. Thus
wold he not lese þe grete habundauns of vertues whech were 28
with-inne him with obstinacye, wherfor he mekly receyued þis
obediens of God and þe comaundment of Goddis vykeᵽ, þe Pope,
trostand for þis obediens to receyue sumtyme þe moᵽ mede, be-cause
he had no grete delectacion to be preferred to swech an office. He 32

---

¹ profl *crossed through.*   ² ly *added in margin.*
³ *inserted above.*   ⁴ *final* e *added in red.*

put his owne wil, his owne profit be-hinde, only for þe welfare and
helth of many othir.   He was ful weel lerned be-fore in þe stody
of *contemplacioñ*, and now be-gan he to lerne who he schuld profith ^{and tried to get the profit}

4 in *ministracioñ* of actiue lyf, for he wold haue þe frute of both lyues, ^{of both lives, the active}
þat is to sey, both actyf & *contemplatif*.   He myth ek moṙ lefully ^{and contem-plative.}
be a dispenser of þoo worldly *goodis* rather þan a-noþir man,
be-cause þe same goodis weṙ his sumtyme.   For he gaf hem to poṙ

8 mon with whech he dwelled as a poṙ man, nowt as a gouernouṙ of
his owne, but as a *procuratour* and a seruaunt of oþer mennes
ricchesse. · For þis cause and many oþer holy toknes & many good ^{Pope Eugenius}
reportes whech weṙ said of him, þe Pope Eugenie had in maneṙ of ^{sorrowed that}

12 an heuynesse[1] þat he knewe neuyr ouṙ ‖ fader Gilbert or þat ^{Leaf 71, back.}
tyme, for if he had knowe him, as he seyde, he wold a promoted ^{he had not}
him to þe archibischoprych[2] of ȝork, whech stood voyd at þat ^{known Gilbert}
tyme.   Thus cam oure fader hom in felauchip long tyme with ^{sooner.}

16 Seynt Malachie, archibischop of Yrland, and Seynt Bernard, abbot ^{Gilbert returned to}
of Clareualle, to whech too men he was so familiar in þat viage ^{England with St. Malachy}
þat in her presens, þorw his denoute prayeṙ, a certeyn man was ^{and St. Bernard,}
mad hool of seknesse whech he had.   He receyued eke toknes of

20 loue both of þe bischop and þe abbot, þe staues of heṙ croses with ^{who gave him presents,}
whech aftirward weṙ doo many myracles; and in *special* Seynt
Bernard gaue him a kerchy, and þerin a *certeyn* relik, as *summe*
sey; but I vndirstand þat þis kerchy was goodly bordred on þe

24 endes, for *orarium* soundith soo in gram*er*.   Thus is he com hom
a-geyn to Sempyngham, frµstrat, as we saide, of his purpos, in
whech, of very meknesse, he had þout to a leyde a-wey þe ȝok fro his
nek, and a put þis office on sum notable ma*n* of þe religio*n* of þese

28 Cistewys; but ouṙ Lord þus with heuenly warnyng, as we suppose,
kept him in þis office as moost parfith & abillest.

[CHAPTER XX.]

cap. xx.[3]

W HAN he was þus co*n*streyned þat he must kepe þis offise ^{He chose men}
32   him-self, ‖ þan chase he owt of his owne religion certeyñ ^{Leaf 72.}
me[n] to beṙ þe birden of gouernau*ns* with him lich as Moyses ^{to govern his order,}

---

[1] sse *inserted above.*   [2] archi *added in margin.*   [3] *In margin,* 20.

ded as we rede be þe councell of Iethro, prest of þe hethen lawe,[1]
he assigned certeyn men to haue gouernauns vndyr him and alle

but attended
to important
matters
himself.

þe grete causes he wold redresse him-self.   Thus ded our maystir;
he chase men of sufficient lettirruŕ, of holy conuersacion, ordered 4
aftir þe custom of þe cherch, whech schuld haue vndyr him þis
gouernauns.   Men weŕ chose for þis cause, for it is moŕ conuenient
þat men be preferred in gouernauns þanñ women.   Letteryd men

These men
were learned.

weŕ chose and no lewed men, þat þei schuld haue cunnyng to 8
tech oþir.   Ordred were þei for þis skil, for þei myth not elles
haue cure of soules[2] lest þan þei weŕ in holy ordre.[3]   Than chase
he men for to gouerne women; letteryd men for to teche þe weye
of Heuene both to men and wommen; clerkis eke, þat þei myth 12
be þe bettyr keperes of þoo scheep whech Crist bowt with his
blood.   All þis ded þis man be holy inspiracioñ of ouŕ Lord
God, and be good councell of holy men and wise men; for, as

Maidens must
have succour
of monks.

þe decres of ouŕ form-faderes beŕ witnesse, þe monasteries of 16
maydenes may not stand with-outen help and socouŕ of munkys,

Leaf 72,
back.

or clerkys, ‖ whech must be spiritual faderes to swech tendyr
soules, to gouerne hem in þe swete ȝok of ouŕ Lord.   But for

But as no
monk may
dwell with
women,

as mech as þe lawes of holy cherch defenden þat no monkys 20
ne clerkys schul dwell with women, but þei schul be feŕ remevyd,
ech of hem fro oþir, so ferforth þat women schuld not come
nyher þe monasterye þan to þe porche of þe same, þis same
prohibicioñ folowyd þis man in þe moost streytest wise, in so 24

Gilbert set
the men's
dwelling far
from the
nuns, and the
canons only
entered the
nunnery to
administer
the sacra-
ment.

mech þat he sette þe dwelling of þe clerkis ferŕ fro þe dwelling
of þe nunnes, as a man schuld sette in o cyte or in o town too
dyuers places of dyuers religioñ.   So weŕ þese chanones feŕ sette
fro þe nunnes, þat þei schuld not come with-inne þe nunnes in 28
no maneŕ but only for ministracion of þe sacramentis.   In þis
mateŕ may be seyd þat habitacioñ of men and wommen in o
place was forfended in eld tyme for grete perell þat fell, moost
specialy for feyned folk þat used her synne vndyr colouŕ of 32
holynesse, as a man may rede in dyuerse places of Seynt Ierom
Epistoles.   Thus ouŕ Lord ful mercyablely and meruelously can
make his seyntes to schyne with grete ioye of consciens in þis

---

[1] *In margin in red,* Exod.   [2] ules *added at margin.*

[3] *added in margin.*

erde, for þem þat he iustifieth he maketh ful gret; for he is ^{God sets His lights on high,}
not wone to lyte a lanterne and hide it vndyr a buschell, but
to sette it vp in heith on a¹ chaundeler, þat all men whech
4 schul ‖ entre in-to þe hous of our Lord may se lith.   Our Lord² ^{Leaf 73.}
wil schew often to þe world what þo men be whech he louyth;
for þe grete dignyte whech þei schal reioyse aftirward, our Lord²
schewith be-fore be grace of myracles, þat þei whech se all þis ^{and shows by miracles who}
8 þing may knowe þe bettyr be very weye of trewth and with ^{shall afterwards be blessed.}
sikyrnesse of hope come to þe lif þat euyr schal lest.   Swech
pite on his seruaunt, Gilbert, hath þe grace of God vsed, first
gyuyng him good werkys with whech he schuld schyne, and
12 aftirward grauntyng vertue of myracles to make his werkes
open.

[CHAPTER XXI.]

H YS paciens a-mong all oþir vertues was to hym a very ^{Gilbert's patience was}
16   crowne, for þat was graunted him of God þat he schuld ^{crown of his virtue.}
want no vertu but þat he schuld be keper of all vertues.   God
wold þat þe onyment of vertue whech was with-inne him schuld
be stered & rolled with many tribulaciones, þat aftyr þat rollyng
20 it schuld haue⁴ þe mor odour.   He wold⁵ eke þat þe smal seed
of mustard schuld be al to-broken whech schuld be þe mor
poynaunt aftir þat grindyng.   Al þis is seyd for our fader Gilbert, ^{He was accused of}
whech was accused to þe kyng Herry þe secunde þat he gaf ^{aiding à Becket in}
24 fauour to Seynt Thomas of Cauntirbyry in his exile and sent ^{France, and}
him in-to ‖ Frauns grete plente of mony.   For whech cause ^{Leaf 73, back.}
Gilbert was endyted and many of his felauchip for fauouryng
of þe kyngis traytour, and writtes wer sent oute þat Gilbert and ^{writs were issued for his}
28 all þe prioures of his ordr schuld be exiled.   And in þis cause ^{exile, though he had only}
our fader was not gilty, þat is to sey, to send mony ouyr þe ^{aided the Saint in}
see; but be-for Seynt Thomas exile, whil þat he was hid in priuyte ^{England.}
in Ynglond, Gilbert gaf him good and sent him to his sustenauns.
32 For, as we rede in þe lyf of Seynt Thomas, a chanon of Sempyngham ^{A canon of his order}

---

¹ candel *crossed through.*   ² *in margin.*
³ *In margin,* 21.   ⁴ *inserted above.*
        ⁵ wold *twice, the first crossed through.*

led St.Thomas
to the sea by
privy ways.

orđr led Seynt Thomas fro Northampton to þe se, þorw many
priuy weyis and fennys onknowe to many men. In þis same
mateŕ, be-cause S.[1] Gilbert was of swech reputacioñ as touching
holynesse, he was reqwyred to come be-fore þe iuges & make 4
þeŕ a bodely oth wheythir he was gilty in þis mateŕ or nowt.

Gilbert
refused to
swear inno-
cence before
the judges.

But þis refused he, for he saide he had leueŕ be exiled þan swere,
for he wold not leue a bad exaumple to hem þat schuld come
aftir him.   Lich on-to þis mateŕ rede we in þe book of Machabees 8
of þe good old man cleped Eleaȝarus whech wold not ete swynys
flesch forboden be þe lawe of Moyses. He saide he wold rather
dye, and whan he was counceled of his frendes þat he schuld
feyne him to ete it he wold not, neythir for feŕ of lesyng of 12

Leaf 74.

his lyf, ne for councell of his ‖ frendes; he seide þat ȝong men
schuld not take exaumple of elde Eleazar to breke þe lawe of
Moyses for feŕ of deth. So was ouŕ old man eke disposed þat

Gilbert was
firm in his
purpose.

he wold not leue þe chirch on-defensed whil he myth leue it, 16
ne he wold not feyne for to leue it; for if he had do soo, he schuld
a be holde a-mongis men hertles; he schuld ha be causeeke þat
oþir men schuld a be moŕ feynt, and moŕ-ouyr, be-fore God he had
runne in grete offens.   20

[CHAPTER XXII.]

cap. xxij.

Then the
king's heart
changed,

IN þis same tyme whill ouŕ fader stood in þis perplexite, ouŕ
Lord chaunged þe kingis hert whech was þan in Normannye,
and letteris weŕ sent fro him ouyr þe se to þe iuges of þis lond, 24

and the
writs were
annulled.

þat þis cause whech touched Gilbert & his bretherin schuld be
differred fro hem to þe kyngis audiens. Mery & glad was ouŕ

Fear turned
into joy.

fader in all þis abydyng, and whan þei alle tremuled for feŕ, as
no wondyr was whañ þei had mad hem redy to forsake kynrod 28
and cuntre and neuyr to come a-geyn. His hert in al þis tyme
was trosting in God, for he þout as Seint Iame seith, a ful grete
ioye was com to him whan he was assayed with dyuers temptaciones.[2] A-noþir vexacioñ had ouŕ mayster whech was not lytyl. 32
Certeyn bretheren of his whech he had conuerted fro þe world ‖

---

[1] *inserted above.*   [2] *In margin in red,* Iacob 1.

and norchid fro her childhod turned in-to malice, were wery of Leaf 74,
her order and of her profession, turnyng all her goostly *conuersa-* back.
cion to lust of etyng and drynkyng and leccherye, so ferforth Some of Gilbert's monks
4 þat þei diffamed our maystir & his felauchip of grete vigour, rebelled, and fell into lust,
and mor-ouyr wrytyn and sent on-to þe Pope, compleynyng and and wrote to the Pope in
allegging many þingis whech wer not soth. Vp-on þis come certeyn complaint.
bullis fro Rome þat þis mater be indifferent persones schuld haue The Pope ordered an
8 his examinacion. Thus was our Gilbert cleped to apper in-to examination;
þe ferþest parties of þis¹ londe, and to answer to þese accusaciones,
not-withstand his grete age and febilnesse. But þis man, ful of
constauns, was not aferd of peyne, ne labour, ne cost, ne þretyng
12 of þe iuges, ne fayre suasiones of oþir; all þese myth not make
him to consent for to goo oute of þe parfith weye whech he had
be-gunne, for he wold sey often he had leuer his þrote wer cut
þan ony þing schuld be left of þe first profession and þe first
16 institucion whech he had mad. But whan þis mater was discussed,
it was founde þat his accuseres wer fals, and þus was þe blessid and Gilbert's accusers were
man proued as metal in þe fornays, and pes sent fro heuene proved false.
on-to þe cherch and his religion. For whan his aduersaries Leaf 75.
20 fayled of her proues & coude with no craft haue þat þei desired,
þei were compelled be God and schame in her consciens to pray They prayed him for
him of forgifnesse, in whech prayer þei desired þat he schuld forgiveness, and asked
sumwhat tempir þe gret hardnesse of religion and suffir hem him to temper the
24 not to be kept so streith as þei wer be-for. The good old man hardness of his rule.
with-outen ony difficulte receyued hem to grace, and in tokne He forgave
of enter loue, he kissed hem all; eke, in þat temperauns whech them and kissed them,
þei desired of all scharpnesse² of religion, partye with auctorite
28 of þe Pope, partye with wise councell of religious men, he
promised hem to fulfill mech of her desir. In þe last ende of and fulfilled their desire.
his age, lich a-noþir Iob whech was smet in his flesch with ful Like Job in
greuous woundes, he was smet with blyndnesse, for he lost þe his age he was smitten, and
32 site of his body. But þis strok was not smet of God as an lost his sight.
enmye, but as a frend prouokyng a man to batayle a[n]d³
behestyng victorie to him. For of þat defaute of blyndnesse in
his body grewe on-to him a grete perfeccion of vnderstanding

---

¹ *Inserted above in red.*   ² MS. schrapnesse, *with* as *over in red.*
³ MS. ad.

His blindness
brought
greater
holiness. in his soule, and he was aftir þat tyme replet with grace of
the Holy Goost moꝛ habunдauntly.   For now wex he absent
to seculer þingis and more present to euerlasting desires, as
a man þat aftir grete laboures had grete delices of contempla- 4
cion ‖.

[CHAPTER XXIII.]

Leaf 75,
back.   cap. **xxiij.**[1]

His daily
occupation
was prayer
and virtuous
talk; H IS occupacion be þe day was[2] in prayeꝛ, or in heryng of good
lessones, or in goostly coumfort of his breþerin, euyr talkyng 8
of uertu; of swech occupacioñ sesed he neuyr, saue swech tymes as
nature requyreth his inclinacioñ; for, saue þo tymes, euyr his mouth
or his mynde was not ydil.   If ony man had interfered wordes
but he spoke
seldom whech weꝛ not plesauns to God, ne soundyng to uertuous lif, þei 12
schuld gretly displese him.   He him-self spak but fewe wordes;
he had moꝛ delite to heꝛ þañ to speke, for aꝉ þat he spak was
soundyug on-to grete profit of vertuous gouernauns.   He þoute
remembering
the words of
David; often of þat verse of þe prophete Dauid, wheꝛ he seith[3]: Obmutui, 16
et humiliatus sum et silui a bonis.   He was down, he seyth, and
meked him-self, and kept silens, þat he schuld not speke good.   It
was þe condicioñ of Dauid, and soo hath be of many holy men, to
speke but fewe wordes and but seldom, for þei were euyr aferd of 20
for, as
Solomon said,
in much
speech sin
wanteth not. þat Salamon seith,[4] þat in mech speche synne wanteth nowt.   This
caused ouꝛ maystir to sey but fewe wordes þat he schuld vse hem
wel.   Euyr was his mynde on-to heuene and euyr bidding soft
bedes, often wold he a-mong his orisones say, Who long Lord schalt 24
Leaf 76. þou[5] ‖ for-gete me?   And woo is me þat my good dwellyngplace
Gilbert
lamented the
distance of
death. is kept so long fro me!   Sum-tyme, whan we supposed he had be
a-slepe, his handis weꝛ cured with his mantel, but his eyne sey we
lift up to heuene, and euyr softe wordes herd we of his mouth. 28
When he had
talked long he
burst out into
his confession. Sumtyme eke whan he sat in talkyng with othir men, if þe talking
were long, he, as in partye aferd þat þeꝛ was do sum excesse of
speche, sodeynly wold brest oute and say his confession, mekly
askyng absolucioñ, and þañ aftir wold he asoile deuoutly þem 32

---

[1] *In margin, 23.*   [2] *was twice, the first crossed through.*
[3] *In margin in red, Ps. 38.*   [4] *In margin in red, Prouer 10.*
[5] *in margin.*

whech were a-boute him þat tyme. Be nyte tyme he was ocupied
moost with orisones and ful pryuyly wold he goo to his rest, first
knelyng longe be-foꝛ his bed.   And whañ his cubiculeres wold
4 loke if he [1] lay wel, þan wold he blame hem þat þei mad his bed no
bettir ouyr-nyth.   Þese wordes were in maner of excusacioñ, for ^{He desired only God and the saints for his night-companions.}
he was loth þat ony man schuld se in what maneꝛ he ꝛested ; for to
þat pryuyte he desyred [2] no moo secretaries but God and seyntis
8 with whom he wold talk þe moost part of þe nyth.   What schuld
we speke of his diete, with what scarsnesse of mete & drynk he
was fed ? He loued so wel þe comoñ refeccioñ þat whañ he was in ^{He would Leaf 76, back.}
gretta langnoꝛ, as it kendly folowith age, he wold not, for no prayer
12 of his breþerin, ete in þe dortouꝛ ; he wold neuyr be absent fro þe ^{never eat in private,}
same hous wheꝛ þei [3] alle had her refeccioñ, not-withstand þat
þe refectorie was fer and many greces þer-too, whech was grete
difficulte to an old man for to clyme.   Whañ he was prayed of his
16 disciples þat he schuld spare his grete age and his seknesse, he
wold in a maneꝛ of a holy ire answeꝛ & sey : Gilbert schal not be
exaumple to his successoures for to ete delicacies in his chambyr.
For þis cause were þei fayn for to bere him, on on þe o side, ^{but was led to the common refectory.}
20 a-noþer on þe othir ; and with grete labouꝛ þus cam he to þe
bord, to whech, whañ he was come, he pyned his body with hungir
rather þan filt it, euyr þinkyng of þe vesselis longing to ouꝛ Lord
and euyr hauyng mynde of his congregacioñ.   Whan he was bore ^{He spent his days in prayer.}
24 fro þe bord a-geyn to his couch, alle þe othir part of þe day he
spent in þe same vse, þat is to say, prayed or herd holy [4] lessones,
or comowned in deuocion.   And þat he schuld haue þe uery ende
of all perfeccioñ, be-cause he had ascended fro o uertue to a-noþir,
28 and eke be-cause he was gretter in uertue þan he supposed ‖ him- ^{Leaf 77.}
self, for he knew weel þat a vertu is neuyr þe lasse þouȝ it defende
not him-self, for þis cause he purueyed pees a-geyns all perelles
whech myth falle to þoo congregaciones mad be him ; eke þat ^{He settled the debate among his lay-people on diversity of foods and had it written in his 'Congre-gations'.}
32 debate whech was a-mong þe lay puple of his ordre for dyuersite
of metis, þis same debate with consent of al his chapetꝛ and in
presens of Hewe, þan biscop of Lyncolñ, he sette in rest and pes,
and oþir menes of pes ordeyned he,[5] and mad hem to be write and
36 kept in his *Congregaciones*,[6] with-oute ende to endewre.

---

[1] *is margin.*   [2] MS. *desered*, y *over in red.*   [3] i *added in red.*
[4] s *crossed through.*   [5] *above in red.*   [6] *is margin in red.*

7

[CHAPTER XXIV.]

cap*itul*um **xxiiij.**[1]

THese be þe myracles whech oure Lord wrout be his s*er*uaunt
Gilbert whil he leued in þis bodely lyff. A chanon of his
þat had be & was euyr i*n* his felauchip whan he went fro o place 4
to a-noþir, whech ma*n*nes name was cleped Albyne, aftir a grete
febilnesse þat he had take of labou*r* in his iornay, fel in a greuo*us*
fevou*r*, in so greuo*us* þat he myte not goo with his maystir as he
was wone to doo, so þat ou*r* maystir was fayn to abyde at a place 8
whech þei clepe þe ylde; þere abode he, abydy*n*g þis ma*n*nes
recur*yn*g, and went no ferther. And whan ou*r* good fader had loy
þere longe and wex wery, desiri*n*g to fulfille ‖ his iornay, he sent
a messanger on-to þis man,[2] comau*n*dyng him in vertue of obediens 12
þat he schuld no mo*r* suffir þe fevyr to come on-to him, but þat he
schuld with-oute ony letty*n*g[3] come on-to his maystir in a*ll* hast.
Be þe same messang*er*, eke, he commau*n*ded on-to þe feueres þat
þei schuld no[4] mo*r* be bold to vexe his s*er*uaunt.   Wha*n* þis 16
message was doo, þis same Albyne inclyned his hed to þat p*r*ecept,
as religious ma*n* schuld do, saying þat he was redy to obeye his
maystir in a*ll* þing. The next day cam, and eke[5] þe ou*r* in whech
þe fevyrues were wont to take him, and all þe toknes we*r* come, as 20
schakyng, akyng of þe hed and swech oþir; þan spak þis Albyne
on-to þis seknesse as to a lyuysch creatu*r*, in swech mane*r*: What
menest þou þat þou wilt now vexe me a-geyn? Hast þou no
mynde who þat my maystir forbad þe þat þou schuld no mo*r* vexe 24
me? But now I commau*n*de þe in my maysteris name þat þou
obeye to his precept and besy þe no mo*r* to my vexacio*n*. A-non,
as he had said þese wordes, he blessed him with þe signe of þe holy
crosse, and sone aftir he felle in a swete slep, and aftir he wook he 28
was delyu*er*ed of þat sekenesse, ne many ʒeres aft*er* was not he
vexed with þe feu*er*ys.

[1] I*n* margin, 24.   [3] *in red in margin.*
[2] MS. letty, *corrected in red.*   [4] *in margin.*
[5] whech *crossed through.*

A canon of
Gilbert's fell
sick with
fever,

to whom

Leaf 77,
back.

Gilbert sent
a messenger,

commanding
him to come
and the fevers
to leave him.

When the
fevers
reappeared
the canon
commanded
them to go,

and they
went from
him.

[CHAPTER XXV.]

cap. **xxv.**[1] Leaf 78.

Aᴺ-oþir chanon was þere of þe place cleped Sixelenses whech had in his feet a violent and intollerable peyne. This man,

4 trostyng in þe grete vertue whech ouᵲ Lord had put in his maystir, made menes to þe minister of ouᵲ maystir þat he schuld kepe him þe watyr in whech onre maystir schuld wasche his feet at eue. For þat was his custom, as þei sey, to wasch his feet euery nyth.

8 As þe man desired, þe water was kept, and he, with grete deuocion, wasched þerin his feet and þerby was mad hool. The grete feith of þe o man and þe clene lyuyng of þe oþir, þorw þe myth of God, browt þis myracle to ende.

12 ¶ Ther was eke a knyt dwellyng a-boute Oxenford, þat, for helth[2] of his soule, was mad a chanon in þe place at Osneye. This man sone aftyr his profession was mad celereᵲ of þat hous, and not long duryng in þat same office, he felle in þat seknesse whech þei clepe

16 podagra, whech is a seknesse, as þei sei, of hem þat haue led heᵲ lyf in grete delicacye; and it causeth swech peyne in þe feet þat it priuyth a man of his walkyng. This man þus hurt, herd telle of þe grete myracles wrout be ouᵲ fader Gilbert, an who many places

20 and what noumbir of persones weᵲ edified ‖ be his doctrine. Of þis fame he coniected in his soule þe veri soth, þat swech þingis myte not be do witȝ-outen vertuous lyuyng. Wherfor, with grete trost of his soule, he conuerted him to God and to þis Seynt, and

24 mad menes on-to hem þat were dwellyng with Gilbert, þat he myte haue a peyre of old sokkys, or pinsones, whech ouᵲ maystir had often wered. He had swech as he desired, and a-non, as he had vsed hem a-while, his feet were hole. A long tyme aftir þis þe

28 same peyne þat was in his feet fel to his handis, and more peyne it was to him þere þan it was in his feet. Thoo took he þe same sokkys and wered hem on his handes, and fro þat day forth both his handis & his feet weᵲ hool.

Margin notes:
A canon of Sixhills(?) was cured of pain in his feet by washing them in water so used by Gilbert.

A cellarer of Osney suffered from gout in his feet.

Leaf 78, back.

He was cured by wearing Gilbert's socks.

His hands were likewise cured.

---

[1] *In margin, 25.*   [2] *fo crossed through.*

[CHAPTER XXVI.]

Cap. xxvj.[1]

A goldsmith in burning fever was cured by drinking from Gilbert's cup.

OWre maystir had a cuppe of whech he drank often, and, as it semeth, it was of tre bounden with siluyr, lich as religious in þis lond vse mech. This cuppe was broke with sum fal and sent on-to Beuyrle, on-to a goldsmyth, for to repayr̄ it. This goldsmyth, whan þe cuppe cam, lay in þe brennyng fevyr, for so happed it þat þat same tyme was þe hour̄ of his seknesse. And

Leaf 79.

whan he herd þat þis was ‖ our̄ maysteris cuppe, and þat of custom 8 he drank often in þe same, he desired gretly to drynk of þis cuppe. So was þe cuppe filt with drynk, and of þat same drynk this man had his helth.[2]

Another man was cured of fistula by Gilbert washing his feet on Maundy Thursday.

¶ A-noþir man, of þe noumbyr of hem þat were no clerkis in þe 12 same ordre, had in his foot a soor whech þei clepe þe fistula. And so happed on Maunde Þursday whan all þe breþerin schuld be waschid, he desired gretly þat our̄ mayster schuld wasch him. So was it ordeyned þat he was sette where our̄ deuoute fader schuld 16 in his cours wasch all þe rowe, þat, be his touching, as he be-leued, veryly þe man myth be hool. The good old man in his cours of wasching cam to þis sek man, and with both his handys con-streyned his sore foot, be-cause he þout it was not clene. [3]Thus he[3] 20 constreyned it[4] with wasching, but in þat same handelyng, corrupt blood ran oute of þe woundys and oþir mater̄ swech as sores haue, and all þis waschid oure fader ful clene with þat same watir of þat holy mynystery. What schal we telle long tale? Be þan he had 24 waschid a-wey þis blood and þis oþir onclene mater̄, all þe foot was hool.

A prioress was saved from death through

Leaf 79, back.

Gilbert's mediation.

¶ There was eke a prioresse of his nunnes þat lay so seek þat euery man loked[4] whan sche schuld deye. He herd telle of hir ‖ 28 þat sche was so ny þe deth, and be a messager̄ comaunded deth þat he schuld not take hir at þis tyme, for sche was ful necessarie on-to þe relygion̄. Sone aftyr þis he visite þis woman him-self, and his bak was but turned fro hir in his goyng þat sche was coumforted 32 a-non, for all þe noyhous humoures went oute fro hir sodeynly be a swet, and eke þe grete constriccion̄ of hir wombe was resolued meruelously.

---

[1] In margin, 26.   [2] in margin.   [3-3] in margin.
[4] inserted above.

[CHAPTER XXVII.]

ca^m xxvij.¹

I N þat same tyme was a grete debate be-twyx Steuene, kyng of
    Ynglond, and Herry, duk of Normannye, aftirward kyng.
4 This debate was so grete and þe parties so strong þat al þis lond
at þat tyme was ny lost.   For þe feldes lay with-oute tilth, þe
smale townes had no dwelleres, þe wallis weꝛ falle down and stretes
distroyed.   Grete townes weꝛ ny desolat; þere wat not elles² but
8 pray and³ þeft and brennyng, euery man a-geyn oþir.   This mad
oure mastiris hert gretly affrayed be-cause he say þe lond ny
distroyed, and in special for þe newe religioñ whech he had be-
gunne was ful likly to renne in desolacioñ.   Vp-on þis sorow and
12 heuynesse þe good man prayed nyte and day þat ouꝛ Lord schuld
haue mercy on his puple ‖ and sende an ende of þis desolacioñ.
Sodeynly, as he lay and prayed, was schewid on-to him a book in
whech book was writyn þe noumbyr of þoo ꝫeres in whech þis
16 desolacion schuld lest.   Whan he had red þis scripture he fel down
plat and mad grete sorow, for he supposed veryly þat alt þese ꝫeres
were for to come.   For if it so were þat þis persecucion schuld last
so longe, alt þis lond schuld, be possibilite, be distroyed.   Tho he
20 þat schewid him þis book gaf him coumfort and notified on-to him
þat þese were þe ꝫeres whech he say of þat hool persecucioñ; of
whech, summe were passed and summe for to come.   There he lete
him haue knowlech who many were passed and who many to come ;
24 and as þis vision schewid, so folowid þe dede, for þat same ꝫere
merked in þe book cesed þat debate and þat desolacioñ.   This
reuelacion was a grete coumfort⁴ on-to ouꝛ fader and on-to oþir
men to whech he opened his councelt.

28   ¶ We knew also in þat same tyme a noble woman⁵ of grete
ricchesse, whech, as often as sche conceyued, þe childyr þat sche
baꝛ weꝛ bore ded.   A-noþir woman dwellyng be-side had a⁶ girdyl
with whech oure fadeꝛ ‖ Gilbert had often be girt next his flesch.
32 This girdil was take be þis woman to þe oþir woman whech myth
not bryng forth childern o-lyue, and sche used it continuely next

Marginal notes: The land was desolate in King Stephen's days, and the people at discord. Gilbert sorrowed, Leaf 80. but he was shown a book telling the duration of the trouble, which comforted him. A woman bore still-born children. Leaf 80, back. and was helped by Gilbert's girdle.

¹ *In margin,* 27.
³ d *added above.*
⁵ *in margin.*
² *a stroke crossed through.*
⁴ t *added in red.*
⁶ gil *crossed through.*

hir flesch. Sone aftyr sche *con*ceyued a child, and þaⁿ a-noþir, whech childyrn leued on-to mannes age and weꝛ worþi men both in honouꝛ and rychesse.

[Chapter XXVIII.]

Cap*itulum* xxviij.[1]   4

THer was a man, eke, of Staunford, at þat tyme had a wyf þat bar no childyrn. So happed our maystir in a iornay to chese his hostel at þis mannes hous. Whan he was com þidir, þe woman herd gret report of his holynesse, and þout [2] þat be his merites sche 8

A woman caused Gilbert to sleep in her bed that she might have children.

myth *con*ceyue, lych as þe woman Sunamite *con*ceyued be þe *pre*sens of Helise. Trostyng þus on þis mannes goodnesse, sche mad our fader Gilbert bed in þat same place wheꝛ hir husband [2] and sche [3] were wone to ly. Gilbert we*n*t forth on his iornay; þe goodma*n* 12 of þe hin cam hom, and in [4] þat same bed, as þe woma*n* be-leued, be meritis of our fadeꝛ Gilbert, sche conceyued [5] a son, and cleped

Her son was Leaf 81. called after the Saint, who sent her a cow.

hym, whaⁿ he was boꝛ, aftir þe name of þe good old man Gilbert. And whan our fadeꝛ herd sey of þis ‖ chau*n*ce, with grete merthe 16 he sent a cow to þe woma*n*, praying hir to norche wel his child.

A place next Gilbert's inn in London caught fire.

¶ It happed on a tyme, eke, our maystir to ly at London; happed soo, þat a place next þe In wheꝛ he lay was sodeynly on fyre. So whan it cam ny his chambir, þei þat were a-boute him cryed up-on 20 him to go þenne and fle swech grete pereł. He wold not him-self remeve ne suffir no þing in þe hous to be caried oute, but comau*n*ded hem þat þei schuld lede him and sette him at þe wyndowⁿ whech he myth best se þe fiꝛ. Whan he was sette þere he [4] be-gan to 24 pray, su*m*tyme loud, su*m*tyme soft, su*m*tyme saying, su*m*tyme

Gilbert refused to leave the inn, and the flames spared it.

singi*n*g. So þe fiꝛ cam so ny þat ałł oþir fled, but he sat stille and meued not, and sodeynly þe flaume of þe fiꝛ, as þouȝ he had dred þe *pre*sens of our maystir, left þat coost and went to oþir 28 place, sparing þat hous wheꝛ he sat and alle þe houses whech longed to þat In. He þat was lord of þat In and keper þankid God ofte sithe, saying with grete feith þat þorw þe me*r*ytes of Gilbe*r*t his place was saued.   32

---

[1] *In margin,* 28.   [2] þout *twice, the second crossed through.*
[2–3] *in margin.*   [4] *inserted above.*   [3] d *added above.*
[6] *in margin.*

[CHAPTER XXIX.]

cap. xxix.

Euene as be þe inobediens of þe first man, Adam, mankynd Adam's lost
lost þe dew dominacioñ ¶ of hym-self and of oþir þingis Leaf 81,
4 þat be vndyr him, rith so be þe meknesse of þe secunde man Crist, back.
þei þat folow his steppis recure swech rite þat þei may haue al domination is regained
þing in subieccioñ. Treuth saith þus to us in þe gospeñ: If ȝe through Christ.
haue feith as grete as a mustard seed, or ellis, If ȝouȓ feith be as
8 a mustard seed, ȝe schal sei on-to þis hiñ, go fro þis place and falle
in-to þe se, and it schal be soo. And in a-noþir place he saith:
I say ȝou treuly, what-so-euy[r]¹ ȝe aske in ȝouȓ prayeȓ, be-leue,
for ȝe schal take it. In ouȓ fader Gilbert haue we þe exibicioñ of As Gilbert was obedient
12 þis precept. Be-cause he was obedient to Him þat mad him, whom to the Lord of the elements
wynde and water obeyen, þerfor ouȓ Lord graunted to him for to he had power over them.
werk many þingis, and to haue comaundment ouyr þese elementis.
For to his preceptis were þese elementis buxum, wynde, se and
16 fire, and alle þei bowed to þe strength of his uertue. O special Once when he should
cronycle wil we allegge in þis mateȓ. Ouȓ fader schuld ones saile have sailed
ouyr þe watir of Humbir for visitacioñ of his flok þat was in þe across the Humber,
prouince of ² ȝork, ³or elles he cam fro ȝork in-to þis cuntre, there was
20 & þat is⁴ moost likly.⁵ The wynd blew oute of the south with a storm.
swech impetuosnesse and mad þe wawe so for to rise, þere durst
no man goo. He was compelled to a-byde at a grange whech þei He awaited its end.
cleñpe⁶ Heseleschop, a-bidyng þe ende of þe storm and coumfort Leaf 82.
24 of fayȓ wedyr. He lay þere long and was wery of þat lyf, and but grew weary,
mech moȓ wery for he had grete hast to see þoo persones whech he
went to visite. He asked of hem þat schuld lede him what wynde
was best to lede him ouyr þe watyr. Thei saide þe north wynd
28 wast best, if it wold blowe. He answered þat he supposed þe
northest schuld be moȓ gracious, but he comaunded hem in ouȓ
Lordis name, in whom was añ his trost, þat þei alle schuld with and asking his people to
a good deuocioñ sei a Pater-noster to ouȓ Lord. This made he pray,
32 hem to do þat no man schuld deme þat he trosted on his owne
merites, and þat he schuld fle þe praysing of men, whech was euyr
his appetite. Aftyr þei had sáyde þis orison he comaunded his

---

¹ MS. euy.   ² god *crossed through.*   ³⁻³ or elles ... likly, *in margin.*
⁴ MS. it.   ⁵ hel *crossed through.*

hors to be sadeled and all his meny to make hem redy. Thus þei
hast to-ward þe brynk of þe watyr, and þe tempest be-gan sumwhat
to cese. The schipmen sayde ech to oþir, lete us take þe watyr in
Mary name ; we ar likly to haue a good freyte. This saide þei of 4
grete sikyrnesse, for þei trostid mech vp-on þis mannes vertue.

Thus make þei redy her schippis, and þe same wynde whech our
maystir desired, þei had ; þei goo in-to ‖ þe vesseles, drawe up her
sailes, and with a fauourable wynde þei londe wher þei desire. 8
The most merueile in þis mater was as þei told þat[1] wher present,
þat whan our maystir was londyd þe same tempest roos a-geyn
& þat same wynd in þat place where he took his schip, þat all
men myth knowe þat þe face of heuene was noth chaunged at þat 12
tyme but be his merytes.

[CHAPTER XXX.]

AFtyr þat tyme þat our maystir was passed oute of this
    world,[1] certeyn dremes were schewid to certeyn vertuous 16
persones, in whech dremes þe tyme and þe hour of his deth was
notified and oppenly declared þat þis man was ioyned on-to þo

seyntis in heuene. For þat nyte in whech he passed fro þe world
swech a vision was schewid on-to a prioresse of nunnes, not of his 20
ordre, but of a-noþir, in þe prouynce of Ʒork. The woman say in
hir vision a grete cherch standyng in a fayr place, and on þe west

side of þe cherch a gret hous, in whech hous many men wer bysi
to aray all swech þingis as longe to byryng of a man, þat is to sey, 24
a bere arayed with cloþis of silk, with candeles and a crosse and

mech oþir þing, as longith to þat solempnyte. And in þis ‖ drem
þis same persone, þis prioresse, had gret merueyle, for sche had
neuyr in all hir lyf seyn no swech solempnyte[3] a-boute no ded 28

man. A-mongis þe puple, whech was gret, as sche þoute,[4] sche
spak on-to on and prayed him to telle hir what maner man þis
was þer ded for whom all þis aray was mad. That same persone
Ʒaue hir þis answere, þat maystir Gilbert of Sempingham was 32

---

[1] *inserted in red above.*   [2] *In margin, 30.*
[3] *part of the word over in red.*   [4] *l crossed through.*

passed fro þe world, and ouꝛ Lord wold þat he schuld be byried
with swech solempnyte. Aftyr þis answere he þat lay on þe bere
rose up, as sche þoute, and took a crose in his hand and be-gan to
4 synge a song in Latyn with a note of swech melodye þat sche had
neuyr herd no swech. The letter to þat same note was þis: Pure
mentis gaudia ostendamus eia in vocis melodia. The Englisch is
þis, as I suppose: The ioye of ouꝛ clene mynde lete us schewe now
8 alt in fere with voys ful of melodye. Whaꝥ he had songe þis vers
alt þe puple folowyng sang þe same, and soo went þei forth on
processioꝥ in-to þat same cherch. Whan þis womaꝥ say þis
bischop þus syngyng and on lyue, sche saide on-to him whech told
12 hir þat Gilbert was ded: Wenest þou þat I knowe ᵹ not maystir
Gilbert? I knowe him ful weel, and he is not ded, for þou saide
he was ded, and he is ᵹondir in þe processioꝥ. Than þe man
saide to hir agayn: Knowist þou nowt what felt to Seint Ion þe
16 Euangelist? Euene as he had þe moder of ouꝛ Lord in kepyng,
so had þis man in gouernauns many persones whech folowid hir
virginite. Tho spak þe nunne to him a-geyn: I knowe wel what
felt[1] to Seyn Ion, for he is þe aduocat of ouꝛ place, and I can his
20 lyf ny be hert. And þaꝥ said þe man to hir[2]: Rith as ouꝛ Lord
hath do with Seynt Ion, rith so wil He do with þis man. In þis
mene-while þe procession went fro þe hous, and sche inqwired of
him whidir it schuld goo. He saide þat alt þe processiones of þe
24 world schuld mete with þat processioꝥ. Thus talkyng, þei[3] entred
þe cherch, and þat processioꝥ stood stille be-fore þe grete crosse.
A-non sche say many processiones entre in-to þe cherch, mo þan
sche coude noumbyr, of whech sche knew many, and þan sche dred
28 hir for þe grete noumbyr þat sche schuld be trode vndir fote. In
þis dred sche wok, and felt so swete a sauouꝛ in hir[4] nase þat sche
had neuyr felt non swech, for al þat day ᵹ and many dayes aftir
þat swetnesse a-bood, with whech swetnesse sche was gretly
32 refrecchid. In þis tyme of her wakyng hir sistir rang to mateyns
& sche roos, gadered alt heꝛ sisteres, and told hem pleynly þat sche
wist be hir drem þat maystir Gilbert was ded. Not long aftir be
a messageꝛ þat was sent to telle hem of his passing, þei knew
36 veryly þat þis was þe houꝛ in whech he passed. It is ful likly

Then she thought that Gilbert arose and began to sing in Latin,

and that she interrogated a man about it,

Leaf 83, back.

who told her Gilbert was like St. John the Evan-gelist. The nun said she knew St. John's life nigh by heart.

She entered the church,

and saw many pro-cessions meet St. Gilbert's.

Leaf 84.

When she awoke her sisters were going to matins, and she told them her dream, which was soon corroborated by a mes-senger.

---

[1] *I crossed through.*

[2] *ir written more plainly above in red.*

[3] *i added in red.*

[4] *MS. his.*

Such visions
occurred at
other times. þat þis visioñ was soth, for we rede þat þe deth of Martyn was
knowe to many sundry *persones* whech dwelt fer, in þat same houſ
of his passing, as to Seynt Seueſ, bischop of Coleyn, and to Seynt
Ambrose, bischop of Melan. Eke Seynt Benet say his sistir*is* soule [4]
boſ on-to heuene þe houſ of hir deth. And Seynt Ierom alsoo
appered on-to Seynt Augustyn in þat same houſ.

[CHAPTER XXXI.]

capl. **xxxj.**[1]

Another
woman
thought she
saw a flock of
angels, Lich on-to þis vision was schewid a-noþir to a noble woma*n* [8]
of vertuo*us* *condiciones* & wif on-to a man lich in vertu on-to
hire. Sche þoute in hir slep þat sche say a grete multitude of
au*n*gellis, with grete noyse of praysing and ful swete song, flye up
in-to heuene.   And aftyr þei were go sche say too grete c*um*panies [12]
Leaf 84,
back.[3]
and a choir of
angels hold-
ing a sheet,
in which were
three chil-
dren. ‖ of blissed spirites[3] wech were so ordeyned þat ech of hem had
face to face, lich as þei haue þat stand in a qweer. Thei held
a-mongis hem a fayre white schete, and in þis schete were thre
naked childirn. On of hem sche myth see fro þe nowle vpward; [16]
he was balled, and ȝet had he a childis face;. þe oþir too say sche
She learnt
that one of
them was
Gilbert of
Sempring-
ham, new-
born to God. but þe schuld*er*is and þe face. Sche inqwired of on in þe c*um*pany
what mane*r* þing þis myth be, & it was answered to hir þat he in
þe myddis was maystir Gilbert of Sempingha*m*, whech was ded to [20]
þe world and þus born to God. Sche inquyred eke if þese to were
chano*n*es of his ordre, and it was answered, nay. Thei [are] not of
his ordre, he said, but good and holy men whech were take oute
This she saw
the night that
the Saint
died, and told
her husband. of þe world and þus led to heſ Lord. This same vision say þis [24]
woma*n*[4] þe same nyte oure maystir deyid, and whan sche wook
sche[5] told þis visioñ to hir husbond; þei both noted þat day and
founde aftir þat it was þe same in whech ouſ mayst*er* went fro þe
world : whidir he was born or wheſ he was sette, was schewid aftir [28]
A canon of
Gilbert's in visioñ to on of his chanones. For a grete tyme aftir þat ouſ
Leaf 85. mayst*er* was ded a chanon of his ordſ say in his sleep ‖ ou of his
order saw in
his sleep one
of his dead
brethren, breþerin þat was ded long be-fore. He þoute þat he inqwyred of

---

[2] *The embellishment of capitals in red omitted from this page.*
[3] *Soules* crossed through and *spirites written above.*
[4] *n crossed through.*   [5] *l crossed through.*

him many sundry þingis, and had answeꝛ ful *conuenient* on-to his whom he asked con-
questiones. Tho inqwired he of þe astate of heꝛ maystir, what he cerning Gil-bert, and who
dede or wheꝛ he was, & his broþir answerd in þis maneꝛ: He is said that the Saint sat
4 not with us; a hyer place holdeth him. For fro þat tyme in high in Heaven with
whech he was take fro þe world, a-non was he set a-mongis þe the virgins.
dauns of virgynes.

[Chapter XXXII.]

cap. xxxij.

8 Ovre blessed Lord, as he magnified Seynt Gilbert in his As during his life, so after
lif with grete meruelous werkis, rith euene soo wold he his death, Gilbert was
schewe þe ioye of him aftir his deth with grete & manifest magnified,
tokenes. And alle þese tokenes, who þat þei cam to þe lite of
12 ouꝛ knowlech, þat þei þat lyue now and eke þei þat schal come
. aftir us haue no doute in þis matere, schortly, as þei were doo,
we wil reherse here. Whan þis man, wel be-loued with God,
was passed fro þe world, þat men schuld know wel his lyf and
16 his merites weꝛ acceptable to God, in þe first ȝere of his deposicioñ and miracles were done at
and so forth oþir ȝeres,[1] weꝛ many myracles doo at his graue.[2] his grave.
But at þat tyme þei whech he had left at Sempingham ¶ were Leaf 85, back.
men drawen in-to secret[3] *contemplacioñ* and had ful lytyl deynte But those of his order were
20 with grete aqweyntauns of þe world, &[4] were necligent, if I schuld reticent,
say so, to dyuulge þese grete myracles whech were dayly wrout
a-mongis hem. Thus þoute þei, of very humilite, be-cause þei
weꝛ his childyr, if þei weꝛ þe first þat schuld puplysch þese grete
24 myracles of heꝛ mayst*er*, men myth sey of hem, as Crist ded of
þe Pharisees,[5] þat þei[6] magnified heꝛ owne hemmys. For þis so that till eleven years
cause, xj ȝeꝛ aftir his deth was no gret pupplicacion mad, not- after his death no pub-
with-stand þat in many sundry place[7] were wroute many sundry lication of his miracles was
28 myracles; and þan þe breþerin at Sempingham þoute þat þe made.
hidyng of þese glorious werkis was displesauns to ouꝛ Lord,
deregacioñ on-to seyntis, and wrong a-geyn þe worchip of þe
cherch; þei as wise men and gouerned be þe councell of wise

---

[1] MS. ȝes, *with* s *crossed through and* res *over in red.*
[2] MS. gra *with* ue *over in red.*   [3] c *added above is red.*
[4] *added above in red.*   [5] *In margin in red,* M[l] 23.
[6] a *added in red.*   [7] oe *added is red.*

Hubert,
archbishop of
Canterbury,
was then told.

men, went up to þe archbischop of Cauntyrbyry, cleped þat tyme Hubbert, and told him all þis þing. Whan þe man herd all þis he wept for very ioye, and þankid God with ful grete deuocioñ þat he wold schewe swech myracles in his dayes. And þouȝ it were so þat he had no doute of þe holynesse of þis Seint Gilbert, ‖

Leaf 86.

be-cause he had know þe man & herd gret reporte of his holy-nesse, ȝet for to satisffye þe opynyon of oþir men, he þoute best to put þis mateȓ in dilacion and tary a-while, in whech he

He com-
manded cer-
tain abbots to
hold inquiry,

myth heȓ more to confermacion of his entent. Vp-on þis poynt þis same archbischop sent down on-to certeyn abbotes of þis same prouynce, comaundyng hem be his letteres þat in þis mateȓ þei schuld make bysy inquysicioñ, and here inqwisicion,

and write the
results,

in what forme it was mad, he wold þei schuld write it on-to him, þat he, þus instruct be her informacioñ, myth write þe

that he might
get Gilbert
canonised.

more sikirly[1] on-to ouȓ fader þe Pope to haue leue of him for to[2] puplysch þe canoniȝacioñ of þis Seynt, aftir þe Pope had doo his part. These abbotes deuoutly receyued þis comaundment, and ioynend on-to hem for moȓ auctoryte many oþir persones

These abbots
and others
went to Sem-
pringham on
January 9,
1201, when
King John
was there.
There they
held inquiry.

of þe cherch, both reguleȓ and seculeȓ. Thus came þei all to þe place of Sempingham, þe ix day of Ianuary, þe ȝere of ouȓ Lord a M ccj, and þat same day þe kyng of Ynglond, Ion, with many of his lordis, visited[3] þe same place. There þei dede rede þe myracles and discussed hem with grete diligens and streyt examinacioñ; þei wrote hem þanne ‖ in her letterys, both

Leaf 86,
back.

on-to þe seid archbischop and to þe Pope. Alle þese letteris

Hubert sent
their letters
to the Pope,

sent þe seid Hubbert on-to þe Pope with his owne episteles,[4] in whech he comended þe grete dedes wroute be þis man, and prayed þe Pope to graunt leue þat he schuld be lyfte fro þe erde and leyde in more honourable place. Eke, be exhortacioñ of þis same man, many notable persones of Ynglond and prelates

to whom
many wrote
also asking
for Gilbert's
canonisation.

wrytyn comendatyf letterys on-to þe court, besekyng þe Pope of þe same. The kyng eke wrote on his side and many of his lordes þat þe Pope schuld þe soneȓ performe here entent.

---

[1] ly *added in red.*   [2] canoni *crossed through.*
[3] MS. vsited.   [4] l *crossed through.*

[CHAPTER XXXIII.]

Capitulum xxxiij.[1]

TO of þe lettered men of þis ordre þoo weʀ sent with all Two Gilbertine clerks
þese letteris to þe court, to whom fel a grete myracle, þat were sent to Rome with
4 not-withstand þei went in þe hoot someʀ in ful grete distempeʀ the letters,
wedir, in whech mech folk deyid of pestilens caused be þat same
hete, for al þis þese men went and cam heyl and sound, not and passed
hurt with þat pestilens. A-noþir þing fel eke in þat iornay, þat safely through pestilence and
8 þei went þorw a buschment of malandrynes, and not aspied, for ambush.
ouʀ[2] Lord sperd þe sith of þoo þeues with a seknesse cleped
acrisia,[3] whech is a febilnesse þat a þing schal ly be-foʀ ‖ a mannes Leaf 87.
eye and not be seyn. Þus weʀ þei saued be meryte of Seynt
12 Gilbert. Thus serued ouʀ Lord[4] þe kyngis men of Surre þat
be-seged Dotaim to kylle Helise, and he appered on-to hem, & þei
knew him nowt.[5] Thus ar þei come hom in good prosperite fro The Pope commanded
þe court, bryngyng with hem þe bulle of ouʀ holy fader þe Pope, the archbishop and
16 with his comaundment to þe archbischop of Cauntyrbyry, to þe others
bischop of Hely, to þe abbot of Borow, and þe abbot of Wardon,
in wheche bulle was enioyned on-to hem þat þei schuld goo to
þe place of his sepultuʀ and þere schuld þei comaunde to þat to go to Sempringham,
20 college of his ordre to faste iij dayes solemply, and in all þoo where, after
dayes þei schuld pray denoutely to God þat he schuld open in three days' fast,
þis mateʀ to hem þe weye of treuth, and more-ouyer, þat þese
bischoppes with þe abbotes schuld ransake streytly þe witnesses all witnesses should be
24 and þe fame opene in þe cuntʀ, &[6] summe scriptuʀ autentik of examined and a record made
þe vertue of þe maneres of þis man and of þe vertue of þe myracles of Gilbert's
doo in his name, all þis schuld þei inqwire bysyly, treuly write it, life, &c., and all this should
and aftir send it up to þe court seled with her seles,[7] be wise men be taken to Rome and
28 and trewe, whech men must swere in þe presens of ouʀ fader sworn to,
þe Pope þat all þis ‖ informacioñ was trewe. All þis comaundment Leaf 87,
of þe Pope was fulfillid in-dede. back.

---

[1] *In margin, .3.*   [2] *ha crossed through.*   [3] *in margin.*
[4] *above in red.*   [5] *In margin in red, 4 Reg. 6.*
[6] *þe crossed through.*   [7] *I crossed through.*

[CHAPTER XXXIV.]

Capl. xxxiiij.[1]

THe sexte kalend of Octobyr, þat is to sey þe day of Seint

On St. Cyprian's day the archbishop and many others

Cipriane and Iustine, þis same archbischop, with þe bischopis of Bathe, of[2] Hely, and of Bangore, with many abbotes & prioures, 4 with summe archdeknes, chanones and officeres of þe cherch of · Lyncolñ, with many famous maysteres and grete puple, came

went to Sempringham

to þe hous of Sempingham; and aftir þei had fastid iij dayes, þei cleped first þe Holy Goost, as men doo at elecciones; þoo 8

and called all the witnesses.

cleped þei, þe witnesses, or witnesseres, religious and seculeres, clerkis and lewed men and women, mad hem to swere þat þei schuld say soth in þat mater in whech inqwisicion schuld be

All their testimonies were sent to Rome.

mad. And all her testimonies þei writyn ful treuly in a dewe 12 forme, and sent hem to þe Pope closed vndir her seles. Ferþermoꝛ, þei writyn certeyn proues of his holy lyf and conuersacioñ and of þe fame of þe cuntꝛ. And whilis þei taried þere iiij dayes

At the same time a young man whose head was turned with

þe treuth was opened of þe mater whech þei soute, be a grete 16 myracle do at his graue, of a ȝong man whos heed with seknesse turned round, of whech turnyng he was oute of hys mynde, and,

Leaf 88.

for uery ‖ peyne, loked euery houꝛ to be ded. Theꝛ was he mad

pain, was cured there, and went to Rome with five priests and others,

hool in here presens, and with þe messageres went in good helth 20 to Rome, and in good helth cam hom a-geyn. For þei sent in þis ambassiat to Rome v. of þe same ordre, prestes, sex simple on-lerned, of whech noumbꝛ summe weꝛ holed fro certeyn seknesse be þe merites of þis Seynt, summe were present whan certeyn men 24

who testified to the truth of the letters.

weꝛ holed. For þis cause weꝛ þei in special sent, þat þe Pope schuld knowe be þe men whech weꝛ þeꝛ[3] þat þe suggestion of þe letteres sent was soth. The messageres go forth with gret[4] ioye, trostyng on ouꝛ Lordes help and þe Seyntes prayer for whom 28 þei goo, mech more with þe betir chere, for þei hadde mery dremes be-fore her iornay, and in her iornay grete prosperite in þe weye, & many oþir good tokenes. And þus, with no grete difficulte, þouȝ it weꝛ so þat Sathanas wold a letted her wey, 32 ȝet, as we saide, with-outen any grete difficulte, þei come to Rome

---

[1] *In margin*, 34.   [2] *inserted above.*
[3] *in margin.*   [4] MS. gꝛt.

on New3ere euen, and aftir þat þe secund day of Ianuari þei come From Rome the mes-
to Anagniam, wheꝛ þe Pope dwelt þat tyme. Ouꝛ Lord gaue sengers went to Anagnis,
hem so grete grace in þe site of ouꝛ holy fader and of þe cardinales, where the Pope was.
4 þat þe x day aftir þei weꝛ come þei were sikyr of alt þat euer
þei desired. ‖ For ouꝛ fader þe Pope had his deliberacion of Leaf 88, back.
þis mateꝛ a-mongis þe cardinales, and say þe wytnesse and þe
iurates what þei weꝛ, apposed hem a-sundyr, and fond gret acord The Pope and cardinals
8 betwix hem; and þou3, as be mannes reson,[1] þe Pope and þe cardi- consented to the canonisa-
nales þout3 þis mateꝛ myth be performed a-non, 3it plesed it to tion, but delayed it.
þe counselt of ouꝛ Lord þat it schuld be dilayed, for he wold þat
his counselt and his help schuld be cleped to þis mateꝛ.

[CHAPTER XXXV.]

12   cap. xxxv.[2]

O nyth with-inne þese[3] ten dayes lay ouꝛ fader þe Pope stodiand One night the Pope
    on[4] þis mater and myth not slepe. He þoute mech[5] of þis
man Gilbert, & was gretly in doute what he schuld do in þe mateꝛ.
16 Thoo prayed he God[6] þat he wold schewe him sum tokne be which[7]
he myte haue knowlech of Goddis wil. In þis þoute slep fel up-on
him, and in þat same slep swech a vision was schewid on-to him.
He þoute he say be-fore him[8] a grete and a hy touꝛ, to whech dreamt he saw a high
20 touꝛ he had gret appetite to goo,[9] and þedyr he went with many tower.
folk aboute him, as he was wone. Whan he was come with-inne
þe touꝛ, he say a bed ful of stre and arayed at þe best; a-boute where he found a bed
þe bed a curteyn of silk, precious I-now, he say hanging, and with a rich
24 þis curteyn, as he þoute, was embrowded with ‖ many ymages Leaf 89.
of seyntes. He stood and merueiled longe on þe beute of þis curtain em-broidered
curteyn, for he had no swech a-boute his bed, and for þat cause with saints' images.
he gan to pulle þe curteyn to him, for he þoute he wold sowe
28 it new and make mete to his bed. And in al þis besynesse he He asked men in
sey a-noþir chambir moꝛ inward and mech folk þere. Whanñ another chamber what
he was com þidir he inqwyred what he schuld do in þe cause, he should do
for whech þe chanones of Sempingham were come and in þe for St. Gil-bert.
32 canoni3ing of þis Seynt. Tho al sodeynly he herd a voys crying
þus: Michael þe archangel, he schal be þi help in þis bisinesse. The answer.

---

[1] b *crossed through.*   [2] *In margin,* 5.   [3] C. 33 b. thesse.
[4] C. studeant of.   [5] C. much.   [6] C. good.   [7] C. wiche.
        [8] *above in red.*   [9] C. for to go.

The Pope
then awoke,
Whan þe Pope had seyn al þis in his slep, sodeynly he wook,[1]
gretely coumforted of þis reuelacioñ, for he vndirstood[2] be þis
þat ouř Lordis[3] comaundment and plesauns was þat þis mateř
schuld be broute to parfite ende.   And a-non, with-oute letting, 4

and made a
special orison
on Gilbert to
be said in his
commemora-
tion.
he mad a special orison of ouř fader Gilbert with a secrete and
postcomun aftir þe forme of þe missale, and whañ he had mad
hem he comaunded þat þei schuld be seyd openly in his *com-
memoracioñ.*   Ferþermoř, þe Pope, as a wise man[3] desiring[4] for 8
to haue þe very certeyn of þis mateř, cleped on-to him a ful

He asked an
abbot to in-
wise man and holy, an abbot, þei cleped hym Reyner, and
Leaf 89,
back.
commaunded him, be vertue of obediens, þat he schuld ‖ be-þink
him of his dreem and telle him þe coniectuř of þat same.   The 12
terpret his
dream,
cause why þat þe Pope uttered his vision to þis man rather
þan to a-noþir, was for he led a solitary lif in þe mountes, and
was in gret opinion both to þe Pope & þe court.   Tho answered
þe abbot a-gayn on-to þe Pope, and sayde þat þis mater neded 16
non auysement, for both þe drem and his interpretacion was
who ex-
pounded it,
like Daniel
and Joseph,
open i-now.   So as a-nothir Daniel on-to Nabugodonosor, or lich
a-noþir Ioseph on-to Pharao, he expowned it[3] in swech declaracioñ:
telling the
Pope that he,
unlike others
before him,
was Pope by
true election.
The fayre touř he seid and þe hye, whech þou say, Ser Pope, 20
is þe grete excellens of þi dignite, to whech þou aspirest; not as
ded many bi-fore þe, but[5] be trew eleccion þou enterest in-to
þe same, and þat is ment in þi drem wher þou þoutist þat þou
weř led in-to þis place witȝ[6] þe handis of many men.   The bed 24
so wel arayed is a clene consciens, in whech a man restith as in
his bed, lich[7] as þe prophete Dauid said in þe Psalme: I schal
wasch, he seith, or ellis, water[8] my bed with my teres.   For euene
as cloþis in whech we rest be mad clene witȝ watyr, so is ouř 28
consciens clensed with repentauns of ouř synnes.   The curteynes
Leaf 90.
a-boute þis bed in whech be impressed ‖ þe faiř figures of seyntes
The figures
on the cur-
tain were the
saints, who
screened men
from tempta-
tion.
are þe commemoraciones of holy seyntis used in þe cherch, be
whech we be schadowyd fro wyndes of temptaciones.   These 32
corteynes aray ful wel ouř consciens whan we, both with hert
and with werk, fulfille heř desir, eþir to honouř hem in God or
elles to folow her steppes.   Thou fader Pope be-gan to sowe þis
curteyn whan þou þout first to sette þis man Gilbert in þe 36

___

[1] C. 33 woke.   [2] C. vnderstode.   [3] *inserted above.*   [4] C. desieryng.

[5] t *added above.*   [6] C. 34 b. wᵗ.   [7] C. lech.

[8] C. I shall wech the fecch or ellis water.

kalende? of seyntes, and I suppose, veryly, he is ful worþi to
be annoted a-mongis hem. Eke swech þing as þou desyred
waking, þou asked in þi slep, and þin answere was gone, þat
4 Mychael schuld be þi help. Noþing a-geyn reson. Michael is
þe propost of Paradys and prince ordeyned be God to receyue
þoo soules whech schul be offered to God. This same Michael
hatȝ receyued þis manne soule and led it to the hye court of
8 blessed spirites, and in þat same court it is determyned þan þis
man Gilbert, fro þis tyme forward, schal be halden in honour [1] and
reuerens as a Seynt. Sowe him In, þerfor, with þi nedel, with
þis power no man hath þat in hand but þou. Ioyne him on-to
12 þe felauchip of seyntis, for it is conuenient þat þe cherch in erde
folow þe ‖ cherch a-boue in heuene.

Leaf 90,
back.

[CHAPTER XXXVI.]

Capitulum xxxvj.[2]

THis interpretacion of þis drem, whan it was þus expressid be
16   þe abbot, plesed þe Pope gretly, for he, with-oute ony tary,
mad calle all þe court of Rome, whech was grete at þat tyme,—and
in special þe archbischop of Reymes was þere present at þat tyme
and bare witnesse of þe holy lyf of Seynt Gilbert, for in his ȝong
20 age he had be in Yngland and knew both þe persone and þe fame.
In þis gret congregacion, whan all men wer sette saue þese
messageres of Sempingham, þe Pope sayde a grete and solempne
sermon of þe holynesse and þe myracles of Seynt Gilbert, rehersing
24 þe witnes þere present, and aftir certeyn wordis whech be pertinent
to þis offise, þere he solemply & openly canoniȝed Seynt Gilbert
with þe comoun assent of al þe cherch, and þer eke he mad a [3] decre
þat þe fest of Seynt Gilbert schuld be seid and songe in þe cherch
28 lich as þe festis of oþir seyntis be. Thus whan þe Pope in his sete
had þus openly schewid on-to puple þis canoniȝacion of þis holy
man, aftir-ward he comaunded þat letteris schuld be mad of þe
same sentens to þe archbischoppis of Ynglond & to þe chapetir of
32 Sempingham, in whech ‖ letteris he rehersed al þe mater fro þe

The Pope
called his
court, and the
archbishop of
Rheims testi-
fied to Gil-
bert's holy
life.

The Pope
then delivered
a sermon,
and canonised
Gilbert,

and sent
word of all
this to Eng-
land,

Leaf 91.[4]

---

[1] C. 34 halden in honor.   [2] *In margin, 6.*   [3] *dc crossed through.*
[4] *The embellishment of capitals omitted from this page.*

begiñnyng on-to þe ende; with all þe inquisicion of his lif and his
myracles he rehersed eke who discretly, who sadly, with what
circumstauns, þis mateꝛ had be [1] treted; wher-for he comaunded in
þe ende of þe bulle þat swech þing as þe Pope with solempnite and 4

and ordered his feast to be kept. with auyse had ordeyned to be kept, þei, as good subiectis, mekly
schuld fulfille and comaunde þe fest of þis holy man to be
solempniȝed be all her prouinces. A special comaundment sent

He also com- manded the archbishop to perform the ceremony, he eke on-to þe archbischop of Cauntyrbyry, be-cause þe place of 8
Sempingham stant in his prouince, þat whan-so-euer þe breþerin
or chanones of Sempingham required him, þat he schuld goo þidyꝛ
and left up fro þe ground þe body of þis holy confessouꝛ, and with
dew reuerens ley it þere whech as þe same breþerin had ordeyned 12
it schuld be leyd. This comaundment of þe Pope was receyued of
þe archbischop and of þe seid chanones as þouȝ it had come fro
heuene; wherfore þei, desiring as good childyrn to fulfill her faderes
comaundment, all þing þat was neccessarie to swech solempnyte 16

and as the Saint was passing out of remembrance, all haste was made. þei purueyed in all hast. And þouȝ þe mynde of þis Seynt, as
haue be of many oþir, was mech oute of rememberauns, eþir for
age or elles, ‖ for necligens of men, or vnkunnyng, or sum oþir
cause; ȝet, as we hope, it was sufficient to us for to be-gynne þis 20
werk, be-cause we had reuelacion first fro God and comaundment
fro ouꝛ holy fader þe Pope, to whos comaundment we be bounde
to obeye as þouȝ it had come fro God. Eke for þe man [2] in his lyf
comaunded us to do þis þing and we eke desired it schuld be do 24
whil we lyue, þis was þe grete [3] hast in þis mateꝛ. For þei þat
weꝛ sent for þis mateꝛ þoute it conuenient to fulfill þe Popes
precept whil he was on lyue and þei eke.

Leaf 91, back.

[CHAPTER XXXVII.]

cap. **xxxvij.**[4]   28

In the vigil of the Holy Cross, 1202, the men of Sempringham ask the arch- bishop to be THe ȝere of ouꝛ Lord Crist a M. cc. ij., þe forseyd breþerin of
Sempyngham, in þe vigil of þe holy crosse, with þe moost
famous men of all þat religion came on-to þe said archbischop
with her maystir, makyng grete instauns þat þe next Sunday aftir 32

---

[1] tred *crossed through.*   [2] *in margin.*
[3] of *crossed through.*   [4] *In margin,* 7.

þe feest of Sein*t* Denys, he wold vouchsaf of his faderhod to be at _{at the trans-}
þe translacioñ of þis holy confessouꝛ Gilbert. The archbischop _{lation of Gilbert.}
receyued hem not but in þe best maneꝛ, and saide he was glad of
4 þese tydannes and redy to fulfille[1] þat solempnyte whech þei all _{He invited his bishops to attend.}
desired, and up-on þis he wrote to þe bischoppes of his prouynce
þat if þei myth haue leyseꝛ þei schuld[2] come to him and ɪ honouꝛ _{Leaf 92.}
þis holy day. Ferþermoꝛ, he desired of hem þat þis schuld be
8 notified þorw-oute her diocise, þat all men whech had deuocion to
þis Seynt myth come to þis fest if þei wold. Thus in þe same day
prefixid, þat is to seyn, þe iij ide of October, all þis mateꝛ is put in _{So it all happened, and}
execucion. And be-side all þe myracles rehersed be-foꝛ in þe Popes
12 presens, eke be-side reuelaciones had fro heuene, and be-side þe seid
witnesses, newe þingis fel þat same day. The nyth of his translacioñ, þat is to sey, þe nyth be-twix þe Satirday and þe Sunday, þe
noble man, þe archbischop with oþir bischoppes and mi*n*istres came
16 on-to þe graue wheꝛ þe holy membres of Gilbertes body was hid,
and with grete worchep þei lifte up þat holy uessel of God, þat, so
waschid and arayed þe next day aftirward, he myte with lesse
tariing be laid in his schrine. Whilis þat þis seruise was do to þe _{wonderful miracles were}
20 body with swete ympnis and songis, summe religiou*s* men þere _{done at the time.}
present, and eke summe seculeres, seyn a grete knot of fyꝛ al
rou*n*d, as þouჳ many candeles had be ioyned to-gidyr, or ellis lich
a grete schiny*n*g sterre ones, twyes, þryes, com down fro heuene
24 and eft-sones goyng up to heuene aboue þe roof of þe cherch,
euene ɪ ouyr þe sepultuꝛ. And at þe þird comy*n*g it semed as _{Leaf 92, back.}
þouჳ it had þirled þe rof & falle in-to þe cherch. Thei þat sey
þis site with-outen told it hem with-inne, þat þei myth goo owte
28 and se þe same, þat is to sey, þe lite of ouꝛ Lord aboue þe cherch.
Lich þing sey oþir men whech had waked at þe graue certeyn
nytes in her prayeres a litil be-foꝛ þis translacioñ, þat is to sey,
a grete lite entꝛ þorw þe rof and thries entre in-to þe graue wheꝛ
32 þe holy body was layd. Swete sauour eke felt þei þere whan þe
stones were remeued be masones for to make space wheꝛ the new⚫
scryne schuld be sette.

---

[1] MS. fulfulle.   [2] d *added afterwards.*

[CHAPTER XXXVIII.]

cap. **xxxviij.**[1]

More miracles
were done at
the transla-
tion,

NOwt only þese myracles rehersed weŕ doo at þis tyme but many oþir testimonies weŕ had in whech men myth know þat þis translacioɴ was plesauɴs to God. Thus whan þei had lifte 4 þe ston fro þe graue þere was founde fayre red pouder of his flesch,[2] swech as þei sey as virgines[3] haue whan þei aŕ ded. The chesible eke in whech þe body was woundyn, of silk, was found hool with-oute corrupcioɴ. Whan aɫɫ þese relikes were lift fro þe 8

Leaf 93.   ground and waschid þe[4] archbischop went a-gayn ǁ to chambyr for
and the arch- to take a rest, for it was fer fro day. Whan he had leyn a litil
bishop be-
came sud-   tyme on his bed sodeynly fel up-on him a greuous sekenesse, and þe
denly ill,   peyne vexed him so sore þat he stood in grete dowt, and in maneŕ 12 dispeyr, þat he myth not fulfiɫɫ þat office for whech he was come, and to whech he had cleped so many persones in special of swech reuerens. For þis secund cause was he moŕ sory þan for his bodely sekenesse. He leyd medicynes to his body, swech [5]as þei[5] tawt 16 him, but al þoo profited nowt. Tho turned he his trost and his deuocioɴ to God and to Seynt Gilbert, þat ouŕ Lord[6] at mediacioɴ of þat good Seynt wold send him myte and strength to performe þis office for whech he was come and many oþir persones. A-non 20

but was cured as þis prayer was fulfilled so sone left him aɫɫ þis peyne, for aftir
through
devotion to   þat same peyne was goo he felt his body moŕ myty and strong þaɴ
St. Gilbert.   it was be-fore. At þis same chaunge cam þe houŕ in whech þe couent rang to mateyns. A-non as þe archbischop herd þe belle 24 he roos him-self and cleped aɫɫ his clerkys, and aɫɫ in fere þei go on[-to] þe chanones mateynis, whech, for þe worchip and loue of

Leaf 93,   þat Seynt for whom þai ǁ were gadered, were ful solemply songe.
back.   In þe morownyng þe archbischop[7] roos heyl and sound, and aɫɫ þat 28 euyr God and Seynt Gilbert had schewid on-to him þat same nyth, with grete ioye he told hem, praysing þe vertue of ouŕ Lord and of þis holy Seynt, whech vertue he felt notablely fulfillid in him. The houŕ is come of þe day þat þis solempnite schal be doo; the 32

---

[1] *In margin,* 8.
[2] wh *crossed through.*
[3] s *added afterwards.*
[4] pope *crossed through.*
[5-5] *inserted above.*
[6] *inserted above.*
[7] MS. pope *crossed through and* archbishop *written over in red.*

bischop is arayed with his mynystres; þe watir is halowed þat Everything is ready for the ceremony,
schal serue in þe office; þe schrine eke is halowed and born
a-boute on þe schulderis of princes aud lordis whech be þere
4 present : a solempne procession is ordeyned, in whech procession
first go þe clergie, nexte princes, lordis and oþir, many beryng þis
halowid uessel in whech þei wil ley him; last of all folow þe
bischoppis. Certeyn seke men þat weꝑ ny and touchid þese relikes more miracles are performed; the Archbishop preaches;
8 weꝑ mad hol þat same houꝑ, as was veryly proued. Theꝑ saide þe
archbischop a ful notable sermone grounded al up-on þe holynesse
and þe myracles of þis holy man Gilbert, and þere mad he rehersaile
of all þe processe, who it [1] was sent on-to þe court of Rome, what
12 answeꝑ þei had fro þe Pope & mech oþir þing. Tho be-gunne þei mass is said : Leaf 94.
a messe of þis same Seynt with ful swe⸗te concent, and in þe last
ende [1] of þat masse, aftir þe bischop had receyued þe holy sacra-
ment, er þat þei song þe postcomoun, þe seide relikes were wounde the relics are wound in silk
16 in fayꝑ silk and þan in a cloth of silk precious I-now whech ouꝑ
fader archbischop had ȝoue to þat same entent, and all þese [2] þus
wounden weꝑ layde in þat same vessel mad for þe same cause. and laid in their vessel,
Thei layde eke with him a grete chartouꝑ in whech was wretyn al with a charter of the Saint's life, duly sealed.
20 his lif, his canoniȝacion eke, and his translacion seled with þe seles
of þe bischoppis & abbotes whech weꝑ þere present. Theꝑ was put
in with him eke a plate of led, in whech plate was wrytyn al þis
þing more compendiously, as I suppose, þat þe rememberauns of al
24 þis werk schuld last euyr. Thus was þat uessel sperd and sette The vessel is closed, and mounted on marble.
up-on a wal of marbil in þe same place where þe seint lay be-foꝑ.
Tho mad þei an ende of þe masse, and aftir ſei had refreschid heꝑ
bodies euery man with ful gret ioye turned a-gayn on-to his owne
28 place. Ouꝑ maystir is layd now in his rest; lete us folow þerfor And so the Saint is at rest.
þe steppes of his good lyf þat we may be translate fro wrecchid-
nesse to ioye and þorw his ledyng come ‖ to þat cuntꝑ wher we Leaf 94, back.
schul haue ioye euyr.

---

[1] *inserted above in red.*   [2] *þis crossed through and þese written above.*

[CHAPTER XXXIX.]

Gilbert's
miracles
attest his
greatness.

NOw of ouꝛ fader Gilbert, who holy was his lyf, who holsom was his doctrine, who grete rewardes weꝛ sent fro God on-to his blessed merites, witnesse þe grete myracles whech aftir his deth 4 wer wroute be ouꝛ Lord God. And of þese myracles now wil we telle all þe maneꝛ lich as þei fell and lych as ouꝛ wel be-loued

Of these we will tell as the Archbishop inquired and discovered.

fader in God, þe [2] said archbischop of Cauntyrbyry, at þe comaund-ment of þe Pope Innocent þe þird with his suffraganes ransaked 8 and inqwired. Lich þat inquysicioñ in sentens & in termes, whech inqwysicioñ þei sent þat tyme to Rome,—þorw whech sond þis canonizacioñ was performed,—lich þat forme wil we write here.

How a clerk, going to school in another town, lay down and slept, and woke with a withered leg,

Ther was a clerk whos name ne place is now on-knowe þat used to 12 go to skole fro o town to a-noþir as in þis lond is grete custom. This clerk in his weye to skoleward fell in grete heuynesse, so þat he must nedis slepe. He layd him down and slept, and aftir slep whan he wook he felt al his rith legge, foot and all, so sered and 16 dryed þat he myth not goo þeron in no maner. So with his staf and his oþir legge he hipped forth as he myte tyl he cam to þe

Leaf 95.

nexte ‖ town. Fro þens was he caryed to a mousasterye whech þei clepe Hauyrholm, for þeꝛ dwelled he iij monthes, euyr vexid with 20 þe same infirmite. That legge, in al þat tyme, down to þe foot was soo insensible and all þe myth þerof go, þat if men had prikkid him with a nedyl or ony oþir scharp þing, he felt no moꝛ þerof þan a man had put þis scharpnesse on-to a stoon or a tre. Eke þe vse 24 of þat legge was as lost, for whan he schuld walk he schuld drawe

which was without feeling:

it after him as þouȝ it had be a braunch of a sere tree, for he was more greued with þe birden þan esed with þe offise. Be-cause he myth not lyft þat foot fro þe ground, but draw it euyr fro þe erde, 28 þe toos were flayn and blody to grete peyn of him & gret pite to all þat seyn him. The prouost of þat place ded make him a hose al of ledir, and þat was wered a-non, in special at þe ferþest ende whech trayled so on þe ground. Aftir þis he ordeyned him a-noþer 32 remedy, for he teyhid his legge fro þe ground with a roop on-to his schulderis, and þus bare he þe legge whech schuld a born him.

---

[1] *In margin, 9.*   [2] MS. þei, *with i dotted underneath.*

To þis same clerk slepyng on a nyte appered a persone of grete how the clerk was told in a
worchip, as he þoute, and saide þus on-to him: If þou wilt be hool dream to go to
þis same day, loke ‖ þou visite þe graue, or elles þe sepultuꝛ, of St. Gilbert.
4 maystir Gilbert at Sempyngham. At þat same houꝛ þe man gat back. Leaf 95,
him a cart and with on[1] of þe breþerin of þat same hous he was He went to the Saint's
brout to þis sepulture, and sodeynly, as he prayed, he fel on slep. grave and slept; had a
In his slep, as he þout, þe same persone whech appered to him vision;
8 be-fore appered a-gayn and sayde on-to him swech wordes: For
what cause liggist þou here so longe? Be-hold þou art mad hool.
With þis visioñ he swette meruelously and be-gan to wayle fyue
sithes, þoo wook he and roos be him-self, loked on his foot and
12 trad with it on þe grouñd for to asay wheþir he myth go with þat
or nowt. Be-cause of þe sodeyn chaunge whech was come so
newly, he stood in grete dowte what he schuld doo. The sexten
þat stood by and perauentuꝛ knew not of þis sodeyñ chaunge mad
16 tokenes on-to him þat he schuld rest a-gayn. He lay down eft- and awoke
sones, and aftir a litil slep wook a-gayn, and þanne he roos and whole.
felt both feet, thy and legge al hool; þus he þrew a-way þis staf
and forsook his cart, and with ful grete lithnesse[1] went wheꝛ he
20 wold. And in tokne þat þis helth cam to him be myracle, in þat
place whech he myth not fele a ‖ nedel prikkid be-fore, now, whañ Leaf 96.
þe natural hete is come a-gayn, he felt sumwhat a peyne in þat same
place wheꝛ þat þe wounde was. A-mongis all oþir þat boꝛ witnesse This man went to
24 of þe myracles do be Seint Gilbert þis man was on, for he went to Rome and gave his
Rome &[2] confessed al þis be-foꝛ þe Pope, and aftir, whan he cam evidence to the Pope.
hom, was mad chanon and prest in þis same ordre, þankyng God
all his lyf and Seint Gilbert of his gracious cure.

[CHAPTER XL.]

28

Capitulum xl.[3]

A Mayde was þere eke in þe strete at Sempyngham þat in The legs of a maid were
both leggis, in þat part whech is be-hinde þe knees, was so contracted,
contract þat sche myth not stand ne goo, for in-stede of hir feet

---

[1] *in margin.*   [2] *inserted above in red.*
[3] *In margin, 4, another figure having been cut away at edge of leaf perhaps.*

whan sche wold remeue hir body fro o place to a-noþir, sche crap
with hir haudys and with hir lendes, or buttokkes. Eke with
grete rankouꝛ of þe soor hir left foot was meruelously disfigured,
for iij grete peces of flesch grew up-on hir foot, ech of hem 4
departed fro oþir, whech semed as þouȝ it had be cut.   More-ouyr

hir left arme[1] had lost þe vertue of felyng and þe hand of þat
arme[1] was lych þe left foot with swech þre cuttyngis of flesch as

we sayde be-fore. Thus hyng it as a[2] onprofitable ‖ byrden fro þe 8
schuldyr downward. This woman herd telle who þat þis clerk[3] of
whom we told last was cured and so cured þat he was strong to

She also went
to the sepul-
chre, and lay
there seven
days,
take his iornay to Rome. So mad sche grete instauns to þem þat
dwelled[4] in þat strete þat þei schuld lede hir to þis sepultuꝛ of 12
Seynt Gilbert and leue hir þere. Ther lay sche seuene days
continuely perseueraunt in hir prayeris, and as sche slept on
a nyth sche þout þat þe ston vndir whech Seynt Gilbert was
closed claf a-sundyr, and he roos up and sat þerupon with ful 16

In a dream
she saw Gil-
bert, who
gave her a
host;
grete lite. Sche þoute eke þat he had in his hand many hostes
and þoo multiplied fast, as to hir site so fast and to so grete
noumbyr þat he myth vnneth hold hem. Too of þoo same hostes
he put in hir mouth, as sche þoute, and aftir þat gaf hir his 20
blessyng. Aftir þis sche a-wook sodeynly and fonde hir body al
on a swet so habundaunt þat it dropped fro hir body and mad þe
pauyment weet; sche felt euene at þat tyme a new chaunge in hir
body, for þat whech was heuy and contract be-fore now sche felith 24
it of swech disposicion þat, as it semeth to hir, sche myth flye for
litenesse. In þis same chaunge sche say who þe lites þat stood

a-boute þe sepultuꝛ of Seint Gilbert ‖ and brent felle down sodeynly,
and þo sche gan to crepe as hir vse was for to amende þoo lites. 28
In hir creping þe senewes whech were contract be-fore in hir[5]
lendes, þei brak and streyned oute to swech largenesse þat sche

roos and stood on hir feet and myth walk and in þat brekyng sche
herd a grete noyse, who þei craked and had ful grete meruayle 32
who þat þe senewes craked whan þei be-gunne to extende hem-self.
In þis same tyme þat þis woman standith þus merueylyng, þe

---

[1] MS. harme. h crossed through in red.   [2] inserted above.
[3] b crossed through.   [4] Word blotted in text and re-written in margin.
[5] but crossed through.

nunne, þe sextenesse, rang to mateyns; þe sisteres be come down The nunnes going to matins saw her standing,
and se þis woman standyng be þe sepultuꝛ: first þei [1] be a-ferd
be-cause many of hem wist not þat sche was þere, for sche was not
4 þere at euen whan þei went to bedde, as it semeth ; þei walk on-to
hir and sche confessith al þe circumstauns of þe myracle euene as and heard her story.
it fel. Þere þank þei God and Seynt Gilbert aꝉ with o *consent*
for þe grete cuꝛ whech now [2] is don. The woman was kept with
8 hem a certeyn tyme for declaracioñ of þe myracle and on-tyl [3] hir
arme [4] and legge had parfitly here use; aftyr þat tyme sche went
hom to þe strete and leued þeꝛ with hir frendis in good helth of
body, þankyng ouꝛ Lord of þat sodeyn chaung. ‖

[CHAPTER XLI.]

12   cap. xlj. Leaf 97, back.

A Knytys wyf þere be-side, a lady of ful noble fame, had swech A Knight's wife could not use her arm,
  seknesse and peyne in *special* duryng *in* hir lyft [5] arme þat
sche myth not mene þat arme ne do with-al no maner werk. This
16 peyn lastid up-on hir fro þe feest of Seynt Petyr, whech þei clepe
in Latyn, ' ad vinculam,' in Englisch, ' Lammesse,' on-to þe natiuite
of ouꝛ Lady. Be-side þis had sche oþir sores whech we name not and had sores,
now. With al þis infirmyte sche is come on-to þe sepultuꝛ of þis She watched a night by the sepulchre and was cured.
20 holy man and aftyr sche had wecchid in deuoute prayeres al a nyte
sche went hom hol fro both sores, euyr-moꝛ hauyng grete trost in
þis holy Seint.

¶ A-noþir woman was þere be-side *contract* & croked whech myt Another woman was deformed and helpless,
24 not go, ne sitte, ne stand, with-oute help of hem þat weꝛ waytyng
up-on hiꝛ. The fadeꝛ and þe modeꝛ of hir, hauyng gret sorow for
þat desese, brout hir on-to þe sepultuꝛ of ouꝛ maystir. The first
nyte sche was þere, at instauns of hiꝛ frendes, þe chanones put She wore Gilbert's scapulary and was eased.
28 up-on hiꝛ þe scapulary of Seynt * Gilbert, and þe woman confessed
þere be-foꝛ hem aꝉ þat in doing on of þat cloth sche felt gret
alleuyauns of hir sore. The nyte folowand appeared on-to hir
a fayre old man with gray heꝛ, as sche þoute in hir sleep, and

---

[1] i *added above.*   [2] her *crossed through and now in margin.*
[3] to *crossed through and* tyl *written above.*
[4] MS. harme, h *crossed through in red.*   [5] b *crossed through.*
[6] a *stroke crossed through.*

in his hand he had a staf, as men walk for age. Thus ⸿ he saide on-to hir: Wilt þou be hool? Sche answered þat gladly sche wold. Tho he blessed hir and said, Thou schal be hool. Sche inqwyred of him what man he was & he answered þat he was maystir Gilbert [4] of Sempyngham. Aftir þis dreem sche a-wook and felt hir-self hool in euery part and þus in helth lyued many ȝeres.

[Chapter XLII.]

cap. xlij.

A clerk was þere eke in þat cuntṝ þat in his breest and in his [8] womble had a meruelous risyng whech bolned soo with-inne his breest þat he fered gretly it schuld drawe on-to ydropesy. Thus al in dispeyṝ of helth he lay in his bed [1] up-on fiftene dayes with-oute hope of ony recuṝ. Certeyn men whech cam to visite [12] hym told him of þe grete myracles whech ouṝ Lord wroute at Sempingham þorw þe merites of ouṝ fader Gilbert. Whan þe seek man herd of þese noueltes he mad a-vow openly þat þat place schuld [2] he visite [2] whan ouṝ Lord wold sende him disposicion and [16] leyser. Sone aftyr þis avow was mad þe man felt him sumwhat amended, þat he myth ryse and walk. For whech cause in grete

hast he took his iornay on-to Sempyngham, and þere in grete deuocioñ he lened up-on þe graue and sayde swech deuoⁱⁱciones [20] as he coude, praying with bittyr teres þat God schuld send him sum reles of his peyne. In þis tyme of prayeṝ he felt þat alł þe boweles of his body weṝ gretly meued and turned, as þei had drawe on-to a-noþer kynde þan þei [3] weṝ be-fore. Tho rose he [24]

fro þe graue and felt him-self in oþir plite, for alł þe bolnyng and eke þe peyne is a-voyded. Thus walkith he in þe cherch, assaying him-self if [4] al be weel, and whan he say veryly þat he was hool he took leue and walkith on-to his wonyng. [28]

⸿ A-noþer prest was waschid in a batth up-on a Fryday and on þe Satirday folowand he fel in so greuous seknesse whech continued a hool ȝeṝ and more, þat alł þe membris of his body had lost her offise; he myte not ete but if he weṝ fed, not goo but [32] if he weṝ led. Thus as a man alł contract with a maneṝ of a

---

[1], [2-2] *in margin.*   [3] i *added in red.*   [4] MS. it, *with* f *written on the* t.

palesie, he kept his bed, neu*er* remeuyng þens but with help. he too went to the sepul-chre,
Thus was he fed and norchid lich a child with his seruau*nt* ordeyned
to his seruyse, for he myth nowt do him-self. This man was brout
4 with grete besinesse on[-to] þe cherch of Sempyngham in a cart,
be-twyx þe myd-day and euensong. Ther at þe graue he mad his
deuoute prayer þat our Lord ‖ be þe merites of Sei*n*t Gilbert schuld Leaf 99.
releue him. That same day was he so hool þat with-outen cart or and was cured.
8 hors he went hom to his owne place.

[CHAPTER XLIII.]

Capi*tu*lum xliij.[1]

I n þat same cuntr[2] and in þat same place at Sempyngha*m* was a A nun going to the kitchen, stumbled,
nu*n*ne whech, at þe comau*n*dment of hir prioresse, went on-to[3]
12 þe kychyn, and be-cause sche went with grete hast and took no gret
consideracion what þing lay in hir weye, sche stombeled at a blok
whech was hid with straw, and þus fel sodeynly. In whech fal sche
was so greuously hurt þat hir foot was fro þe ioynt, and þus[4] sche and injured her foot.
16 lay crying and waylyng for grete peyne þat sche felt. Hir cry
was herd þorw þe place and a-non hir sisteres cam on-to hir,
coumforted hir, lyft hir up with many handis and grete heuynesse,
and bar hir on-to þe infirmarie. Thus bolned þe foot and ranked,
20 þat þei wer compelled to kit hir schoo, elles had þei not gote it of.
Many remedies wer ordeyned to þis foot; it was drawen with All remedies failed to cure her.
grete peyne to bryng it in ioynt ageyn, but it a-vayled not. Thei
layde eke to it playsteres of dyue*rs* herbis, but it profited not, for
24 euyr þe peyne grew mor and mor. Thus lay þe nu*n*ne in þat
peyne ‖ al þat ʒer and þe next, on-to þe day whech we clepe þe Leaf 99, back.
annyuersarie of Sei*n*t Gilbert. Than was sche so febyl þat þei
þoute best to gyue hir þe holy anoyntyng whech is last of all þe
28 sacrame*n*tis. Tho sche reqwyred hem to make a kandel of wax[5]
aftir hyr length, and þat same kandel and hir-self eke sche desired She was taken to the sepul-chre,
þei schuld bere on-to þe sepultur of Seynt Gilbert. This was doo
in dede, for whan sche was broute þedyr þe prioresse took þe same
32 lynand cloth in hande whech lay up-on þe breest of þis holy con-

---

[1] *In margin, 4 and part of 3 at edge of leaf.*
[2] *was crossed through.*   [3] *to above in red.*
[4] *a written above.*   [5] *in margin.*

fessour swech hour as he schuld dey. In þis same cloth wonde
þe prioresse þe soor foot of hir sister often rehersed. Thus lay
sche wakyng þere be þe sepultur all þat anniuersary day, þe nyte
folowand, and þe next day tyl it was noon, for þan fel sche in sleep. 4
And in þat same sleep sche þoute þat sche say many men, clad al
in white, comand in-to þe monasterye and bysy to araye þe auter
as þouჳ a preest schuld go to masse. Be-bynde hem al came Seynt
Gilbert, as sche þoute, arayed lich a prest, and his chesibile was al 8

red. He turned him to þat woman whech lay þus seek; he blessed
hir þryes, and at euery blessyng he mad a tokne on-to hir þat sche
schuld ryse. ¶ Sche þout in hir slep þat sche roos and wold haue
hold him be þe clothis, but hir hold fayled and sche fel down gruf 12
up[1]-on þe ground. As sche þoute in hir slep so fond sche whan
sche a-wook, for sche lay þus still on þe pauyment sor astoyned.
In þis mene-tyme come þe prioresse and hir sisteres fro mete with

her grace, and a-non þis same woman told hem who sche was 16
mad hool be þe help of Seynt Gilbert, eke[2] of al hir dreme and
appering of þe Seynt sche mad at þat tyme open declaracion.
Tho þe prioresse took hir be þe hand and felt wel þat sche was
hool, for hir-self, with-outen ony leder, sche went agayn to þe 20
infirmarie, and euyr aftyr was þat foot as fayr and as hool as ony
foot myth be.

[CHAPTER XLIV.]

cap, xliiij.[3]

WE rede eke þat, be touching of þe clothis of our fader 24
Gilbert, and eke be drynkyng of þat water in whech his
ded body was waschid, þat many vertues wer wroute þerby and
many sores holed. For þere was a prioresse of þat same ordre
whech was vexed with seknesse xv dayes and þat greuous maledy. 28
Remedye cowde sche non haue of no bodely medycynes, wherfor

sche turned hir trost to þe help of God and þis Seynt, and with
a gret feyth drank of þat water ¶ in whech his body was waschid,
and sone aftyr was sche hool, for þe cuppe was not so sone fro hir 32
mouth þat hir body was hool, as many of hir sisteres bore witnesse
whech were þere present.

---

[1] MS. ut.   [2] *in margin.*   [3] *In margin,* 44.

¶ A-noþir woman eke was þere fast by whech trauayled in byrth ^{and a woman in child-birth} of a child too dayes, so greuously vexed with peyne þat euery man had pite of hir. Sche drank eke of þat[1] watyr in whech þe tonsure
4 of his berd was wette, and sche was mad hool.

¶ Eke þe same ȝere þat oure fader deyid, on of þe nunnes, as ^{and a nun who had swallowed a fish-bone.} sche sat in þe[2] refectory and ete fysch with hir sisteris, þe bon of a fisch left in hir þrote and stood so fast þat sche myth be no weye
8 remeve it, not-withstand þat sche myte touch it with hir fynger. Sche drank often sithes be þe councell of hir sisteres, but it a-mended nowt, for þe penauns was so grete in hir drynkyng þat sche cast þe likour, but þe boon a-bode stille. Hir felawes ded all
12 her craft to drawe it owt, and al a-vayled not. This cuÞ, as myn auctouÞ seith, was reserued to a-noþir maner drynk and an-oþir werk. Thus lay sche, hir peyne euyr encresing fro myd-day tyl euen. Hir sisteres þan, takyng a sadder councell, ledde hir in-to
16 þe cherch, & broute hir on-to þe auteÞ and þere alle þei fell down ^{Leaf 101.} on knees, deuoutly prayng to God and to Seynt Gilbert for helth of hir.[2] Tho mad þei hiÞ to drynk of þat water in whech þe body of þat holy confessouÞ was wasch in. A-non, as sche had dronk
20 þat watyr, sodeynly sche was delyuered of þat peyne, but sche coude nevyr haue knowlech wheÞ þis bon be-cam.

[CHAPTER XLV.]

cap. xlv.[3]

OF þat same ordre eke a chanon had swech peyne in his nek ^{A canon wraps his sore head}
24 and þe aftir part of his hed þat he myte not suffir þat place be touched, not with his owne handes. This peyne lastid eyte dayes, þat he myth neuyr turne his hed but if he turned al his body. On of his breþerin, whech was his keper,[4] gaf him þis
28 counsel, þat he schuld wynde his hed with a certeyn cloth of ^{in a linen cloth of Gilbert's,} lynand whech Seynt Gilbert wered. I suppose veryly it was his awbe, for my auctoÞ heÞ setteth a word 'subucula' whech is both an awbe and a schert, and in þe first part of þis lyf þe same
32 auctouÞ seith þat þis holy man wered next his skyn non hayer, as for þe hardest, ne lynand, as for þe softest, but he went with

---

[1] was crossed through in red.
[2] In margin, 45.
[3] in margin in red.
[4] r added in red.

wolle, as with þe mene. Whan þis man had wounde þus þis

Leaf 101,
back.
cloth a-boute his hed,[1] whech cloth Seint || Gilbert had used at

and suddenly
became
whole,
solempnite of messe, as we seid, a-non and sodeynly þis man was
hool. This was at euen, for on þe morow he was purposed to entr 4
þe infirmary þat he schuld not inqwyet his breþerin with[2] clamour
whech he mad for peyne. For þis cloth was not so sone put
a-boute his hed, and he þat wond it a-boute his hed was not
go fro him thre or four passe, or he cleped him a-geyn, saying þat 8
al his peyne was goo and he felt no maner greuauns. He leyd his
hand to þe place whech was sore, groped it, and touchid it with sad
felyng, and he felt no sor. His hed myte he turne on what side he
wold, not mevyng his body; flesch, skyn and nek, al was hool. 12

and followed
his usual
course of
life.
The same nyte he slept qvyetely, and, to merueyle of all his
felawchip, roos to mateyns, þere fulfillid all his office[3] in redyng
and synging as he of vsage was wone to doo. In þe morownyng
and non er he told his breþerin al þis myracle, who he was mad 16
hool be þe[3] lynand cote of Seynt Gilbert.

[Chapter XLVI.]

cap. xlvj.

A woman
with a swollen
knee
EKe a woman of good report dwelled þere be-side, whech in hir
kne and legge had swech a passion þat a month hool sche 20

Leaf 102.
myte not goo on þe rite foot, so bolned and rankyd was hir || kne.
Thus with grete bysynesse of hir seruauntes sche was horsed, for in
sykyrnesse þis is hir desire, þat sche wol be caried to Sempyngham,
trosting in þe merites of þis holy confessour þorw whech sche 24

goes to Sem-
pringham,
wears Gil-
bert's hose,
and is cured.
schal be hool. Whan sche was come on-to Sempyngham aftir hir
desire, þei broute hir þe hose of Seynt Gilbert; sche put hir legge
in þat same hose and sodeynly sche was hol, so parfithly cured
þat sche went þat same day a myle on hir feet hom to her owne 28
hous.

A woman was
sick after
childbirth;
¶ A-noþir woman eke aftir delyuerauns of a child had a greuous
seknesse fourty wekys and too. For hir womb was bolned to swech
quantite men supposed sche schuld deye. Many holy places visited 32

---

[1] in crossed through in red.   [2] ch crossed through.
[3] inserted above.

sche for hir helth and was not hool. So was sche inspired at þe last to visite þe sepultuᵽ of ouᵽ fader Gilbert, and þeᵽ was sche mad hool. For sche was cured þere sone aftir sche was com, euene 4 in þe fest of Seynt Cruce, þe ix houᵽ of þe day. And þan with ful glad hert sche went hom, schewing to hir frendis hir body wheᵽ þei myth parceyue þat al þat swellyng was goo.

she visited Sempring-ham and was cured.

[CHAPTER XLVII.]

capl. xlvij.

8 THe þrote and eke the hed of a-noþir man þere be-syde was so risyn and bolned with seknesse whech þei ⫶ clepe þe swynesye, and eke so greuously knottid, þat viij dayes continuely he was compelled for very peyne with-outen mete or sustenau� to 12 kepe his bed and suffyr þe maledye. The last too dayes was his drynk secluded fro him, so closed weᵽ his pipes with violens of þat soᵽ. Than fel on-to him moᵽ greuauᵽ, for in þe myd houᵽ of þat last nyth of þoo viij days he lost his spech, whech priuacion lastyd 16 on-to þe euyn of þat day folowand. Thaᵽ supposed þei all whech weᵽ aboute hym þat he schuld dye. For to heᵽ couᵽfort and consolacioᵽ he myte in no wyse gyue non answeᵽ. The small issewes of his þrote myte ful euel receyue wynd in-to his body. 20 Than, at grete instauᵽ of his wyf, þe girdill of Seynt Gilbert was broute, and water eke, whech he halowyd. With þe girdill þei girt his nek ful deuoutly, and þe watyr þei pored in-to his mouth. Eke þei waschid þe bolnyng of his þrote with þat same watyr, and 24 þan be-gan þe man fele sumwhat reles, for wyth þat wasching he voyded wynd, and aftyr þe wynd o grete blody drope went oute fro his mouth. Thus be-gan he to releue in so mech þat or euen he spak and ete, and ⫶ wyth-inne iij dayes he receyued parfite hele, so 28 sodeynly cesed his peyne.

Another Leaf 102, back. man's throat and head were swollen, and he had to fast. The girdle of Gilbert was brought, and water which he hallowed; and through these he was healed. Leaf 102.

[CHAPTER XLVIII.]

Cap. xlviij.

ON of þe nunnes of þat same ordᵽ xxx. ȝere continuely twyes ¹ or thries in þe ȝere had meruelous seknesse with-inne 32 hir body, for a-bowte hir hert and in hir left syde was swech

A Gilbertine nun was frequently sick,

¹ *ones crossed through, and twyes written above.*

pressuꝛ þat whan it cam, þe woman, ny ded for uery peyn, lost
hir mynde. And in þis peyne sche had swech strength þat many
of hiꝛ sisteres myth not at þat tyme hold hiꝛ ne kepe hir in
rest. Thus on a day whan þe seknesse had caute hir þus violently 4
þei sent aftir prestes of þe same ordre for to be a-boute hiꝛ in
tyme of hir deth, for all loke þei whan sche schal passe.

A-mongis þese prestis cam in þe maystir of Sempingham, þat
same mayster whech was next successouꝛ aftir Seynt Gilbert. 8
Theꝛ fond he þe woman bownden and holden as a furiose person
is wone to be seruyd. Tho he inqwyred of hem þat weꝛ þere[1]
if ony part of Seynt Gilbertis watyr weꝛ in þat hous. Thei
had it redyly, and at þe comaundment of heꝛ prelat, þei pored 12
of þe same watyr in-to hir mouth. A grete merueyl was seyn
þere, for þat watyr was not so sone entered in-to hir þrote but
sche be-gan to chaunge all þat wode rage, and hir veyl, whech
was pul|led down to hir schulderis, in ful religious maneꝛ sche 16
redressid, and hid hir face and hir eyne as sche was wone to
doo. And þoo in þe presens of þe maystir & many folk whech
stood with him, sche cryed in þis maneꝛ : O moder of mercy,—What
schuld we tell long tale ?—As þouȝ sche had be in a trauns 20
ʄsche be-gan to knowe hir-self, and be processe of tyme sche was
restored to parfite helth, for aftyr þat tyme had sche neuyr more
þat seknesse.

¶ A-noþir woman was þere with dyuers seknesse vexed, þat 24
is to seyn dissentyrie, govte, and vomyte dayly folowand. Dis-
sentyrye þe Grekys clepe þis sekenesse whan a mannes guttys
be hurt so þat þei be slitte or cutte. Othir sekenesse had þis
woman dyuers, whech sche was a-schamed to confesse and for 28
whech sche was compelled be debylite to kepe hir bed fro þe
fest of All Seyntis on-to iij dayes be-foꝛ Candell-masse. Than
was told hir þat too of hir neybouris, women bothe, on def,
a-noþir bedred, infect with a maner of palesie, þat þei weꝛ led 32
on-to þe toumbe of Seint Gilbert and þere weꝛ þei maḍ parfitly
hool. Of þese tydanes sche caute a coumfort, and a-non sche let[2]
make a candel aftir hir mesuꝛ, and in a cart with þat same was

---

[1] *inserted above.*

[2] led *crossed through in red, and* let *in black in margin.*

sche caried on-to þe sepultuꝛ of ouꝛ fadeꝛ. ‖ Theꝛ wook sche Leaf 104.
in þrayer al þat nyte, & þe next day a-boute nyne of clok was went to the sepulchre and was cured.
sche mad hool of all þoo maledies rehersed be-forə.

[CHAPTER XLIX.]

Capitulum xlix.

4   Anoþir woman was þere whos kne was soo contract þat too Another woman had a contracted
     monthis sche myth not goo. Sche was brout eke in a cart knee, went to Semprling-
on-to þe toumbe of Seynt Gilbert wheꝛ sche wook to nytes in ham,
8 ful devoute prayeres. The secund nyte sche þoute in hir dreem
þat oute of a ymage mouth whech stood be þe graue, mad in
worchip of ouꝛ Lady, fell a fayꝛ red flouꝛ, and eke þat same had a dream of Our Lady,
flouꝛ, as sche þoute, fell up-on hir soꝛ kne. Sche a-wook and
12 felt hir kne hool, for þis sodeyn helth, as sche vndirstood weel, and was healed.
was goue hir be þe mediacion of ouꝛ Lady and þe merites of Seint
Gilbert. Than with ful grete denocioñ sche kissid þe feet of
þat same ymage, and þus in parfite helth sche is goo hoom.

16   ¶ Theꝛ was a-noþir woman eke in þat cuntꝛ whos rite eye A woman with bad eyes
be-gan to wax seek, þat is to sey, al red of colouꝛ with peyne prayed by the tomb,
folowand. Sone aftir þe lift eye was in þat same plite, for þat
eye in special bolned soo þat iij dayes sche myth se no lite.
20 In all þis peyne sche cam to þe toumbe of ouꝛ fadeꝛ Gilbert,
with a candell brennaund and a petous hert. Theꝛ ‖ a-bode Leaf 104, back.
sche stedfastly in prayeꝛ whilis þat þe priouꝛ of þat same place
sayde masse þere. Aftir sche had herd þat masse sche went
24 hom in hope of helth, and þere fell sche on sleep. Aftir hir
sleep sche felt neythir passioñ in eye ne hed, and or þe sunne
went to rest þat bolnyng was voyded and hir site restored. Day
be day aftyr þis hir site wex bettyr and bettir tyl it cam to þe and was healed.
28 same perfeccioñ whech it had be-foꝛ.

[CHAPTER L.]

Capitulum l.

   Aconuerse of þat same orꝺꝛ, in þe vigile of Seynt Mathie On a Saint's vigil a weaver
     þe apostell, whech was a weueꝛ of cloth, aftyr þe euensang continued weaving,
32 sayd of þe same apostel, sat stille in his craft weuyng. Othir of

his feláuchip warned him þat at reuerens of þat feest he schuld sese, but he wold not. The same nyte, aftir his first slep, he

and his right
arm was
smitten.

felt þat al þe myte of his rite arme was lost fro þe cubyte on-to þe hand; eke þe same rite hand was turned wrong, and myte 4 in no maneȝ haue recors on-to his natural office. This peyne lastid iij wekys and iij dayes. So in þe feste of Seynt Benet he asked leue of þe priouȝ of þat place in whech he was conuerse þat he myte goo visite, with oþir too felawes ioyned on-to him, 8

Leaf 105.

þe sepultuȝ of ouȝ fader Gilbert. Thidir he cam with a hand ‖ of

He went to
the sepulchre
of Gilbert,

wax, and mad his offeryng; þere abod he certeyn tyme in prayeȝ & wakyng, lyuand euyr in hope þat he schuld haue reles of his

and at first
became worse.

peyne. The fyrst nyte folowand his hand was rather apeyred þan 12 amended, so was þe hand of ouȝ Lord agreued up-on him. The man be-þoute him and remembred þat þe soȝ of his soule, per-auentuȝ, as often is sene, was cause of his bodely seknesse; wherfor he þoute best to þrowe a-wey his synnes, þat he myte 16

He then con-
fessed his sins,

þe soneȝ purchase grace of his desire. Vp-on þis he went to a prest, & with good rememberauns he confessid his synnes fro his ȝong age on-to þat same day, took his penaunce mekely and ful-fillid it deuoutely. So aftir þis up-on þe nyte next þe anun- 20 ciacion of ouȝ Lady he set his hope only in him[1] þat wold þat same day be incarnate for ouȝ helth, and in hir eke, þat blessed virgine, of whom he took both flesch and blood; moȝ-ouyr he put his trost in his fader Gilbert, whech in his lyf exercised þe 24 weyis both of chastite & of mekenesse: in al þis trost he desired with certeyn lite for to wake al a-lone at þe sepultuȝ of his fader

and after-
wards watch-

Gilbert. Ther lay he & sayde his seruyse swech as is assigned

Leaf 105,
back.

on-to ‖ conuerses of þat order. He prayed instantly for helth 28

ed by the
grave, and
fell asleep.

on-to his fader and many oþir seyntes, and in his prayeȝ as he lened up-on a ston þat lay ouyr þe graue, he fel on slepe, and

He awoke
healed.

so rested a tyme. Whan he a-wook he felt certeyn prykkingis in his arme ny his cubite; he drow his hand on-to him, and say 32 wel þat þe crokednes þerof was a-mendid, for he myte strecch it oute as he wolde. All þe senewis & all þe fyngeres weȝ so restored on-to helth þat he myte meue hem; eke in his arme felt he no moȝ peyne.   36

---

[1] MS. þat wold þat wold, *the first two words crossed through in red.*

[CHAPTER LI.]

cap. lj.

There was a woman eke þat for seknesse fel in a frenesie, A woman behaved as if mad.
or ellis in swech maner passioñ whech was lich frenesie.
4 For as a[1] wod creatuᵹ sche spak, gnacching with hir teth, and
voydyng hir spatil in oþir mennes faces & women. So was sche
vexed in swech wilde rage þat þei bounde hir fast, and þus lay
sche bownde fully a monthe. Sche was broute þus bownde in She was brought to the sepulchre and was cured.
8 a carte be labouᵹ of hir husband and hir frendis on-to þe toumbe
of Seynt Gilbert, and þere abood in prayeres iij dayes and
nytes; þoo complet sche went hom heyl and sound, euer þankyd
be God.
12   ¶ Lich on-to þis myracle fel on-to a-noþer woman þat too A similar miracle.
monthis and a half was distraut, and whan sche was broute Leaf 106.
on-to þe graue and lay þere too dayes and nytes, þe þird day
a-boute þe þird ouᵹ sche was mad hool.
16   ¶ Eke at a monastery cleped Watbone a pore man, kept in At Watton a madman
þe hous mad for poᵹ men, had swech a seknesse too monthis
þat he fel in-to a maner of frenesy so was his mynde alienat.
The seruauntis of þat infirmarie had ful grete pite and compassion
20 up-on him and leyd him[2] in an old hors bere in whech ouᵹ fader was laid in St. Gilbert's bere,
Gilbert was caried sumtyme whan he myte not wel walk for
grete age and febilnesse. Many seke men had be layde in þat
same bere, and caut heᵹ helth be þe merites of þis man whech
24 used it sumtyme. The man was layd þer-in, and be-cause he
was wilde þei bond him to þe bere; so lay he too dayes and and so was cured.
too nytes, and on þe þird day was he mad hool and turned on-to
helth a-geyn.

[CHAPTER LII.]

28
cap. lij.

Eke a noble woman, as þei sey, dwelled not fer þens, and A noble-woman had great pain in her eyes.
sche had a greuous passioñ[3] in hir eyne, so greuous þat
sche myte se but litil or ellis nowt, speciali on day lite. Be-side

---

[1] *inserted above in red.*   [2] *inserted in red above.*
[3] *s crossed through.*

þis had sche oþir seknesse, so þat sche was compelled to kepe hir bed. There had sche a vision, þat if sche wold goo on-to ‖ þe tumbe of þis holy fader, sche schuld be releued of þat peyne. Sche mad a candell be þe mesuꝛ of hir body, and to þe graue 4 sche is come, wheꝛ sche drank of þat same watir in whech þe holy confessouꝛ body was wasched; sone aftir þat drynk sche was mad sodeynly hool.

¶ The sun of þis same woman eke receyued helth of his eye,[1] 8 whech was ny ouyrspred with a webbe, be drynkyng of þat same watyr.

¶ Eke a-noþir woman þat myte not heꝛ no maneꝛ þing, not þe sound of grete bellis, aftir sche had wakid in deuocioñ at 12 þis sepultuꝛ o nyte, first receyued coumfort þat sche myte heꝛ þe noyse of bellis, and aftyr, þe speche of men.

¶ A-noþir man of ful grete fame, cleped Herry Biset, a ful long tyme was seek, and aftir þat seknesse had a grete & greuous 16 bolnyng of his wombe. This same peyne lastid him too ȝeꝛ or moꝛ. The bolned womb roos on-to so grete quantite þat whan he was sette he myte not se passing too vnch of his thy. Thus in dispeyre of all helth, for medycynes myte not help, he sent 20 his wif and his douteres to Sempingham, to dwelle þere and haue a-qweyntauns, for he supposed not elles but ‖ for to deye. The wif cam hom a-geyn to se hir husband and broute with hir a lynand[2] girdil with whech ouꝛ fader Gilbert was sum-tyme 24 girt; sche broute eke of þat same watir in a crowet in whech þe holy confessouꝛ body was wasched. And whan þe man had drinkyn of þat watyr and was girt with þat girdill, a-non he bo-gan to qwake & gnach with teth, but he wex no þing hoot. 28 Thoo fel he in a sleep, and in þat same sleep, merueyl to here, he fel on a swete, for he had no swete of al þe tyme in whech he was seek. But now swetith he horribily. His wif, þat sat by, sey þe ȝelow dropes who þei[3] stilled fro him and þoo were 32 grete and had ful euel sauouꝛ. Whan he wook he aspied þis him-selue, and felt þe same sauouꝛ. He loked up-òn his wombe and say wel þat al þis bolnyng was fled downward fro þe girdill ny half a fote. For þe skyn whech was be-forn his sleep so 36

---

[1] wa *and part of* s *crossed through.*   [2] gil *crossed through.*
[3] i *added afterwards.*

pressed oute þat he was aferd it wold brest, now is it voyde as
a empty bagge. Aftir al þis not long tyme þe man recured all
þis seknesse and cam to parfite helth, myte ryde and goo as man *and finally cured him.*
4 of armes, for as it semeth be myn auctour he was a knyte.||

[CHAPTER LIII.]

Cap. liij. *Leaf 107, back.*

A Woman eke was in þat cuntř whech had a greuous sekenesse *Another woman cured*
with-inne hir boweles all a hool ȝere. Hir wombe bolned *of an internal complaint*
8 not, ne no maner risyng had sche of skyn ne flesch, but fretyng
and prikkyng, speciali a-boute hir hert and sum-tyme in hir sides,
þat sche supposed veryly for to deye. Wherfor[1] sche was schryue
and hoseled and took all maneř obseruaunces whech long to men
12 whan þei schal passe, and be-cause sche abode still in lyf aftir
all þis do, þerfor hir husband, of grete deuocion, caried hir in
a cart on-to þe hous of Sempyngham, trostyng in þe merites of
þis holy confessouř. Whan sche was come on-to þat place sche
16 receyued þe sacrament newly a-geyn, and þan þei mad hir to *by means of the water.*
drynk of þat watir in whech þe body was waschid of þis holy
confessouř, Gilbert. Thus a-bode sche stille praying at þe graue
of þis Seynt iij dayes; in þe þird day sche had a great vomyte
20 of corupte blood, and with þis corrupcion cam oute a grete long
worme. Thus iij dayes & ij nytes had sche þis purgacion. Aftir
þis went sche hom, and þus day be day þe vomyte sumwhat cesed,
and þe grellte peyne was fully relesed. *Leaf 108.*

[CHAPTER LIV.]

24 capl. liiij.

I n þat same hous of Sempingham was a nunne[2] whech our *A nun at Sempring-ham had leprosy.*
fader Gilbert had receyued him-self. This woman was infect
with leprosite, whech encresed in hir so horibily þat all hir body
28 was infect. The her fled frq hir hed, hir browes and hir eyne
weř so infect þat sche myte not lift hir ey-ledes for to loke.[3]

---

[1] l *crossed through.*   [2] non *crossed through and* nunne *in margin.*
[3] his *crossed through.*

Hir handes eke so sore þat sche myte in no maneꝛ put mete
or drink on-to hir mouth.   Thus lay sche in þe infirmarye xij
ȝere, euyr serued be a woman whech was hir bodely sistir, whech
woman ofte tyme wold [1] sey [2] þat sche sey [2] neuyr man ne woman 4
so horribily infect.   Be-cause þat þis same woman was so conuersaunt with hir and had often tymes vsed to a-noynt hir naked
body with certeyn medycynes, þat þe soꝛ schuld be moꝛ tollerable,
for þis cause, þe nunnes of þat hous fled þe comunicacion of þis 8
same woman, so weꝛ þei aferd for to be infect.   To þis woman
þat ley þus greuously hurt with þis horible seknesse appered
in sleep a worchipful lady, comaundyng hir þat sche schuld
be caried to þe sepultur of Seynt Gilbert, for þere schuld sche 12
receyue helth.   Thus ¶ is sche brout on-to þe graue and þere, aftir
deuoute prayeres, sche fel in a slep, in whech slep þe same
honourable lady appered to hir and saide þese wordes: A-rise, for
þou art hool; and be-for þese wordes þe lady, as sche þoute, sprad 16
a fayre mantell of purpill a-boute þe graue, with [3] whech mantel
sche cam in, and eft-sones sche sayde on-to þe sek woman: A-rise,
for þou art hool.   Than in þat same dreem semed it to þat seek
woman þat sche was hool, and sche herd þe couent syng Te Deum 20
Laudamus for hir helth.   Thus lay sche dremyng on-to þat tyme
whan þe conuent rang to mateyns; þan sche awook and returned
a-gayn to þe infirmarie.   In hir rising sche voyded gret humores
and in grete quantite, but with-inne iij dayes sche was parfitely 24
hool, for al a weke aftir, þe swames fell fro hir body as þei had
be scalis of a fisch, & þus with-inne fewe dayes aftir, hir flesch
was restored lik þe flesch of a ȝong child.

Marginal notes:
She lay years without use of her limbs,
and was isolated.
She sleeps by the sepulchre,
Leaf 108, back.
has a dream,
awakes as the matins are rung,
and is subsequently cured.

[Chapter LV.]

Capitulum lv.   28

CErteyn men of þis lond sayled ouer þe see whech is be-twix
Inglond and Normandye.   In her sayling ros a grete tempest
whech þei skaped with ouꝛ Lordes mercy.   Whan þe tempest ¶
was sesed and down, þan had þei no wynd for to sayle, but likly 32

Marginal notes:
Some men crossing the Channel were becalmed,
Leaf 109.

----

[1] *inserted above.*
[2] MS. say *with a* dotted *underneath and* e *written above.*
[3] *in margin.*

weꝛ þei al þat nyte for to trauase þe se. Many þat weꝛ þeꝛ drede and many dreaded the peril of the sea.
mech þe pereł of þe se, specially be nyte cared mech, but remedy
coude þei non. A man was a-mongis þem[1] þei cleped Ion, con-
4 stable of Chestir, a man of noble birth & grete fame; he cleped
a prest on-to him whos name was Ancelme, whech was his Anselm brings out Gilbert's scapulary,
chapeleyn, and prayed him þat he schuld bryng forth þe scapularie
of Seynt Gilbert whech þe successouꝛ of Seynt Gilbert had[2] ȝoue
8 him,[3] and whech he kept for a gret relik. This Ancelme ful
deuoutly arayed him in holy uestimentis lich a prest, waschid
his handes, and oute of his lordes cophre took oute þis scapulary, and, holding it aloft, prays for wind.
lyft it up in þe eyre, and þus he prayed þat þei all myte here:
12 Lord God omnipotent, Lord Almyty, if it be so þat þe lif and
þe conuersacion of Seint Gilbert weꝛ wroute ou-to þi plesauns,
schewe now þat þorw his merites we may come to sum hauene
in[3] whech we may be saf fro perel. A-non, as þese wordes weꝛ
16 said, a fayre soft wynd blew in þe scapulary, and fro þe scapulari A wind arises, and they 'oversail' other ships. Leaf 109, back.
it ascendid on-to þe sayl and euyr multiplied, þat in þat same
day[4] þei ouy[r]took schippes ı þat sailed with hem and ouyrsailed
hem, were eke in Normaanye long or þei; for summe schippis
20 þat were in þat viage cam not to Normanie neythir þat day ne
þe next day. Many oþir tokenes were do be þe myracles of ouꝛ Many other miracles are forgotten, and some are not attested.
fadeꝛ Gilbert whech be not touchid in þis present werk, for summe
of necligens ar forgotin, summe were not approued be swech
24 notable witnesse as þese were, summe weꝛ eke wroute aftir tyme
þat þis book was mad, wherfor þei be not ȝet browte in-to þis
forme. And be-cause þat we be in no dowte þat þese weꝛ do
in þe same forme, þerfor haue we wrytin hem in swech lungage
28 as we coude, to þe praysing and ioye of ouꝛ Lord God in whos
name þei were wroute, to þe worchip of holy cherch and profite
of hem þat schul rede or here þis lif, for whom þese notable þingis
weꝛ do, to þe worchip eke of þis holy man be whom þese myracles
32 weꝛ doo, whech man with his merites and pray[er]es schal com-
mende us to þat Lord whech is hiest of all Lordes, and bryng
us eke on-to þoo ioyes þat be eterne, wheꝛ we may rest fro all
labouꝛ with-outen ende, Amen.

---

[1] *inserted above.* [2] *in margin.*
[3] ne in *inserted above.* [4] h *crossed through.*

[CHAPTER LVI.]

Capitulum lvj.∥

Leaf 110.
Innocent III
ordered Gil-
bert's canoni-
zation,

and preached
a sermon
about it,
which he sent
to England.

The gist of the
sermon.

OWre holy fader, þe Pope Innocent þe þird, ordeyned þat þe canoniȝacion of þis same fader Gilbert schuld be solempniȝed in þe cherch, and eke his translacion, of whech canoniȝacion he 4 him-self at Rome, be-for al þe clergye and þe puple, mad a ful solempne sermon, whech sermon he comaunded it schuld be wretyn and sent on-to þe archbischoppis and bischoppis of Ynglond in bullis, and eke on-to þe chapiter of þe hous of 8 Sempingham, of whech sermon þis is þe sentens: For-as-mech as treuth seith in þe gospell þat no man litith a lanterne & hidith it vndyr a buschel mette, but settith it up-on heith, þat all þat dwelle in þat hous may haue coumfort of þat lite, for þis cause, 12 we þink þat it is a dede of grete pite and of equyte þat þoo men whom our Lord God hath crowned for her merites & goue to hem honour in heuene, þat we in erde schuld worchep hem, prayse hem & make ioye of her exaltacion, specialy whan our Lord, for 16 swech worchip as we do hem, is þe more magnified of us, be-cause þat scriptur seith: Our Lord is preisable, or praysid, and glorious in seyntys. To þe grete vertue of pite longith ∥ þe grete behest, nowt only of þis present lyf but of þe lyf eke þat is eterne, as our 20 Lord saith be þe prophete on-to hem þat deye in holy lyf: I schal make ȝou þat ȝe schal stand in swech opinion of þe puple þat þei schal gyue to ȝou praysyng & honour, þe ioye þat ȝe haue schal I gyue ȝou. And in a-noþir place of scriptur þus is seide of[1] 24 seyntis: Ritefulmen schul schyne as þe Sunne in þe kyngdam of her Fader. For our Lord oft-tyme, þat he schuld schewe[2] meruelously þe myte of his uertu, and þat he schuld werk merci-ablely þe cause of our helth, þoo same trewe seruauntis whech 28 he rewardith in heuene often-tyme he honourith in þis world, and at þe places where her bodies rest þere reysith he grete tokenes and myracles be whech[3] þe wikkidnesse of heresies is confundid and þe trew cristen feith confermed.　32

Leaf 110,
back.

---

[1] MS. seide of seynt of seyntis; *only* seynt *crossed through in red.*
[2] MS. schewe þe uertue meruelously; *only* uertue *crossed through.*
[3] *a character crossed through.*

[CHAPTER LVII.]

capĺ. lvij.

THerfor we, as we may not as we schuld, sende þankinggis ^{The Pope's} on-to Almyty God þat in oure dayes to þe confirmacion of ^{sermon on Gilbert.}
4 cristen feith and confusion of wikkid heresie hath mad now his
tokenes newe and chaunged hem meruelously, makyng þe seyntis
now in oure dayes to schyne with myracles, whech seyntis as is
now sene kept þe trewe cristen ⁋ feith, not only with mouth but ^{Leaf 111.}
8 with werk. A-mongis whech seyntis maystir Gilbert, fundouꝛ and
be-gynneꝛ of þe ordꝛ of Semyngham, whech in þis world was myty
in grete merites, now liuand in heuene, schynyth with grete
miracles, for it is ful conuenient þat his holynesse schuld be
12 approued with open & manifest tokenes.   And þou3 it be soo þat
fynal perseuerauns is sufficient i-now to proue þat he or ony oþir
þat deyith in goodnesse schuld be a seynt be-for God in þat cherch
a-boue whech hath ouyr-come her enmyes, witnesse of treuth þat
16 seith: He þat is perseueraunt in goodnesse, in-to þe last ende schal
be saf. And in þe Apocalipse wheꝛ he seith þus: Be trew on-to
þe last ende, and I schal gyue þe þe crowne of lyf; 3et þat a man
schuld be hold holy in þe opinion of men, and here in þis cherch
20 whech lyueth in continuel batayle with hir enmies, too þingis to
þis mateꝛ be ful necessarie: Vertue of good maneris, & vertue of
tokenes, þat is to sey, good werkys and myracules, þat ech of hem
schuld bere witnesse to oþir. For good werkis be not sufficient
24 with-oute myracules, ne myracules sufficient with-oute good werkys
to bere very witnesse of ony ⁋ mannes holynesse; for as we rede, ^{Leaf 111,}
sumtyme þe deuele, whech is cleped þe aungel of Sathan, may ^{back.}
transfiguꝛ him-self lich to aungel of lite, and summe men as we
28 rede all heꝛ good werkis whech þei do, þei do hem for þis entent
þat þei schuld be knowe a-mongis men as for holy leueres. Eke
of þe wicchis þat dwelled with Pharao rede we, þat þei wroute
meruelous tokenes; and Anticriste whan he comth schal werk so
32 meruelous þingis þat, if it myte be, þoo soules þat be chosen to
heuene schuld be meued and led in-to errour be þe same tokenes.
Wherfor we conclude þat þe testimonie of good werkis be him-self
a-lone is sumtyme fals and deceyuable, as may be sen openly in
36 þese ypocrites, eke þe testimonie of myracles be him-self sumtyme

is deceyuable, as is sene in þese wicchis þat dwellid with Pharao. But whann good werkis go be-foꝛ in ony persone, and aftir þoo folowyn glorious miracles, þan haue we[1] a very certificacion of mennes holynesse, þat þoo too þingis schuld lede us þe rite wey to 4 honouꝛ þat persone whom þat ouꝛ Lord hath offered on-to us to be worchiped, with good werkis going be-foꝛ and miracles folowand.

Leaf 112. These to ar notabely touchid in þe ‖ Euangelist Mark wheꝛ he writith þus of þe aposteles: Thei walkid forth in þe world and 8 prechid, ouꝛ Lord werkyng and helpyng her sermones and sigues or ellis myracles folowid aftir þat.

[CHAPTER LVIII.]

Capꝉ. lviij.

Continuation of the sermon. And þouȝ it be soo þat oure weel be-loued childyrn in God, þe 12 priouꝛ and þe couent of Sempingham, haue instauntly mad heꝛ postulacion on-to us þat we schuld graunt þat maystir Gilbért schuld be wrytyn in þe cathaloge of seyntis and be a-noumbered a-mong seyntes, whech Gilbert was be-gynner of her ordre,[2] and 16 whech man, as þei sey, be-foꝛ his deth had exercise of good werkys, and aftir his deth wroute many grete myracules, ȝet wold we not The Pope will inquire into Gilbert's life; graunt heꝛ peticion but we wil be fully enformed of[3] his lyf and of his myracles, not-with-stande[4] þat ouꝛ noble & worchipful son 20 in Crist, Ion, kyng of Ynglard, with his lordes, and ouꝛ broþir,[5] archbischop of Cauntybyry, Hubert, with his suffragauis, eke þe priouꝛ of þe seid couent, with oþir abbotes and priouures, wrote on-to us in þis mateꝛ of þe vertuous lif of þis man and of þe 24 tokenes do at his graue. Wherfor we wil in þis mater do grete Leaf 112, back. diligens to haue þe very treuth, ‖ and for þis cause we haue wrytyn and has written to various clerics to proclaim three days' fast at Sempringham, and comaunded be oure letteris to ouꝛ welbeloued breþerin, archbischop of Cauntirbyri, þe bischop of Hely, and to ouꝛ welbeloued 28 sones, abbot of Borow & abbot of Wardon, þat be ouꝛ auctorite þei schal go to þat place of Sempyngham and, in vertu of obediens, comaunde al þat college of men and women þat þei schul fast iij dayes and crien on ouꝛ Lord God whech is weye, treuth and lyf, 32

---

[1] *inserted above in red.*   [2] *inserted above in red.*
[3] *MS. of of.*   [4] *a character crossed through.*
[5] *er crossed through.*

þat he wil open þe treuth of þis mateƿ on-to þe knowlech of his
seruauntis. Ferþermore we wil þat þei ransake þe wytnesse and
þe fame spred in þe cuntƿ, and make al þis to be writyn be scriptuƿ
4 autentik of þe [1] vertue of þe maneris, of þe vertue of þe myracules
of þis man, and al þis þing þus writyn, seled with heƿ sealis, send
up on-to us be feythful and trewe men whech may swere in ouƿ
presens þat al þis þing be trewe, þat we, þus pleynly informed,
8 may þe moƿ sikirly procede in þis mateƿ,—whech is to moriɴg of
þe ioye of oure Lordis name and a grete confirmacioɴ of cristen
feith.   And if it be so þat alle þese men assigned may not be at
þis examinacioɴ, we wil at þe lest þat iij of hem schul fulfille þis
12 dede.

and to gather
and examine
evidence,

and send it
with witnesses
to Rome.

[CHAPTER LIX.]

Capitulum lix. [2]

Thus þese same men fulfillid ouƿ comauɴdment ful treuly, and
be-cause on of hem myte not be þeƿ for a grete and a
16 neccessarie cause, þerfor iij of hem had þis examinacion in ouƿ
name, þat is to seyn, þe forseid archbischop, and þe bischop of Hely,
with þe abbot of Borow ; þese iij went on-to þat place and fulfillid
al þat was conteyned in ouƿ comauɴdment, for with gret diligens
20 þei examined all þe witnesse and mad hem for to swere þat þei
schuld non informacion make but soth; þei mad clepe religious
men, seculeƿ men, clerkis, lay men, men and women generali, whos
attestaciones and witnesse þei wrytyn treuly, and vndyr her seles
24 closed, sent al þis þing to us, whech sondes þouꝫ þei were euydent
and certeyn, be-cause þei wery many and dyuers, we wil not at þis
tyme sette hem in oure wrytyng. Thei mad eke grete inqwysicioɴ
of his conuersacion and of his maneres, whech was open on-to alle
28 men ; þei cleped in dyueres religious men, whech were famyliar
with him at dyuers tymes, and whech knew of his pryuy conuersacion : all þese men with on acord bore wytnesse þat his lyf was
ondefyled and holy.   For he was a meruelous man in abstinens,
32 a clene man in chastite, a deuoute man in orison, mech vsed to
wakyng; ouyr þat flok of his congregacioɴ with grete prouision

Leaf 113.

The clerics
did as they
were bidden,

called wit-
nesses, and
examined
them,

and recorded
their evi-
dence.

They inquired
into Gilbert's
life,
and learnt of
his virtues.

Leaf 113,
back.

---

[1] MS. þe þe, *the first dotted underneath in red.*
[2] Leaf 113 *has heading.* Item lix.

and discrecion *euer* bysy ; certeyn houris whan he myte haue ony

leyser in contemplacion, quiete.   So as it semeth, whil he was in
erde he departed treuly his lyf, sumtyme *in* good werkis of actyf
lyf, sum in holy rest of *contemplatif,* lich on-to þe patriarch Iacob 4
þat sey aun*gelles* in þe ladder goyng up and goyng down.   And
whan he had ony collocucion with his breþeriu or sisteres, it myte
be seid of him, as it was seid of Samuel, þere feff not a word of his
on-to þe erde.   For aftir þe doctrine of þe holy apostel, ydil wordes 8
were ful seldom in his mouth, but þoo wordes whech he spak were
to edificacion of our feith, for he was good in þat same, and þerfor
his wordes wer ful of grace on-to þe hereres.   And þouȝ many oþir
þingis mad his lyf to be *in* grete comendacion, þis was ȝet a principal 12
þing longi*ng* to his *perfeccion,* þat he wold chese wilful pouerte, and
aff his possessiones whech wer left him be herytage, he wolde assigne
for euyr ‖ to meynteyn þe breþerin and þe sisteryn [1] whech he had
institute and set vndyr a vertuo*us* reule of religion.   For his 16
succession in processe of tyme grewe, be þe goodnesse of our Lord,
to so gret a noumbyr þat he byled nyne monasteries of wome*n* and
four of chanones reguler, in whech monasteriis þat tyme þat he
deyid he left, be-side þe religio*us* men, a þousand and fyue hundred 20
sisteres þat seruyd God our Lord with-oute vylonye.

[CHAPTER LX.]

Capitu*lum* lx.

MOre-ouyr, to strength of þis mat*er* and to a gretter cautel,
fyue of þoo breþerin of þat forseid order whech wer sent 24
on-to our *presens,* we haue charged hem with grete oþis þat þei
schuld informe us with þe soth, & þei haue told us mech mor, both
of his meke werkys and of his glorio*us* myracules.   Wherfor we,
of þis man*nes* lyf and myracules be sufficie*nt* witnesse þus informe 28
and set in a man*er* of sikirnesse, aftir þe testimonie of þe aungel
þat seid to Tobie, it is good to hydyn þe sacrame*nt* of þe by kyng,
but þe werkis of God to open and confesse is gret worchip,—eke
for þe Psalme seith [2] þat God schuld be praysed in his seyntis,—for 32
þese causes ‖ haue we ascribed and anou*m*byred Seynt Gilbert in-to

---

[1] whom *crossed through.*
[2] *inserted above and written again in margin.*

þe cathaloge of seyntes, and ordeyned þat his memory schal be So Gilbert is canonised.
songyn a-mongis oþir seyntes.　All þese be þe Popes wordes; now
folowith þe autouꝛ.　Thus aftir þe comaundment of ouꝛ fader þe
4 Pope, whan þe translacion of Seynt Gilbert was broute to an ende,
and þe holy relikes weꝛ layd in þe vessel arayed for hem, but or it
was closed þe bischoppes and þe abbotes þat weꝛ *principal* fufilleres The clerics put a charter with his body,
of þis werk, layde a char*tour* up-on his breest, in whech chartoꝛ and a plate describing
8 was *conteyned* all þe maneꝛ of his translacion, of þe myracles and him.
of þe canoniȝacion; eke þei layde *þere* a plate of led, in whech led
was wrytyn certeyn þing whech schuld neuyr be oute of mynde.
The scripture of þat plate was þis : Heꝛ lith Seynt Gilbert, þe first
12 fader and foundoꝛ of þe order of Sempyngham, whech was translate
in-to þis schrine¹ be ouꝛ fader & lord, Hubert, archbischop of
Cauntyrbury, be þe comaundment of ouꝛ holy fader, Pope Innocent,
²þe þirde yde of October, the ȝere of ouꝛ Lord, a þousand, too
16 hundred and on.　This is þe wryting of þe chartoꝛ layde be him
in his schryne: In þis schryne ar *conteyned* þe relikes of ‖ Seynt Leaf 115.
Gilbert, prest and confessouꝛ, þe first fader and begynneꝛ of þe ordꝛ The charter tells of his
of Sempyngham, whos lyf, þouȝ it be so þat many þingis mad it life,
20 comen*dable* & honourable, þis was þe principal and moost excellent
cause whi he schuld be in mynde, þat wilfully he chase honest
pouerte and all his temporal goodes þat God had sent him he freely
relesid to þe neccessite and sustentacion of þoo breþerin and sisteres
24 whom he sette vndyr reguler discipline and kept hem ful bysily.
And to þis same Gilbert in *processe* of tyme ouꝛ Lord God graunted
swech grace and uertue þat he mad fouꝛ houses of chanones and his work,
nyne monasteries of nunnes, in whech houses þat tyme þat he
28 deyid and went to ouꝛ Lord, be-side al þoo þat were ded be-fore,
he left of religious men on-to a vij hundred, of sisteres a þousand
and fyue hundred, whech ful bysily ded seruyse to God.　He deyid his death
in his best age,³ more þan a hundred ȝere old, þe ȝere of þe incarna-
32 cion of ouꝛ Lord Ihesu, a þousand, a hundred⁴, eyty and nyne, þe
day be-foꝛ þe nonas of Februari, þe tyme of þe worchipful kyng
Herry þe Secu[n]d.　And þus, be-cause of his owne merites and be his miracles,
‖ testimonie of many myracles folowand, and reuelaciones eke, þat Leaf 115, back.

---

¹ *in margin in red.*
² MS. þe þird þe þirde ; þe þird *crossed through in red.*
³ *a stroke crossed through.*　　　⁴ *final d added in red above.*

and his
canonization, cam fro God, he was canoniȝed and wryten in þe cathaloge of
seyntes of ouꝛ holy fader Pope Innocent þe þirde, be þe general
cort of Rome at Anagniam, be-for þe clergy and þe puple, þe ȝere [1]
of þe incarnacioñ of ouꝛ Lord a þousaud too hundred and too, þe 4
þirde idus of Ianuari, þe ȝeꝛ of þe kyngdam of þat [2] worþi man,
Ion, kyng of Ynglond, þe þirde, *president* to þe see of Cauntirbury
þe worchipful archbischop Hubert, whech aftir þe comaundment of
þe said Pope, with his felawis as in [3] þat act, bischop of Hely, 8
Eustace, & abbot of Borow, Acarius, had mad diligent inqwisicion
up-on þe miracules wroute be þis man, and wrytyn alle þis mateꝛ
treuly, and sent it up to þe court.   Be whech examinacioñ ouꝛ
fader þe Pope receyued þe very treuth, both of þe holynesse of þis 12
man Gilbert and eke of his tokenes, and for þis cause he anoumbered
him a-mongis seyntis, þe ȝere of his papate, þe fourte.   [4] And þat
same ȝere, be þe comaundment of þe seide Pope, he was translate of
þe seid archbischop in-to þis schryne, þe þirde ide of Octobir, 16
Leaf 116. standyng by, þese wor‖chipful men, bischop of Norwich, bischop of
and who offi-
ciated at it. Hereforth, bischop of Landaue, and oþir abbotes and prelates and
nobel-men of Ynglond, with mech prese of [5] clergy and puple.
And to perpetuel memory of þis þing þus don, þe seid archbischop 20
and þe oþir bischoppis & abbotes sette her seles on-to þis chartoꝛ,
and in þis schrine þei put it, to þe praiaing of ouꝛ Lord God
Almyty, whech schal enforme us with þe exaumples of þis man, and
reise us fro synnes to grace with help of þe prayeres of þis man ; 24
and eke þe same Lord schal lede us fro peyne to ioye wheꝛ he
So ends this
book, trans-
lated in A. D.
1451. lyuyth and regnyth euyr moꝛ.   Amen.   Thus endith þe lif of
Seint Gilbert, translat in-to ouꝛ moder tonge, þe ȝere of þe
incarnacioñ of ouꝛ Lord a M cccc lj.   28

---

[1] *re added above.*   [2] MS. *þat þat, the first crossed through.*
[3] *inserted above.*   [4] E *crossed through.*   [5] MS. *of of.*

A Treatise of the Orders under the Rule of St. Augustine

FROM A SERMON PREACHED BY

JOHN CAPGRAVE

AT CAMBRIDGE IN 1422.

And here begynnyth a tretis of tho[1] orderes þat be
vndyr þe reule of oure fader Seynt Augustin, drawe oute
of a sermoñ seyd be freᵲ Ion Capgraue at Cambrige,
þe ȝere of ouᵲ Lord a M cccc xxij.

WE may likne ouᵲ fader Seynt Augustyn on-to þe holy ^{Augustine is like Jacob.}
patriark Iacob for many causes. On is for interpreta-
cion of his name, for Iacob is ǁ as mech to say as a supplanteᵲ ^{Leaf 116, back.}
4 or a deceynour, for he, at þe comaundment of God, supplanted his
broþir, bying his fader blessing for a mese of potage and aftirward
apperyng to his fader in Esaues cote. So may ouᵲ blessid fader
Augustyn be cleped a supplanter of þe Deuel, for whan þe same
8 Deuel ha hold him in his seruyse xxx ȝere, pañ ran he fro þe
Deuel and took up-one him þe swete ȝok of ouᵲ Lord Ihesu Crist.
For xxj ȝere was he in paganite, and ix ȝere in þe heresie of þe
Manychees. He may[2] be cleped Iacob also, for euene as Iacob
12 sey ouᵲ Lord God fas to[3] fas, so ouᵲ maystir, with secret contemplacioñ, was as ny God as ony erdely man myte be, as may be
wel perceyued be þe labouᵲ whech he had in inuestigacion of þe
godhed in þe bokes whech he mad of þe Trynyte. This Iacob
16 had xij sones, to whom aᵭ þe lond of byhest was distribute and
departed be Moyses & Iosue. And þis Augustin hath xij religious ^{He founded twelve reli-}
cumpanies, be whech xij aᵭ holy cherch heᵲ in erde is replecchid. ^{gious bodies like the twelve sons.}
We wil at þis tyme on-to ȝouᵲ deuoute eres open þese Hebrew
20 names of þese xij tribus, and referᵲ hem to dyuers religions ǁ whech ^{Leaf 117.}
lyue vndir Seynt Austyn reule.
   ¶ The first be-goten child. hite Iudas. ⁴For Iudas is as mech
to sey as a preyseᵲ, and þese men preise God nyte & day in holy
24 songis & ympnis whech þei continuely be vsed too.⁴ And þis

---

¹ MS. who *crossed through and tho written above.*
² b *and part of* l *crossed through.*   ³ *inserted above.*
⁴—⁴ *passage written at top of page and marks of insertion made.*

10

Judas like the
Heremits. Iudas eke[1] may be referred on-to þoo heremites þat Seynt Augusti*n*
mad ny iij ȝere be-foᵲ þat he was bischop[2] at Ypoᴜe, and mad þere
chanones. This mateᵲ is proued with grete euydens i*n* þe book
Capgrave's
English and
Latin books
on the sub-
ject. whech I mad to a gentil woman in Englisch, and in þe book whech 4
I mad *to* þe abbot of Seynt Iames at Norhampton in Latin, whech
boke I named Concordia, be-cause it is mad to reforme charite
be-twix Seynt Augustines heremites and his chanones. In þese
same bokes may men se þe names of þe first faderes of .þis order of 8
heremites, whech heremites Simplicia*n* sent witȝ Augusti*n* on-to
Affrik.

Reuben like
the Secular
Canons. ¶ The second child of þis Iacob, he hite Ruben, and þis Ruben is
referred on-to chanones seculer swech as be in cathedral cherchis. 12
For Ruben is as mech to sey as seing in þe myddis, or seing be þe
myddis. What schal we calle bettir þe myddis þa*n* þis *present*
lif? What was be-for þis lif ordeyned for us is on-knowe. What
we schal haue aftir þis lif it is in doute, saue we hope veryly, be þe 16
good menes of þis myd lif, to come sumtyme to Goddis *mercy*.
Leaf 117,
back. But ‖ men wil merueyle peraᴜentuᵲ whi þat I sette seculer chanones
be-for reguler, and þis [is] my cause. Thoo chanones þat dwelled
with Seynt Augusti*n* whan he was bischop we*n*t in cloþis of dyᴜers 20
colouris and in *preciouᴜ* furres and with girdel[3] & barres of[3] syluᴇr
and gilt, as is manifestly writyn in his *sermones*,[4] Ad fratres in
heremo, and þis aray long not to reguleᵲ chanones.

Gad like
Canons Regu-
lar. ¶ The þird son of Iacob he hite Gad, and his name is as mech to 24
sey as a man þat is[5] wel girt. Girdyng in holy scriptuᵲ is take
for restreynyng of ouᵲ body fro uices, and þis may be applied in
þe best maneᵲ to chanones reguler, whech, with holy obserᴜaᴜnces
girdyn heᵲ bodies fro sinful werkis & here soules fro foule desires. 28
If þese me*n* be-gu*n*ne with Augusti*n* in his cherch in þe same
degre as þei stand now, su*m* me*n* haue doute; but I wyl not
stryue. I be-leue wel þat þere had þei heᵲ begi*n*nyng but þe
hardeᵲ distinccio*n* fro þe first ordᵲ was mad sithe be oþir holy 32
Monks of the
Charterhouse. faderes,[6] as þe mu*n*kis of Charturehous cam oute of þe blake
ordᵲ.[7] Many euydens haue I mad [8] in my book *Concordia* [8] þat

   [1] *inserted above.*   [2] MS. preest *crossed through and* bischop *written over.*
   [3]—[3] *in margin.*   [4] wri *crossed through.*   [5] *inserted above.*
   [6] s *added above.*   [7] *in margin.*   [8]—[8] *in margin.*

Sei*n*t Ruffus not be-gu*n* þis ordꝛ, but þat he refoꝛmed þis ordre.
So may I wel be-leue þat her first fundacion cam fro Augusti*n*.

¶ The iiij son of Iacob, he hite Aser. Aser is as mech to ⸗ sei Leaf 118.
4 as blessed, and þis blessing is referred to þe grete nou*m*bir of þat Asher like the Dominicans.
holy congꝛegacion whech Seynt Do*m*i*n*ice gadered a*n*d ordeyned,
to þis entent, þat þei schuld labouꝛ in þe world and with here
prechi*n*g distroy synne in þe puple and plant vertue. This ordre
8 be-gan Sey*n* Do*m*i*n*ice þe ȝeꝛ of oure Lord a M cc xvj.

¶ The v. son of Iacob hite Neptalim, as mech for to sey as Naphtali like the Knights of St. John.
gret brede; be þis vndirstund we þe knytes of Seynt Ion whech
begu*n*ne first at Ierusale*m*, and now ar þei spred þorw-oute all þis
12 world. Her institucion is to defende Cristen feith a-geyn Turkes
and Sarsines. And all þoo possessiones whech þei haue in londis
of pees pay tribute to þe hous of Rodes.

¶ The sext son hite Manasse, and he is for [to]¹ sey as obliuious. Manasseh like the Knights of Prussia.
16 This son be-tokneth þe heres of Pruce whech weꝛ institute to þe
same entent to defense of þe bordures of cristen men a-geyn þe
enmyes of þe crosse. Obliuio*us* be þei cleped be-cause þei must
forȝete þe delectable lyf of þis world a*n*d put² heꝛ bodies in grete
20 perel for þe honouꝛ of Crist. The differe*n*s of þe habite of þese
too knytes is þis, þat þei of Seynt Iones haue blak mantell with
a crosse, and þei of Pruce white mantell with a crosse.

¶ The vij son of Iacob, he hite³ Simeon, whech ⸗ soundith in ouꝛ Leaf 118, back.
24 tonge heuynesse or pencifnesse, and þis may be applied with grete Simeon like the Gilbertines.
conue*n*iens on-to þat ordre þat was founded at Sempyngham be
þe solicitude of Seynt Gilbert, of whech Seynt, be-cause I mad
a special tretis on-to þe maystir of þat ordꝛ, þerfor in þis place
28 I touch no moꝛ of him.

¶ The viij son of Iacob, he hite Leui, þat sou*n*deth in owre Levi like the Premonstratensians.
langage a moryng or a multipliyng of þing þat was be-gu*n*ne,
and be þis name we vndirstande þe ordꝛ of Pꝛemonstraoense*s*,
32 whech be-gan in Fraunce vndir a holy man þei cleped Norbertus,
þe ȝeꝛ of ouꝛ Lord a M and a hundred, and be-cause þat I mad
his lyf in Englisch to þe abbot of Derham þat deyid last, þerfor as
now I wil no lengeꝛ tarie in þat fundacio*n*.

36 ¶ The ix son of Iacob, he hite Ysacar; he sou*n*deth in ouꝛ Issachar

---

¹ MS. a *crossed through*.   ² MS. but.   ³ be *crossed through*.

langage grete mede for laboure; þis wil we applie to þat ordre whech þei clepe þe Freres of þe Crosse,[1] for þis cause, for þat crosse on heꝛ breest schul make hem so to labouꝛ in þe weye of Crist þat þei schuld come aftir heꝛ labouꝛ to euyrlasting mede. 4 Off þis ordre haue I as ȝet no certeyn knowlech, who was heꝛ foundoꝛ, or vndir what Pope, or kyng, þei be-gunne.

¶ The x son of Iacob, he hite ȝabulon, and in ouꝛ langage it may be cleped a dwellyng-place of strength. ‖ Ful wel longith þis 8 interpretacion on-to þe ordꝛ of Seynt Bryde; þei haue a mansion of strength, for þei be sperd fro vanites of þe world, whech vanytes ar ouyr open to many men. This holy woman Bryde be-gan þis order and went to Rome for confirmacioñ; who wil se hir lyf and 12 hir reuelaciones he may diffusely se it in hir book, as now I haue no tyme to tary lenger in þat mateꝛ.

¶ The xj son hite Ioseph, and he is to sey[2] a moring or augmentacioñ; þis is applied to certeyn chanones of þat hous whech be[3] 16 of þe ordꝛ of Seynt Victoꝛ. This hous of Seynt Victour is in Paris, to whech I trowe þei longe. We haue in ouꝛ libraries many sundry bookes þat to chanones of þat hous mad; on of hem hite Hewe, þe oþir hite Richard, notabel clerkis þei weꝛ and men of 20 holy lyf.

¶ The xij son hite Beniamin; he is þe son þat longith to þe rite hand, as euery religious man with þe mercy of God doth. This son, be-cause he is ȝongest of age, is likned on-to an ordre whech 24 is not in þe world, as þei sey, but in Northfolk. Fouꝛ houses had þei and on of hem is fall on-to þe[4] kyngis hand, & he gaue it to Walsingham; þe hous hite Petirston: oþer informacioñ of hem haue I not at þis tyme.   28

---

[1] O *crossed through.*   [2] y *in red above.*
[3] *inserted above in red.*   [4] *inserted above in red and written in margin.*

NOTES

p. 3, l. 14. *Comagene,* the region north of Syria and Cyrrhestica between the Euphrates and the Taurus Mountains.

p. 3, l. 15. *Nussie,* perhaps Tuscany or Russia. Achay is Achaia, properly the northernmost part of the Grecian peninsula; Macedonia, north of Thessalia and Epirus; Dalmatia in Illyricum on the Adriatic seaboard.

p. 3, l. 18. *Jeugis,* i. e. Zeugitana, the northern part of modern Tunis, and east of ancient Numidia. Tripolitane is Tripolitana, modern Tripoli, minus Fezzan; Getuly is Gaetuli, south of Numidia; Gaetuli Darae was on the Atlantic coast south of the Atlas mountains, and part of Mauritania.

p. 3, l. 27. *hated þe Grɐke letteris and loued weel þe Latyn.* *Confessionum,* ed. P. Knöll, Lipsiae in aedibus B. G. Teubneri, 1909, Book i, p. 14, l. 21 : 'Quid autem erat causae, cur graecas litteras oderam, quibus puerulus imbuebar, ne nunc quidem mihi satis exploratum est. Adamaveram enim latinas, non quas primi magistri, sed quas docent qui grammatici vocantur.'

p. 4, l. 3. *Cathegories,* or 'Predicamentes', see 11/28; not by Aristotle. Augustine says he understood the book freely and without master. *Confessionum* iv, p. 70, l. 29.

p. 4, l. 10. *good and rich kynrod.*—Not so; in the *Confessions,* ii, p. 26, l. 13, Augustine describes his father as a poor freeman of Tagaste : 'municeps Thagatensis admodum tenuis.'

p. 4, l. 18. Conversion of Patrick, *Conf.* viiii, p. 182, l. 27.

p. 4, l. 23. A brother is mentioned in *Conf.* viiii, p. 185, l. 25.

p. 5, l. 25. *redy eke on-to ire.* *Conf.* viiii, p. 181, l. 6 : 'erat vero ille praeterea sicut benevolentia praecipuus, ita ira fervidus. Sed noverat haec non resistere irato viro, non tantum facto, sed ne verbo quidem. Iam vero refractum et quietum cum opportunum viderat, rationem facti sui reddebat, s forte ille inconsideratius commotus fuerat,' etc.

p. 6, l. 18. The mother-in-law, *Conf.* viiii, p. 181, l. 28.

p. 6, l. 29. The orison, *Conf.* viiii, p. 190, l. 12.

p. 7, l. 8. *Seint Gregorie telleþ in his Dialoges :—Dialogues,* Book iv, ch. xix. The tale is told by Robert of Brunne, *Handlyng Synne,* p. 161, from William of Wadington's *Manuel des Pechiez,* which follows St. Gregory. The child in this tale was torn away from his father's bosom and carried to hell, when five years old, for cursing.

p. 7, l. 17. Childhood's sin, *Conf.* i, p. 5, l. 23, p. 6, l. 10, p. 8, l. 1, p. 8, l. 17.

p. 7, l. 27. *put to skole, Conf.* i, p. 10, l. 22.

p. 8, l. 5. *lerned lesse þat he schuld or myth a lerne, Conf.* i, p. 11, l. 20 : 'et peccabamus tamen minus scribendo aut legendo aut cogitando de litteris, quam exigebatur a nobis . . . delectabat ludere et vindicabatur in nos ab eis qui talia utique agebant.'

p. 8, l. 8. *Mandauris*, i. e. Madaura, *Conf.* ii, p. 26, l. 9.

p. 8, l. 11. *sekenesse in his stomake, Conf.* i, p. 12, l. 29.

p. 8, l. 12. *þe fader wold not suffir it, Conf.* i, p. 13, l. 11—p. 14, l. 2.

p. 8, l. 20. Goes to Carthage, *Conf.* ii, p. 26, l. 11 ; iii, p. 35, l. 1.

p. 8, l. 22. Tullius Cicero, &c., *Conf.* iii, p. 38, l. 26. Cicero is mentioned only in connexion with *Hortensius.* See note to 9/13.

p. 8, l. 26. *tauernes and stewis.* Capgrave's interpretation of Augustine's reference to the 'cauldron of shameful loves'—'sartago flagitiosorum' (iii, p. 35, l. 15)—and to the stage-shows—'spectacula theatrica' (iii, p. 36, l. 12); and to his joys of passion (iii, p. 36, l. 8).

p. 9, l. 7. *an appil-tre, Conf.* ii, p. 29, l. 12.

p. 9, l. 13. *Hortencius, Conf.* iii, p. 39, l. 21 : 'liber ille ipsius [Cicero] exhortationem continet ad philosophiam et vocatur Hortensius.'

p. 9, l. 18. *name of Crist, Conf.* iii, p. 40, l. 24.

p. 9, l. 22. *holy scriptuꝛ, Conf.* iii, p. 41, l. 1. The reference to St. Paul is not in *Confessions.*

p. 9, l. 27. *þe Maniches, Conf.* iii, p. 41, l. 14 : 'Itaque incidi in homines superbe delirantes, carnales, nimis et loquaces,' &c.

p. 10, l. 1. *ix ȝere, Conf.* iii, p. 51, l. 2.

p. 10, l. 11. *a faiꝛ tre, Conf.* iii, p. 50, l. 4.

p. 11, l. 1. *consolacioñ be an holy bischop.* The bishop is not named. *Conf.* iii, p. 51, l. 11.

p. 11, l. 22. *impreuded sche.* 'The Latin is, *Conf.* iii, p. 52, l. 5 : ' quod illa ita se accepisse inter conloquia sua mecum saepe recordabatur, ac si de caelo sonuisset.' This ends Book iii.

p. 11, l. 28. *Predicamentis.* See note to 4/3.

p. 11, l. 31. *bokes of philosophie,* &c. In *Conf.* iiii, p. 72, l. 30, Augustine speaks only of the ' so-called liberal arts '.

p. 12, l. 3. *he cam first hom.* The chief dates of Augustine's life are as follows : born, Tagaste, 354; lived at Carthage, 371-373 ; went to Rome, 383, and taught rhetoric for a short time; went to Milan and met St. Ambrose, who baptized him in 387. In 388 he returned to Tagaste, and lived in quietude for awhile. He became bishop of Hippo in 395. The date of the *Confessions* is 397. He died in August, 430, at Hippo.

p. 12, l. 7. *resorted a-geyn to Cartage. Conf.* v, p. 82, l. 16 : p. 88, l. 7.

p. 12, l. 9. *Hermes.* Capgrave's misreading of Hierius, *Conf.* iiii, p. 66, l. 23 : 'Quid est autem, quod me movit, domine deus meus, ut ad Hierium, Romanae urbis oratorem, scriberem illos libros ? ' [*De Pulchro et Apto*].

p. 12, l. 11. *þei are not in hand now.* Cf. *Conf.* iiii, p. 66, l. 21 : 'non enim habemus eos [libros de P. et A.], sed aberraverunt a nobis nescio quomodo.'

p. 12, l. 14. *Faustus, a grete snare of þe deuele. Conf.* v, p. 74, l. 7 :

'Iam venerat Carthaginem quidam Manichaeorum episcopus, Faustus nomine, *magnus laqueus diaboli.*' The latter phrase is one of St. Paul's, 1 Timothy iii. 7, and 2 Timothy ii. 26. It is also used by Augustine elsewhere in the *Conf.* concerning the *Manichees*, iii, p. 41, l. 15, '*laquei diaboli.*'

p. 12, l. 18. *Contra Faustum.*

p. 12, l. 20. *Conf.* v, p. 79, l. 26.

p. 12, ll. 32–33. *a fayr-spoke man eke, but not greily grounded in sciens,* *Conf.* v, p. 8, ll. 26-31; p. 81, l. 5; p. 81, l. 18.

p. 13, l. 2. Defeat of Faustus. *Conf.* v, p. 81, l. 29 : 'Quae tamen consideranda et discutienda protuli, modeste sane ille nec ausus est subire ipsam sarcinam. Noverat enim se ista non nosse nec eum puduit confiteri.'

p. 13, l. 6. *no deynte in her bokes, Conf.* v, p. 82, l. 11.

p. 13, l. 11. Augustine goes to Rome, *Conf.* v, p. 83, l. 5.

p. 13, l. 17. *more liberte yous on-to skoleres, Conf.* v, p. 83, l. 14.

p. 13, l. 22. *His modir folowid him, Conf.* v, p. 84, l. 12.

p. 14, l. 8. *greuous seknesse, Conf.* v, p. 85, l. 13.

p. 14, l. 11. *bryng him forth,* &c., *Conf.* v, p. 86, l. 9.

p. 14, l. 13. *not for to telle veyn tales, Conf.* v, p. 86, l. 20.

p. 14, l. 14. *sche prayed for him, Conf.* v, p. 86, l. 13.

p. 14, l. 17. Augustine whole again, *Conf.* v, p. 87, l. 3.

p. 14, l. 21. Goes to Milan, *Conf.* v, p. 91, l. 7.

p. 14, l. 23. *meyr of Rome, Conf.* v, p. 91, l. 8 : 'ad praefectum urbis.'

p. 14, l. 28. Ambrose. *Conf.* v, p. 91, l. 13 : 'et veni Mediolanium [Milan] ad Ambrosium episcopum, in optimis notum orbi terrae, pium cultorem tuum,' &c.

p. 14, l. 31. Augustine hears Ambrose preach, *Conf.* v, p. 91, l. 24.

p. 15, l. 9. *þe incarnacion.* Cf. *Conf.* vi, p. 97, l. 24.

p. 15, l. 24. *þe feith of Crist, Conf.* v, p. 93, l. 18.

p. 15, l. 27. *his moder sowt him, Conf.* vi, p. 94, l. 2.

p. 16, l. 3. *Beth of good coumfort,* &c. Capgrave's embellishment of the incident. *Conf.* vi, p. 94, l. 2 : 'Iam venerat ad me mater pietate fortis, terra marique me sequens et in periculis omnibus de te secura. Nam et per marina discrimina ipsos nautas consolabatur, a quibus rudes abyssi viatores, cum perturbantur, consolari solent, pollicens eis perventionem cum salute, quia hoc ei tu per visum pollicitus eras.'

p. 16, l. 9. *sche hopped,* i. e. leapt. But Augustine says distinctly that she was not unduly excited. *Conf.* vi, p. 94, l. 17 : Nulla ergo turbulenta exultatione trepidavit cor eius,' &c. Later on, after the *Tolle lege* passage, she does 'leap for joy'. *Conf.* viii, p. 166, l. 2 : '*exultat* et triumphat et benedicebat tibi.'

p. 16, l. 18. *Sche loved Ambrose,* &c., *Conf.* vi, p. 94, l. 30.

p. 16, l. 20. *fluctuaction.* Direct from the Latin, *Conf.* vi, p. 95, l. 2.

p. 16, l. 25. *for-bode hir be þe keper.* In the Latin, *Conf.* vi, p. 95, l. 8, 'ab ostiario,' by the door-keeper.

p. 17, l. 4. Alipius and Nebridius, *Conf.* vi, p. 103, l. 21 ; p. 110, l. 1.

p. 17, l. 11. *wyxes.* The idea was to form a society of about ten. Some however, already had wives; and some, including Augustine, intended to have : hence the difficulty. *Conf.* vi, p. 115, l. 14.

p. 17, l. 17. Augustine's maid. *Conf.* vi, p. 114, l. 26.

p. 17, l. 23. Alypius arrested. The story appears somewhat mutilated in Capgrave's text. Alypius was studying under Augustine at the time, and was repeating, as he walked in the market-place, some rhetorical exercise. The thief was a youth, not the boy who recognized the axe. The friend who intervened was an architect (p. 108, l. 4).

p. 18, Chapter xiii. In this chapter Capgrave goes on with Book viii, making practically no use at all of Book vii.

p. 18, l. 30. Simpliciane, *Conf.* viii, p. 144, l. 18.

p. 19, l. 11. Victorinus, *Conf.* viii, p. 144, l. 22.

p. 19, l. 12. *a statua.* From the Latin. *Conf.* viii, p. 145, l. 7.

p. 19, l. 27. *sette to serue God, Conf.* viii, p. 150, l. 15.

p. 19, l. 30. Pontitianus, *Conf.* viii, p. 153, l. 13.

p. 20, l. 17. *grete Antonie, Conf.* viii, p. 153, l. 28. The story of Anthony's conversion, as told by Capgrave, follows.

p. 21, l. 5. Augustine's sorrow, *Conf.* viii, p. 155, l. 26.

p. 21, l. 14. 'What suffir we?' &c. *Conf.* viii, p. 157, l. 17 : 'Quid patimur! Quid est hoc, quod audisti! Surgunt indocti et caelum rapiunt, et nos cum doctrinis nostris ecce ubi volutamur in carne et sanguine! An quia praecesserunt, pudet sequi et non pudet nec saltem sequi !'

p. 21, l. 21. *labour of his tunge, Conf.* viii, p. 157, l. 24.

p. 21, l. 32. *a figge-tre, Conf.* viii, p. 164, l. 16.

p. 22, l. 1. *O blissed Lord, who longe? Conf.* viii, p. 164, l. 20 : 'et tu, domine, usquequo ? Usquequo, domine, irasceris in finem ? . . . Iactabam voces miserabiles : "Quamdiu, quamdiu, 'cras' et 'cras'? Quare non modo? Quare non hac hora finis turpitudinis meae !"' The italicized portion is from Psalm vi. 3 (4 in Vulgate).

p. 22, l. 5. *whil he lay pus, Conf.* viii, p. 164, l. 26.

p. 22, l. 8. *Tak and rede. Conf.* viii, p. 164, l. 29 : 'Tolle lege, tolle lege!'

p. 22, l. 15. *Non in comessacionibus,* &c. *Conf.* viii, p. 165, l. 13. Capgrave's text does not exactly follow the Augustinian. The passage is from Romans xiii. 13.

p. 22, l. 20. *schalful dedis,* 'wantonness' in authorized version, 'non in impudicitiis' in *Conf.*

p. 22, l. 32. Monica. *Conf.* viii, p. 166, l. 1. This ends Book viii.

p. 23, l. 3. Leaving the rhetoric school, *Conf.* viiii, p. 167, l. 15.

p. 23, l. 10. *heruest dayes. Conf.,* vintage vacation, viiii, p. 167, l. 21 : 'ad vindemiales ferias.'

p. 23, l. 18. *a feld pei cleped Cassiate. Conf.* viiii, p. 169, l. 29, a country-seat called Cassiciacum, or villa (*Conf.* viiii, p. 171, l. 27).

p. 23, l. 26. Plato. This expression of Capgrave is based on a statement made by Augustine concerning the 'Academics, as they are considered, doubting everything and fluctuating between all.' *Conf.* v, p. 93, l. 9 : 'Itaque Academicorum more, sicut existimantur, dubitans de omnibus atque inter omnia fluctuans . . .'

p. 24, l. 26. *Psalmis of Dauid. Conf.* viiii, p. 171, l. 24.

p. 24, l. 29. *In pace, in idipsum,* &c. *Conf.* viiii, p. 174, l. 20, from Psalm iv. 8.

p. 25, l. 4. *neknesse . . . of þe teth. Conf.* viiii, p. 175, l. 6 : ' dolore dentium,' &c.

p. 25, l. 14. Letters to St. Ambrose, *Conf.* viiii, p. 175, l. 23.

p. 25, l. 20. *Ysaie, Conf.* viiii, p. 175, l. 27.

p. 25, l. 25. Goes to Milan. *Conf.* viiii, p. 175, l. 19, then ending his rhetoric teaching.

p. 25, l. 26. Baptism, *Conf.* viiii, p. 176, l. 3.

p. 25, l. 35. Te Deum. This story of the making of *Te Deum* is, of course, quite apocryphal.

p. 26, l. 4. Adeodatus, *Conf.* viiii, p. 176, l. 7.

p. 26, l. 11. *he had neuer no woman but hir.* Not so; in Book vi Augustine relates how when his concubine left him for Africa, he turned to another woman; p. 115, l. 30: ' et illa in Africam redierat vovens tibi alium se virum nescituram relicto apud me naturali ex illa filio meo. At ego infelix nec feminae imitator, dilationis impatiens, tamquam post biennium accepturus eam quam petebam, quia non amator coniugii sed libidinis servus eram, *procurari aliam,* non utique coniugem.'

p. 26, l. 27. *De Quantitate Animae.* The book mentioned in this connexion by Augustine is *De Magistro, Conf.* viiii, p. 176, l. 16.

p. 27, l. 1. Songs of St. Ambrose and Justina. *Conf.* viiii, p. 177, l. 1. The remarks concerning the hymnology of Ambrose, ll. 11–12, are apparently a specimen of Capgrave's 'pertinent' ideas. Augustine himself quotes from one of Ambrose's hymns in this same Book viiii, p. 89, l. 6: ' Deus, creator omnium,' &c. Augustine describes, in connexion with Justina, the discovery of the bodies of Gervasius and Protasius, and the consequent miracles. This Capgrave leaves unmentioned.

p. 29, l. 10. Monica desires to go home. Augustine says, *Conf.* viiii, p. 178, l. 20, that he and Euodius and others desired to go where they might best serve God, and so started to return to Africa; and that on the way, at Ostia Tiberina (Ostia), Monica died. In Chapter xx, p. 28, our text is first made up by systematic use of the Sermons, which henceforward continues to the end of the narrative, except for Chapters xxii–xxvi.

p. 30, l. 31. Monica, ' a very moder,' &c. *Conf.* viiii, p. 183, l. 3.

p. 31, l. 2. *Tussie,* i. e. Tuscany.

p. 31, l. 15. Wyclif. ' Was there ever,' writes Mr. G. M. Trevelyan on a card to me, ' a persecuted sect of whom that was not said !' ' Be thou as chaste as ice,' &c.: it is an old story.

p. 31, l. 29. Ostia. *Conf.* viiii, p. 183, l. 15.

p. 32, l. 2. The window. *Conf.* viiii, p. 183, l. 13. The garden did not belong to Monica, as Capgrave says, but to the house where Augustine and his party rested.

p. 32, l. 11. *Son, as to my part,* &c. *Conf.* viiii, p. 185, l. 11: ' fili, quantum ad me adtinet, nulla re iam delector in hac vita. Quid hic faciam adhuc et cur hic sim, nescio, iam consumpta spe huius saeculi. Unum erat, propter quod in hac vita aliquantum inmorari cupiebam, ut te Christianum catholicum viderem, priusquam morerer. Cumulatius hoc mihi deus praestitit, ut te etiam contemta felicitate terrena servum eius videam. Quid hic facio?'

p. 32, l. 18. Fever. *Conf.* viiii, p. 185, l. 20.

p. 32, l. 33. *No-ping is fer fro God. Conf.* viiii, p. 186, l. 29.

p. 33, l. 1. *reise me*, i. e. resurrect me. *Conf.* resuscito.

p. 33, l. 12. *Thi seruaunt, Lord. Conf.* viiii, p. 190, l. 1: 'famula tua,' l. 3.

p. 33, l. 23. *Entyr not with hir in-to þi dom. Lete þi mercy flete above þi dom. Conf.* viiii, p. 190, l. 28 : 'ne intres cum ea in iudicium. Superexultet misericordia iudicio.' From Psalm cxliii. 2, and James ii. 13.

p. 33, l. 30. *Inspire, Lord, &c. Conf.* viiii, p. 191, l. 29. Here ends the debt of our text to the *Confessions.*

p. 35, l. 15. *De Magistro.* See note to 26/27.

p. 37, l. 6. *Euodio, &c.* Notice the retention of the Latin case-ending.

p. 46, l. 33. Cf. note to 4/10.

p. 52, l. 27. Donatists, called from Donatus, one of their leaders. These men rebaptized converts from the Catholic Church, hence the 'Rebaptiȝatores' of l. 30.

p. 53, l. 2. *wepun.* Note the plural without the plural ending, a survival of O.E. neuter *wæpen.*

p. 54, l. 9. *leuand.* The early Midland form of the present participle ending was *ende*, later *inge.* *ande* was characteristically Northern, but was fairly common in Midland.

p. 54, l. 30. *þe other tonge*, i. e. Greek.

p. 56, l. 6. St. Thomas Alqwyn, i. e. St. Thomas Aquinas.

p. 61, l. 1. This 'maystir of þe order' was Nicholas Resby, or, as Capgrave spells it, Reysby, known to be master in 1445, and receiver in that year of Henry VI's exemption of the houses of the order from aids, subsidies, and tallages, &c. See Rose Graham's *St. Gilbert of Sempringham & the Gilbertines,* 1903, p. 155.

p. 61, l. 7. See before, p. 1/15.

p. 61, l. 12. See after, p. 145.

p. 62, l. 31. Gilbert's father was Joceline, a wealthy Lincolnshire land-owner ; his mother, a Saxon woman of inferior position,—*inferioris conditionis* ; the '*non*' prefixed to this in Cotton Cleop. BI f. 37, being an interpolation. Dugdale retains the *non*, vi, pt. II, p. vi*. (See Graham, 3.)

p. 63, l. 28. *þat despised of þe world.* Gilbert was afflicted with some sort of deformity, which rendered him repulsive, and was despised even by the serving-men.

p. 63, l. 30. Gilbert was not a very willing pupil in his young years ; and he left England for France to study letters—a fact which Capgrave omits to mention.

p. 64, l. 28. It may not be amiss to refer the reader to what Dean Stanley had to say concerning this 'Athanasian' *Quicunque Vult, Eastern Church,*

p. 247, Everyman edition: 'the ancient hymn, "Quicunque vult," . . . throughout the middle ages and by our own Reformers, was believed to be the Creed of S. Athanasius. The learned world is now fully aware that it is of French or Spanish origin. It not only contains words and phrases which to Athanasius were unknown, but it distinctly and from the first asserted the doctrine of the Double Procession of the Spirit, which never occurs in the writings of Athanasius.'

p. 65, l. 33. Of Robert Bloet, Miss Graham says, *S. Gilbert*, 7, 8 :—'Like many of the bishops of that age, Robert Bloet was a royal official who had received a bishopric as a reward, and he continued to serve the King rather than the Church. He was a chaplain of William the Conqueror, and was with him when he died at Rouen. Immediately afterwards he set out for England with William Rufus, to carry the letter sent by the Conqueror to Lanfranc, bidding him crown Rufus king. Until 1092 Robert served Rufus as chancellor. In the first week of Lent in that year the king lay sick unto death at Gloucester ; his bishops and nobles came to him and implored him to repent of his evil deeds. In terror of death, Rufus gave the archbishopric of Canterbury to the unwilling Anselm, Abbot of Bec, and the see of Lincoln to Robert Bloet. Robert resigned the chancellorship, but under Henry I he held the more important office of justiciar. He was famed for the splendour of his household. "When I beheld the glory of our Bishop," wrote Henry of Huntingdon, one of his archdeacons, "honourable knights, noble youths, costly horses, gold and gilded vessels, the number of dishes, the splendour of his servants, the purple raiment and the torches, I could think of nothing more happy." In the last year of his life he was twice impleaded by King Henry on the charge of an inferior justice ; he was disgraced and condemned to pay a heavy fine in both instances. He retired to his palace at Lincoln overwhelmed with grief. "As I reclined by his side at dinner," said Henry of Huntingdon, "I saw him shedding tears, and asked him the reason. ' Once,' he said, ' those who stood around me wore costly raiment ; now the fines of the king, whom I ever sought to please, have compelled them to put on lambs' wool.' " Robert Bloet died on January 10, 1123. "The King was riding in his deerfold at Woodstock, and the Bishop Roger of Salisbury on one side of him, and the Bishop Robert Bloet of Lincoln on the other side of him ; and they were there riding and talking. Then the Bishop of Lincoln sank down, and said to the King, ' Lord King, I am dying.' And the King alighted down from his horse, and lifted him betwixt his arms, and caused him to be borne to his inn ; and he was then forthwith dead ; and he was conveyed to Lincoln with great worship, and buried before S. Mary's altar. And the Bishop of Chester, named Robert Pecceth, buried him." '

p. 66, l. 1. *Mad a chapeleyn*. Not so, at first. A chaplain, Geoffrey, was appointed by Bloet, as Gilbert was not ordained. It was Alexander, Bloet's successor, who made Gilbert a priest, against his will, and subsequently offered him the archdeaconry. See l. 23.

p. 67, l. 6. This is what the worthy Fuller, *more suo*, has to say of Gilbert and his order :—' *Gilbertine Monks*, may be the third, a *mongrel Order*, observing some *Select Rules* partly of S. *Bennet*, partly of S. *Augustine*. So named from *Gilbert* (son to *Joceline* a Knight) Lord of *Sempringham* in *Lincoln-shire*, where 1148, first they were planted. Whereupon, this Order may *boast*, that it alone is a *native* and *Indegena*, (whereas *Benedictines* are by original *Italians* . . .) pure *English* by the *extraction* thereof. This *Gilbert, unhandsome* but not *unlearned*, erected this order, (contrary to *Justinians* constitution, who forbade *double Monasteries*) wherein men and women lived together, (though secluded) under one roof. He survived to see *thirteen Houses* of this his own Order, and in them *Seventeen hundred Gilbertine Brothers and Sisters*. Yet I finde no *Writer* of this *Order*, conceiving them so well busied with their *Company* in their Convent, they had little leisure for the *writing of Books*,' pp. 268-9, Book vi. Fuller's *Church History of Great Britain*, fol. 1655. Not very generous this.

p. 67, l. 9. Of these maidens, one was the daughter of a poor parishioner of Sempringham, in whose house Gilbert, and Geoffrey, the chaplain, dwelt. (Graham, 6.)

p. 67, l. 12. St. Andrew's Church is the last relic of Gilbert's Sempringham. The picture of the south doorway forms the frontispiece to Miss Graham's *S. Gilbert*. The maiden's dwelling was by the north wall.

p. 69, l. 32. No 'veyn tales' by the way. Unlike Harry Baily, we presume, and his motley wayfarers.

p. 72, l. 21. This was Roger, Prior of Malton, one of Gilbert's first canons, at whose hands, as Capgrave remarks, l. 25, Gilbert received the canon's habit.

p. 73, l. 17. Gilbert suffered, however, from ague.

p. 76, l. 5. *Cadney*. This was on Christmas night, 1188. Miss Graham, quoting *Monasticon*, vol. vi, pt. II, p. xxii*, says Gilbert received extreme unction at the monastery of Newstead-on-Ancholme.

p. 76, l. 11. *sum man of gret myth*. The real danger feared was lest some other church or monastery should become the resting-place of Gilbert's remains.

p. 77, l. 21. *at laudes, at mateyns*, the phrase *at laudes* being added above. As *at mateyns* is not cancelled by Capgrave, we let it stand. See l. 26.

p. 78, l. 34. This was in the priory church of St. Mary.

p. 81, l. 20. *De Constructione Monasteriorum*, now lost.

p. 81, l. 28. Tyrington, i. e. West Torrington.

p. 82, l. 1. See note to 67/9.

p. 83, l. 32. Alexander, successor to Bloet, and nephew to Roger, Archbishop of Salisbury.

p. 85, l. 24. *þe auctour of þis lif*, i. e. the canon of Sempringham who wrote of Gilbert's life and miracles at the command of Roger, Gilbert's successor.

p. 89, l. 13. *Cystewys*, the Cistercians, meeting in congress at Cîteaux, in 1147.

p. 90, l. 5—p. 91, l. 24. The Latin text is as follows, Dugdale's *Monasticon*, vol. vi, Pt. II, pp. viii*-ix*, from MS. Cot. Cleop. BI :—

' *Quod commissum est ei a Domino Papa Regimen Ordinis sui.*

' Data est igitur et iniuncta beato Gileberto a sancto Papa Eugenio collecti gregis custodia, quia non inveniebatur, nec inveniri poterat melior conservator, quam is qui fuerat conquisitor, nec fortior esse poterat boni status zelator; quam qui primus et summus fuerat ad statuendum laborator. Verumtamen vir sanctus, ad tanti pondus regiminis virgentis aetatis causabatur importunitatem, ad honorem; indignitatem, ad magisterium; imperitiam ad praelationem suam praetendit humilitatem. Timuit namque suam, quibus praeferendus erat imparitatem; timuit placide mentis suae soliditatem dissipandam; timuit delecti sui secreti et assiduae contemplationis dulcedinem debellaturam occupationem: quae omnia devotae humilitatis apologetica intellexit, ut erat vir prudens dominus apostolicus, et eo proclivius et securius pastoris ei deputavit officium, quo nullum vidit illi inesse praelationis appetitum: propositum enim eius erat semper humilibus adhaerere (vel humilia appetere) et Domini fuit voluntas, illum se semper humiliantem amplius exaltare.

'Cognoscens autem beatus Gilebertus divinum circa se exactum iudicium, non est ausus diu supernae reniti dispositioni, quae illud ad hoc opus asciverat; sed ne caeteris, quibus pollebat, se privaret virtutibus, si pertinaciter obsisteret, amplexatus est devote obedientiam Dei, eiusque vicarii papae, ampliorem inde sperans mercedem, quia nullam ex hoc habuit delectationem; suique, solius postposuit utilitatem, ut multorum adipisceretur salutem. Contemplationis studiis iamdudum eruditus, piae actionis nunc consensit inservire operibus, ut utriusque vitae meteret fructus: Porro licite poterat earum rerum fieri dispensator, quarum pristinus fuerat possessor, quoniam pauperibus ea conferens, et ipse pauper effectus, ut minister sibi credita, non ut dominus propria gubernavit. Propter haec et huiusmodi sanctitatis signa, et multorum consona testimonia, doluisse fertur Papa Eugenius, quoniam virum antea non novisset, eo quod voluisset, ut dixit, illum sullimasse in archiepiscopum Eboracensem, cuius sedes tunc vacabat, si fama meritorum eius illi prius innotuisset. Beatis quoque Malachiae, Hyberniensi archiepiscopo et Bernardo Clarevallensi abbati, in illo itinere adeo factus est familiaris, ut illis solis praesentibus, ipse quoque praesens adesset, ubi per orationem eorum fertur sanitas collata cuidam aegroto. Insignia etiam amoris, baculum scilicet tam praesulis, quam abbatis, accepit ab utroque; in quibus quaedam factae sunt virtutes; et orarium cum manipulo ei dedit abbas in monimentum sui.'

p. 91, l. 17. *Clarevalle*, i. e. Clairvaux. See the Latin passage above for the origin of Capgrave's form.

p. 93, l. 24. This was in 1164. For a full account of the incident see Miss Graham's *S. Gilbert*, pp. 16-19.

p. 97, l. 32. The debate among the lay-people. The leaders were Ogger and Gerard, who spread defamation throughout the neighbourhood, and demanded less labour and better food. They then left England, and journeyed to Alexander III, whom they convinced of the justice of their case. Henry II, Hugh the papal legate, William, Bishop of Norwich, however, and other influential men, stood by Gilbert in his adversity. Ogger and Gerard were seen to be false, finally returned to Gilbert, asking forgiveness and the mitigation of the harshness of the order. Gilbert received and forgave them. See MS. Cot. Cleop. B L. f. 896, &c., and Graham's *S. Gilbert*, p. 21.

p. 98, l. 5. *Albyne*. This was Albinus, Gilbert's chaplain.

p. 99, l. 18. Oseney Abbey. See the *English Register* of the place, edited by Dr. Andrew Clark, pt. I, E. E. T. S., 1907. I find no mention of this particular cellarer.

p. 100, l. 5. *Beuyrle*, i. e. Beverley, in Yorkshire, 7½ miles north-west of Hull.

p. 101, l. 7. *wat* = was. The same form occurs in *Cursor Mundi*, ed. Morris, p. 1576, l. 29185 :

'Þar was a woman hight mari,
Þat sum time *wat* wit me-selri,'—

again followed by a monosyllabic ending in the dental.

p. 106, l. 13. The dream of angels carrying the soul to heaven is not infrequently met with in mediaeval monkish books. Compare the story of how the Oxford student died, and of his friends watching the bier, and,

'As hi slepe, hem þoȝte boþe : þat hi angles meniee iseȝe
Here felawes soule þat þer lai ded : to heuene lede heȝe
Oure leuede as to teche þe weye : hire silue ȝeode bifore
And openede þe dore of heuene : þat þe soule were in ibore.'

Early English Poems and Lives of Saints, ed. Dr. Furnivall, 1862, p. 41.

p. 118, l. 20. *Hauyrholm*, i. e. Haverholm, given to Gilbert in 1139 by Alexander of Lincoln.

p. 141, l. 16. The Latin text is as follows, Dugdale's *Monasticon*, vol. vi, pt. II, p. xix* :—

'*Rescriptum Cartae, in Feretro positae, hoc est.*

' In hac capsa continentur reliquiae beati Gileberti presbyteri et confessoris, primi patris et institutoris ordinis de Sempringham ; cuius vitam, licet multa praeclaram reddiderint et commendabilem : hoc tamen praecipue eum insignivit, quod spontaneam eligens paupertatem, omnia temporalia, sibi a Deo praestita, fratrum et sororum, quos sub regulari disciplina prudenter instituit et sollicite custodivit, necessitatibus deputavit : cui processu temporis tantam Deus adauxit gratiam et virtutem, quod quatuor canonicas regulares, et ix. monasteria sanctimonialium construit : in quibus eo tempore, que migravit ad Dominum, praeter innumeros antea defunctos, circiter septingentos viros religiosos, mille et quingentas sorores iugiter Deo famulantes reliquit. Obiit autem in senectute plusquam centenaria ; anno incarnationis Domini MC. lxxxix, pridie nonas Februarii, tempore incliti regis Anglorum Henrici secundi. Exigentibus vero propriis meritis, attestantibus miraculis multis, et suadentibus revelationibus divinis canonizatus, cathalogo sanctorum est ascriptus a domino papa Innocentio tertio, per generalem curiam Romanam, apud Anagniam, coram clero et populo, anno Verbi incarnati MCC. ii, tertio idus Ianuarii, anno regni illustris regis Iohannis tertio, praesidente sedi Cantuariae venerabili archiepiscopo Huberto ; qui de mandato memorati summi pontificis Innocentii tertii, cum collegis suis Heliensi episcopo Eustachio, et abbate de Burgo, Achario, diligentem super miraculis per eum divinitus patratis fecerat inquisitionem, et ipsi eorum attestationes fideliter in scripturam redactas, sub sigillis suis, clausas, ad sedem apostolicam transmiserunt ; unde.

certioratus dominus papa de sanctitate eius, et signis, ipsum sanctis Domini decrevit annumerandum, anno pontificatus sui quarto. Et eodem anno per mandatum praefati papae, a praedicto archiepiscopo Huberto translatus est in hunc loculum tertio idus Octobris, assistentibus viris sibi venerabilibus Norwicensi, Herefordensi, et Landavensi episcopis; et abbatibus, aliisque ecclesiarum praelatis plurimis, cum maioribus et nobilioribus Angliae, magno ibi praesente coetu cleri et populi : ad cuius rei perpetuandam memoriam, iam dictus archiepiscopus, et coepiscopi sui, et abbates, sua signa huic scripto appenderunt, et in hoc loculo reposuerunt.'

p. 142, l. 9. *Acarius.* This is Acharius, Prior of St. Alban's, called Zacharias by Hoveden; he became abbot in 1200 and died on the 2nd of the ides of March, 1210. See *Monasticon*, I, p. 354.

p. 145, l. 1. The following is the account of this sermon in Tho. Gibbon's *Historical Collections*, Harley MS., 980; fol. 120 :—

' Gilbert (the son of a Norman knight that came in with the conquerour and of the Lady of Sempringham) was the first founder of the Gilbertines of the ordere of Sempringham. He builded nine monasteries of women & fower of chanons reguler in which monasteries he left at the time of his death of religious women 1500 and of men 700. He died ann. 1189 And was translated by the command of Innocent 3 Ann. 1201. Vid. Joh. Capgraue in Vit. Sti Gilberti manuscript ex Museo Rbt Kemp Milit. Gissing.

The religious which liued vnder the rules of St Augustine wer in number 12.

The first of Hermites made by St. Aug before his being bishop of Hippo.

The second of Cannons seculer when he was bishop.

The Third Canons reguler which were begun by him but a distinction hath been made since by others (as by St Ruffus) and so the monks of Charterhouse came out of the black order.

The 4th The Dominicans begun Ann. 1216.

The 5 Knights of St Johns of Jerusalem.

The 6 Heres of pruce, the same with St John but that they of St John haue black mantles with a cross and they of Pruce white with a cross.

The 7 the Gilbertines of Sempringham order.

The 8 Premonstratenses begon in France by Norbertus ann. 1100.

The 9 the friers of the cross ther foundat incertan.

The 10 The order of St Bridget.

The 11 the canons of St Victor in Paris.

The 12 An order onely in Norff which had 4 house[s] one of them is faln into the Kings hand and he gaue it to Walsingham hite Peterston.

Joh. Capgrave in vii sermon at Cambridg Ann. 1422 et ex museo supra-dicto.'

p. 148, l. 20. Hugues and Richard de St. Victor, two of the most famous theologians of the middle ages. Richard was a Scotchman.

p. 148, l. 27. This appropriation of Peterston to Walsingham took place in 1449.

GLOSSARY

ABBREVIATIONS USED

A

a, *inter.* ah ! 24/30.

a, *v. t. inf.* have 8/5, 57/17, 68/5, 69/6, 84/22, 23. *See* have.

abiden, *v. i.* 3 *pl. pres.* abide 15/6.

abod, abood, *v. i.* 3 *s. p.* abode 8/23, 10/1, 28/2; abod, abood, *v. i.* 3 *pl. p.* 23/21, 27/26, 28/28; abood, *v. t.* 3 *pl. p.* awaited 32/1.

a-boue, *adj.* above 2/29.

absens, *n.* absence 29/4.

absolucion, *n.* 75/25.

abstined, *v. i.* 3 *s. p.* abstained 70/11.

Achay, *n.* Achaia, Greece 3/15.

acordith, *v. i.* 3 *s. pres.* accordeth 2/3; acorded, *v. i.* 3 *pl. cond.* accorded, agreed 17/14.

acrisia, *n.* 109/10.

Aduent, *n.* Advent 70/14.

aferd, a-ferd, *adj.* afraid 16/2, 32/34.

afore, *adv.* before 13/2.

aftir, *adj.* hinder, back 125/24.

aftir, *prep.* after 1/8.

a-gayn, a-geyn, *adv.* again 6/33, 19/16.

ageyn, *prep.* against 12/17.

a-knowe, *pp.* made known 47/5, 57/16. *See also* I-knowe.

akyng, *n.* aching 98/21.

al, *n.* all 19/23.

Alani, *np.* Alans 58/18 (Latin *Alani*).

a-legge, *v. t.* 1 *s. pres.* allege 63/4; alleggid, *pp.* 37/5.

alienat, *pp.* alienated 131/18.

Alisaundr, *n.* Alexandria 64/30.

allegaunce, *n.* 43/15.

alleuyauns, *n.* alleviance 121/30.

ambassiat, *n.* embassy 110/22.

ambicius, *adj.* ambitious 57/30.

amitted, *pp.* admitted 90/19.

a-mongis, *prep.* amongst 1/27.

a-mys, *adv.* amiss 10/26.

amyse, *n.* amice 46/30.

an, *conj.* and 19/4.

an, *prep.* on, at 64/22.

anachorites, *np.* anchorites 38/10.

and, *conj.* if 87/33, 69/5.

annexid, *pp.* annexed 21/24.

annoted, *pp.* recorded 113/2.

apeyred, *pp.* impaired 73/9.

apostell, *n.* apostle 1/7; apostoles, *np.* 30/1.

appechid, *pp.* appeached 17/20.

appelles, appillis, *np.* apples 9/9, 10.

appil-tre, *n.* apple-tree 9/7.

apposed, *v. t.* 3 *s. p.* opposed 111/7.

approximat, *adj.* approximate 3/29.

aproximacion, *n.* 64/7.

aqueyntauns, aqweyntauns, *n.* acquaintance, friends, 36/9, 52/2.

arayed, *pp.* arrayed 38/28.

archibischoprych, *n.* archbishopric 91/14.

aretten, *v. t. inf.* ascribe, reckon 66/18.

argew, *v. i. inf.* argue 26/19.

armur, *n.* armour 53/2.

arowys, *np.* arrows 2/24.
arametrik, *n.* arithmetic 11/32.
articules, *np.* articles 9/3.
a-schamed, *adj.* ashamed 21/11.
a-sikir, *adj.* safe 36/26.
asined, *v. t. 3 s. p.* assigned 19/3;
   assined, *pp.* assigned 9/2.
asken, *v. t. inf.* ask 26/19.
aspie, *v. t. inf.* aspy, perceive 11/11;
   aspied, *v. t. 1 s. p.* 11/15.
aspying, *n.* 31/8.
assoyle, *v. t. inf.* assoil 71/25; assoiling, *pres. p.* 71/28.
astate, *n.* estate, authority 66/5.
astates, *np.* estates 51/36.
astoyned, *pp.* astonished 25/13,
   124/14.
attached, *pp.* apprehended 18/21.
auoter, aucter, auteȓ, *n.* altar 14/12,
   32/26, 124/6; aucteris, *np.* 16/24.
auctorite, *n.* authority 95/27.
auotouȓ, *n.* author 38/10; auctoris,
   np. authors, 1/27, 2/27.
audiens, *n.* audience 53/24.
auditorye, *n.* auditory, pupils, hearers 65/18.
aungellis, *np.* angels 1/6.
autentik, *adj.* authentic 109/24.
auysement, *n.* advisement 76/8.
a-vised, *adj.* advised 49/35.
a-vow, *n.* vow 20/37.
avowe, *v. t. inf.* 78/16.
avowid, *v. t. 3 pl. p.* dedicated 21/4.
awbe, *n.* alb 125/30.
axid, *pp.* asked 83/32.

B

bagg, *n.* bag 30/10.
bakkes, *np.* backs, 65/29.
balled, *adj.* bald 106/17.
baptem, *n.* baptism 8/15, 24/17.
baptisterie, *n.* baptistery 25/31.
baȓ, *adj.* bare 48/27.
barbaȓ, *adj.* barbarian, foreign, 3/25.
barres, *np.* bars 28/21.
batayle, *n.* battle 8/20, 63/16.
be, *conj.* but, 40/31.
be, *prep.* by 4/19, 19/18.
be, *v. i. 2 pl. pres.* be 38/16; ar, aȓ,
   be, *v. i. 3 pl. pres.* are 2/10, 14/9,
   23/7, 28/34; beth, *v. i. 2 pl. imper.*
   be 16/3, 52/10; was, wast, wat,
   v. i. 3 s. p. was 19/19, 101/7,
   103/28; be, ben, *pp.* been 7/8,
   15/16, 20/6, 27/4.
Beamoundis, *np.* Beaumonts 63/8.

bedred, *adj.* bedridden 79/19, 128/32.
be-forn, *prep.* before 132/36.
beginne, be-gynne, *v. t. inf.* begin
   1/23, 20/30; begynnyth *v. t. 3 s.
   pres.* 5/11; be-gunne, *v. t. 3 pl. p.*
   12/15.
be-had, *v. i. 3 s. p.* behaved 68/19.
be-hest, *v. t. inf.* promise 85/16; behestyng, *pres. p.* 95/34.
beleue, *n.* belief 10/30.
bellis, *np.* bells 132/14.
benyngly, *adv.* benignly 64/12.
beȓ, *v. t. inf.* bear 39/8; berith, *n. t.
   3 s. pres.* 67/1; beren, *v. t. 3 pl.
   pres.* 62/23; bare, *v. t. 3 s. p.*
   bore 72/30, 84/29; bare, *v. t.
   3 s. p.* 7/2; boȓ, bore, *pp.* born
   3/2, 20/1, 26/12; boȓ, *pp.* borne
   67/8.
beȓ - baytingis, *sv.* bear - baitings
   65/22.
berke, *v. i. inf.* bark 24/22; berk,
   v. i. 3 pl. pres. 52/26.
beryng, *n.* bearing, behaviour 66/6.
besekyng, *pres. p.* beseeching 108/31.
besi, bisi, *adj.* busy 6/23, 10/8.
besily, bisily, *adv.* busily 21/19,
   24/16.
besinesse, bisinesse, *n.* business
   13/28, 19/5.
bete, *pp.* beaten 7/27.
bettir, *adj.* better 1/20.
be-twix, *prep.* between 6/6.
beute, *n.* beauty 83/19.
Beuyrle, *n.* Beverley 100/5.
bittirnesse, *n.* bitterness 25/2.
blak, *adj.* black 28/21.
blasphemes, *np.* blasphemies 56/19.
blisse, *v. t. inf.* bless 73/1; blessed,
   v. t. 3 s. p. 75/3.
blodis, *np.* bloods 63/11.
blow, *pp.* blown 31/14.
bodely, *adj.* bodily 5/1.
bok, booke, *n.* 5/2, 20/6, 8, 23/24;
   booke, bokes, bokis, bokys, *np.*
   2/34, 3/31, 20/4, 53/33.
bolstering, *n.* bolstering (of bed)
   71/20.
bon, boon, *n.* bone 125/6, 11.
bond, *v. t. 3 s. p.* bound 33/27;
   bounde, bounden, boundyn,
   bownde, *pp.* bound 6/13, 51/2,
   100/2, 131/7.
bord, *n.* board 20/4, 47/23.
bordred, *pp.* bordered 91/23.
bordures, *np.* borders 147/17.
Borow, *n.* Peterborough, 79/28,
   142/9.

11

bowt, *v. t. 8 s. p.* bought 92/13.

boystonsly, *adv.* boisterously 46/17.

breke, *v. t. inf.* break 20/38; brak, *v. t. i. 3 pl. p.* 120/30; broke, *pp.* 6/16.

brent, *v. t. 3 s. p.* burnt 21/11; brennyng, *pres. p.* 2/17; brennaund, brennyng, *adj.* burning, 1/28, 100/6, 129/21.

brest, *v. i. 3 s. p.* burst 96/31.

bringgist, *v. t. 2 s. pres.* bringest 5/5.

brith, *adj.* bright 16/17.

broches, *np.* 87/18.

bropir, *n.* brother 4/26.

brout, *v. t. 1 s. p.* brought 37/12; brout, brovt, browt, *pp.* 1/22, 16/19, 19/25, 21/8, 28/14.

brynk, *n.* brink, shore 14/3.

bullis, *np.* bulls (papal) 38/7, 95/7.

buschell, *n.* bushel 93/2.

buschel mette, *n.* bushel measure, 136/11.

buschment, *n.* ambush 109/8.

buttokes, *np.* buttocks, 120/2.

buxum, *adj.* obedient 28/33, 103/15.

bye, *v. t. inf.* buy 49/31.

byled, *v. t. 3 s. p.* built 140/18.

byleue, *n.* belief 52/19.

biried, byried, byryed, *pp.* buried 16/25, 32/25.

byrying, byryng, *n.* burying 32/28, 79/23.

Byʒance, *n.* Byzantium 3/19.

C

caceh, *v. t. inf.* catch 5/28.

Cam, *n.* Ham 3/9.

cam, *see* cum.

can, *v. t. 1 s. pres.* know 105/19; coude, *v. t. 3 s. p.* 39/10; coude, *v. i. 1 s. p.* could 1/26; cowde, *v. i. 3 s. p.* 30/12.

cap, *n. capitulum*, chapter 3/3.

capitle, capitule, *n.* chapter 1/2, 26/3.

capitoll, *n.* the Capitol at Rome 56/18.

carde, *v. i. 3 pl. pres.* card 55/18.

caryage, *n.* carriage, journey 76/12.

cast, *v. t. 3 s. p.* purposed 15/23, 25/26.

cathaloge, *n.* catalogue 80/1.

cathecume, *n.* catechumen 9/1.

caue, *n.* cave 20/25.

cautel, cautele, *n.* precaution 50/18, 140/23.

cedr, *n.* cedar 50/22.

celerer, *n.* cellarer 99/14.

celles, *np.* cells 67/13.

cenobites, *np.* 88/10.

cese, *v. i. inf.* cease 28/11.

cessacion, *n.* 23/13.

chalange, *n.* challenge 51/4.

chamel skynnys, *np.* camel skins 38/30.

chanones, *np.* canons, 6/15.

chapetir, *n.* chapter 113/31.

charite, *n.* charity 1/29.

chartor, chartour, *n.* charter 141/7, 16.

chast, *adj.* chaste 83/14.

chateryng, *adj.* chattering 6/20.

chaundeler, *n.* chandelier 93/3.

chekis, *np.* cheeks 21/21.

cher, chere, *n.* cheer, 10/13, 10/14.

chere, *v. t. inf.* cheer, entertain 44/27.

cherch, chirch, kirk, *n.* church 19/17, 19, 94/16; cherchis, *np.* 67/33.

chese, *v. t. inf.* choose 17/9, 39/16; chase, *v. t. 3 s. p.* 70/31; chase, *v. t. 3 pl. p.* 39/17; chose, *pp.* chosen 19/29.

chesibile, chesible, *n.* chasuble 116/7, 124/8.

childhold, *n.* childhood 4/21.

childyr, childyrn, *n.* children 4/23, 7/15.

chois, *n.* choice 30/2.

cite, cyte, *n.* city 2/30, 20/26, 31/15; cite, *n.* city, people 25/32; cytees, *np.* 87/22.

citeceynes, *np.* citizens 41/25.

clad, *pp.* 55/19.

claf, *v. i. 3 s. p.* cleft 120/16.

clamour, *n.* 64/18.

Clareualle, *n.* Clairvaux 91/17.

clatering, *adj.* 85/5.

clauser, *n.* cloister 83/28.

clennesse, *n.* cleanliness 7/24.

clepe, *v. t. 1 pl. pres.* call 38/6; clepe, *v. t. 2 pl. pres.* 20/9; clepith, *v. t. 3 s. pres.* 23/30, 38/7; clepe, *v. t. 3 pl. pres.* 4/27; clepid, *v. t. 3 s. p.* 1/3; cleped, *v. t. 3 pl. p.* 12/9; clepyng, *pres. p.* calling 33/20; cleped, *pp.* called 3/7.

clepyng, *n.* calling 75/8.

clerkis, *np.* clerks, monks 36/20.

clopis, *np.* clothes 10/12.

cloystirer, *n.* cloisterer 66/8.

clyme, *v. t. inf.* climb 97/15.

coeterne, *adj.* coeternal 31/25.

cold, *n.* coldness 45/15.

collectes, *np.* collects 80/4.

college, *n.* brotherhood 29/18.

collocucioñ, *n.* conversation 140/6.

comendatyf, *adj.* commendatory 108/31.

comminaciones, *np.* commination 66/5.

comoun, *v. t. inf.* commune 11/4; comound, *pp.* 18/1.

compendiously, *adv.* 117/23.

complacens, *n.* 84/8.

compleynt, *n.* complaint 6/29.

compowned, compownyd, *pp.* compounded 2/27, 2/28.

comprehendid, *pp.* comprehended, contained 38/33.

compromisse, *n.* promise 58/5.

compunct, *adj.* constrained 20/28.

comyng, *n.* coming 19/30.

conceytes, *np.* conceits, ideas 38/34.

conclaue, *n.* 83/11.

condicioñ, *n.* behaviour, demeanour 5/26.

conformite, *n.* 70/32.

confundid, *pp.* confounded 136/31.

congrue, *adj.* congruous 77/16.

coniected, *v. t. 3 s. p.* conjectured 99/21.

consciens, *n.* conscience 9/8.

consent, *n.* accompaniment (of tunes to words) 27/14.

conservacion, *n.* conservation 69/4.

constrewyng, *n.* construing, grammar 8/17.

constriccioñ, *n.* constriction 100/34.

conuentual, *adj.* 67/33.

conuercion, *n.* conversion 21/1.

conuerse, *n.* convert 129/30.

conuicte, *v. t. 3 s. p.* convicted 41/21.

conyng, *n.* cunning 26/16.

coost, *n.* side, part 102/28.

cophre, *n.* coffer 135/10.

corage, *n.* courage, disposition 63/32.

corteynes, *np.* curtains 112/33.

cosyn, *n.* kinsman 5/13; cosynes, *np.* 5/7.

cote, *n.* coat 70/25.

couetyse, *n.* covetousness 36/3.

councell, *v. t. inf.* counsel 50/30.

coynoures, *np.* coiners 17/29; coynouris, *np. gen.* coiners' 17/32.

craft, *n.* ability 125/12.

craked, *v. i. 3 pl. p.* cracked 120/32.

crap, *v. i. 3 s. p.* crept 120/1.

credens, *n.* credence 78/2.

crien, *v. i. inf.* cry 138/32.

cristen, *adj.* Christian 2/18, 5/9, 29/13.

cristendam, cristendham, *n.* Christianity 20/12, 29/4.

croked, *adj.* crooked 70/28.

crokednes, *n.* crookedness 130/33.

crowet, *n.* cruet, phial 132/25.

cubiculeres, *np.* cubiculars 97/3.

cubyte, *n.* elbow 130/3.

cum, *v. i. inf.* come 12/19; comth, *v. i. 3 s. pres.* 5/19, 17/30, 42/7, 58/32; cam, *v. i. 3 s. p.* came 3/26, 13/36, 20/2; cam, *v. i. 3 pl. p.* 3/7; comand, *pres. p.* 63/30, 124/6.

cumpany, *n.* 24/10.

cunnyng, *n.* ability 13/3.

cuntî, cuntre, *n.* country 3/2, 12/4, 23/18.

cuntre-man, *n.* countryman 20/10.

cure, *n.* care, charge 43/18, 89/16.

cured, *pp.* covered 17/32, 96/27.

cura, *v. t. inf.* curse 51/1.

curyng, *n.* 74/25.

custumablely, *adv.* by custom, usually 4/29, 41/11.

cyssyng, *n.* kissing 79/7.

Cystewys, *np.* Cistercians 89/13.

D

daliauns, *n.* daliance 15/6.

daî, *v. t. 1 s. pres.* dare 1/9; durst, *v. t. 3 s. p.* dared 13/4.

dauns, *n.* dance 77/30.

debate, *n.* strife 6/19.

debylite, *n.* debility 128/29.

deces, *n.* decease 79/26.

deceyued, *v. 3 s. p.* 13/31.

dedis, *np.* deeds 5/27.

dedly, *adj.* mortal, subject to death 25/28.

defautes, *np.* defaults 7/25, 75/26.

defenden, *v. t. 3 pl. pres.* forbid 92/20.

defouled, *pp.* defiled 36/7.

defraude, *v. t. inf.* 79/15.

del, *n.* part 70/19.

delectabily, *adv.* delectably 27/14.

delectable, *adj.* 28/23.

delectacionis, *np.* delectations, delights 19/9.

delicasises, *np.* delicacies 70/15.

delices, *np.* delights 96/4.

delite, *n.* delight 15/6.

delt, *v. t. 3 s. p.* dealt 65/17.

deme, *v. t. 3 pl. pres.* judge 41/17.

denouns, *v. t. inf.* announce 48/6.

departed, *pp.* divided 3/3.

dere, *adj.* dear 26/31.

deregacioñ, *n.* derogation 107/30.

desolat, *adj.* 23/10.
despect, *adj.* despised 4/9.
determyn, *v. t. inf.* determine, settle 58/3.
detour̃, dettour̃, *n.* debtor 1/3, 1/11.
dettis, *np.* debts 1/12.
deuele, *n.* devil 7/9, 56/30.
deuocyoñ, *n.* devotion 24/26.
deute, *n.* duty 33/26.
dew, *adj.* due 6/13, 103/3.
dewid, *pp.* dewed 24/23.
deye, *v. i. inf.* die 4/18, 27/27.
deyid, *v. i.* 1 *s. p. and* 3 *s. p.* died 5/4, 32/14, 35/17.
deynte, *n.* esteem 12/13, 13/6.
deynte, *n.* regard 107/19.
dialoge, *n.* dialogue 26/27.
diffuncioñ, *n.* conclusion 24/12.
diffusely, *adv.* 61/11.
dignyte, *n.* dignity 61/4.
dilacioñ, *n.* 86/23.
diosise, *n.* diocese 43/27.
dirkly, *adv.* darkly 57/14.
dirknes, *n.* darkness 77/20.
disceptacioñ, *n.* disceptation, debate 42/6.
disoerne, *v. t. inf.* 7/12.
disciplens, *np.* disciplines 9/24.
disport, *n.* 20/22.
dissentyrie, *n.* dysentery 128/25.
disseyued, *v. t.* 3 *s. p.* deceived 18/23.
dissolue, *v. t. inf.* solve 54/10.
dissoluer̃, *n.* solver 54/9.
distraut, *adj.* distraught 131/13.
dite, *v. t. inf.* dight, prepare 70/16; dite, *pp.* 89/25.
diuturne, *adj.* diuturnal 71/16.
do, *v. t. inf.* do 6/13; ded, dyde, *v. t.* 3 *s. p.* 7/17, 27/28, 66/16; dede, *v. t.* 3 *pl. p.* 6/17; do, don, doo, *pp.* 4/16, 7/13, 33/25, 34/17, 67/17; doyng, *n.* doing 74/23.
dobiled, doblid, *pp.* doubled 87/15, 17.
dobyl, *adj.* double 67/4.
doctour̃, *n.* doctor 1/18, 7/17; doctouris, *np.* 2/10.
dom, *n.* doom, judgment 33/24, 89/7; dome-place, *n.* doom-place, judgment-place 18/1.
dor̃, *n.* door 31/33.
dormytori, *n.* 69/26.
dortour̃, *n.* dortor, dormitory 97/12.
Dotaim, *n.* Dothan 109/13.
doutir, *n.* daughter 6/24, 31/1; douteres, *np.* 132/21.

dowte, *n.* doubt 19/6; doutes, *np.* 13/1.
dramme, *n.* dram, drachma 82/4.
dred, *v. t.* 3 *s. p.* dreaded 34/12, 57/30.
dred, *n.* dread 16/1, 81/16.
drenchid, *pp.* drowned 21/17.
dronk, *v. t.* 3 *pl. p.* drank 16/33; drinkyn, *pp.* drunk 132/27; drynkyngis, *np.* drinkings 65/21.
dropesie, *n.* dropsy 79/19.
drow, *v. i.* 1 *s. p.* drew 29/24; drow, drowe, *v. t.* 3 *s. p.* 86/18, 130/32; drawe, *pp.* drawn, withdrawn 60/19.
dul, *adj.* dull (wit) 85/9.
dwelt, *v. i.* 3 *pl. p.* 21/2.
dysmittid, *pp.* dismissed (*Latin:* dismittere), 23/15.
dyuers, *adj.* divers 12/3, 20/15.
dyuulge, *v. t. inf.* divulge 107/21.
dyuynes, *np.* divines 56/3.
dyuynite, *n.* divinity 40/17.

E

ech, *pron.* each 1/8, 65/16.
edifie, *v. t. inf.* 29/33.
edifiyng, *n.* edifying 37/23.
eft-sones, *adv.* eftsoons, soon afterwards 115/24.
eke, *adv.* also 1/21.
eld, elde, *adj.* old 4/3, 6/22, 70/27.
ellis, *adv.* else 6/29.
elmes, elmesse, *n.* alms 14/13, 69/33.
elmesse-houses, *np.* alms - houses 67/29.
elmesse - ȝeuyng, *n.* almsgiving 82/15.
embrowded, *pp.* embroidered 111/24.
emolliment, *n.* emolument 60/20.
emperease, *n.* 27/17.
emperour̃, *n.* emperor 20/21.
encenseris, *np.* censers 62/6.
encreser, *n.* increaser 2/33.
endewid, *v. t.* 3 *s. p.* endowed 41/13; endewid, endewyd, *pp.* endowed 1/9, 65/19.
endewred, *pp.* endured 49/16.
endyted, *pp.* indicted 93/26.
endytyng, *n.* inditing 12/16.
enforsyng, *pres. p.* enforcing 53/18.
ensaumple, *n.* example 41/5.
enspired, *v. t.* 3 *s. p.* inspired 19/20.
entent, *n.* intention 20/38.

entent, *n.* understanding 4/4.
enter, *adj.* entire 95/26.
entr, *n.* entry 55/29.
epistil, *n.* epistle 2/11; epistoles, *np.* 20/9, 57/2.
equyte, *n.* equity 136/13.
er, *adv.* ere 68/4.
erdly, *adj.* earthly 32/7, 81/6.
eres, *np.* ears 14/4, 28/6.
ergo, *adv.* 19/18.
errouris, *np.* errours 19/6, 25/15.
eryng, *n.* hearing 67/14.
est, *adj.* east 8/9.
estern, *adj.* easter 28/29.
esy, *adj.* easy 1/13.
ete, *v. t.* 3 *pl. pres.* eat 47/15; ete, *v. t.* 3 *s. p.* ate 47/11.
ethimilogie, ethimologie, *n.* etymology 2/1, 2/26.
epir, *conj.* either 112/34.
euel a-vised, *adj.* ill-advised 5/31.
euyr, *adv.* ever 1/6.
euyr-lestyn, *adj.* everlasting 32/4.
ex, exe, *n.* axe 17/31, 18/3.
excedid, *v. i.* 3 *s. p.* exceeded; became wrathful 5/29.
excellens, *n.* excellence 1/28.
excusaciones, *np.* excuses 90/18.
exemplary, *n.* 61/23.
exequies, exequiis, *np.* exequies 33/4, 78/23.
exhortacion, *n.* 19/8.
exorted, *v. t.* 3 *s. p.* exhorted 67/27.
experiens, *n.* 26/17.
experiment, *n.* declaration, proof 73/28.
expounne, *v. t. inf.* expound 85/31.
eyer, *n.* heir 63/3.
ey-ledes, *np.* eyelids 133/29.
eyne, *np.* eyes 21/22.
eyr, *n.* air 9/30, 58/6.
eyty, *n.* eighty 77/25.

F

fader, fader, fadir, *n.* father 1/6, 3/5, 4/17, 5/20; fader, fadir, faderes, *n. gen.* father's 7/10, 63/11, 84/4.
faderles, *adj.* fatherless 66/29.
faderly, *adv.* fatherly 29/30.
falle, *pp.* fallen 8/25.
fals, *adj.* 19/9.
fantastical, *adj.* 9/29.
fas, *n.* face 145/12.
fast, *prep.* near 17/5.
fayr, *adj.* fair 13/5.
fayr-spoke, *adj.* fair-spoken 12/33.

feble, *n.* feeble (people) 66/30.
Februarij, *n.* 77/24.
fecch, *v. t. inf.* fetch 20/26.
fedyng, *n.* feeding 24/7.
feer, *n.* fear 16/1.
feest, fest, feste, *n.* feast 1/22, 2/11, 4/30, 5/8.
feith, *n.* faith 19/23.
felauchip, felawschip, *n.* fellowship 8/25, 12/29, 26/29.
felawes, felawis, *np.* fellows 2/22, 20/18.
feld, *n.* field 23/18; feldes, feldis, *np.* 31/3, 101/5.
fennys, *np.* fens 94/2.
fer, fer, *adv.* far 18/26, 28/34, 38/13; fer, *adv.* far (dissimilar) 4/6; fer, *adj.* far 21/27.
fer, *n.* fear 42/26.
fer, fere, *n.* comradeship 30/30, 31/28.
ferd, *v. i.* 3 *s. p.* fared (?) 41/3.
ferforth, *adv.* farforth 55/31.
ferme, *adj.* firm 43/6.
feruent, *adj.* 80/9.
feuerys, ffevyrues, *np.* fevers 59/17, 79/19.
feyne, *v. t. inf.* pretend 94/12; feyned, *v. t.* 3 *s. p.* 13/24.
feynt, *adj.* faint 94/19.
ffrer, *n.* frere, 62/3.
figge-tre, *n.* fig-tree 21/32.
filt, *v. t.* 3 *s. p.* filled 14/4, 97/22; filt, *pp.* filled 100/10.
fistula, *n.* 100/13.
flayn, *pp.* flayed 118/29.
fle, *v. t. inf.* flee 70/33; fle, *v. t.* 3 *pl. pres.* 38/27.
fleschly, *adj.* carnal 24/7.
flete, *v. i. inf.* fleet, pass 33/24.
flour, *n.* flower 129/10; flouris, *np.* 62/24.
fluctuacion, *n.* 16/20.
folowand, *adj.* following 121/30, 122/30, &c.
folowyn, *v. i.* 3 *pl. pres.* follow 138/3.
fond, fonde, *v. t.* 3 *s. and pl. p.* found 9/18, 20/3, 26; found, founde, foumden, *pp.* 4/15, 28/31, 30/11.
forboden, forbodyn, *pp.* forbidden 47/24, 94/10.
fore, *conj.* for 4/28.
for-gete, forgetyn, *pp.* 33/7, 27.
forgif, *v. t.* 2 *s. imper.* 33/22; for-3oue, *pp.* 52/15.
forhed, *n.* forehead 21/21.
form-faderes, *np.* forefathers 92/16.

fornays, *n. furnace* 95/18.
forsaid, *adj.* 24/6.
forsok, *v. t. 3 s. p.* forsook 27/4; forsok, *v. t. 3 pl. p.* 45/27; forsakyn,
pp. 28/33.
foundour, *n.* founder 29/4.
fourt, *adj.* fourth 77/23.
fre, *adj.* free 5/25, 23/4.
fre-hertet, *adj.* free-hearted 36/34.
fremanly, *adj.* free, composed of
freemen, 63/20.
frenesie, *n.* frenzy 131/2.
fretyng, *n.* fretting 133/8.
freyte, *n.* freight 104/4.
fro, *prep.* from 21/8.
frustrate, *v. t. inf.* frustrate 61/18.
frutes, *np.* fruits 2/16.
fulfillid, *pp.* replete 27/5; fulfilt,
pp. fulfilled 16/12.
furris, *np.* furs 38/28.
fynde, *v. t. inf.* find 30/10.
fyred, *pp.* fired 1/29.
fytyn, *v. i. inf.* fight 51/4.

G

gadered, *v. t. 3 s. p.* gathered 21/29;
gadered, *pp.* gathered 14/19,
21/10.
gaderer, *n.* gatherer 90/8.
gaf, goue, *see* ȝeue.
Galile, *n.* Galilee 3/14.
gardeyn, *n.* garden 21/24.
garmentis, *np.* 47/2.
gat, *v. t. 3 s. p.* got 11/29, 41/8;
goten, *pp.* got 41/3.
gayler, *n.* jailor 84/28.
geaunt, *n.* giant 58/17.
gelosie, *n.* jealousy 42/27.
gemetrie, *n.* geometry 11/32.
gendres, *np.* genders, kinds 29/22.
gentill, *adj.* gentle 1/15.
gessid, *pp.* guessed 57/4.
gest, *n.* guest 66/29; gestis, *np.*
44/29.
gilty, *adj.* guilty 33/19.
girdil, *n.* girdle 28/21; girdilis, *np.*
38/29.
girdyn, *v. t. 3 pl. pres.* gird 146/28;
girt, *pp.* 28/20.
glade, *v. t. inf.* make glad, gladden
70/3.
glorius, *adj.* glorious 2/8.
gnach, *v. t. inf.* gnash 132/28; gnacching, *pres. p.* gnashing 131/4.
go, goo, *v. i. inf.* 13/13, 13/25; go,
v. i. 2 s. imper. 11/19; go, *v. i.*
1 *pl. imper.* 19/21; go, i-goo, *pp.*
gone 16/7, 21/12, 77/20.

god, *adj.* good 29/27.
god, godis, *np.* goods 34/10, 37/23.
goost, *n.* ghost 12/28.
goostly, *adj.* spiritual 24/7.
Gothi, *np.* Goths 58/18.
gouernauns, *n.* governance, control,
5/27.
govte, *n.* gout 128/25.
gramer, *n.* grammar 2/2, 30/9.
greces, *np.* steps 97/14.
gret, grete, *adj.* great 1/1, 2/32,
4/30; gretter, *adj. comp.* 8/18.
gretly, *adv.* greatly, 6/31, 12/33.
greuauns, *n.* grievance, injury 8/14.
greue, *v. t. 3 pl. pres.* grieve, hurt
7/16; greued, *v. t. 3 s. p.* grieved,
pained 7/1.
greuous, *adj.* grievous 14/8, 25/4.
griffid, *pp.* grafted 68/30.
groped, *v. t. 3 s. p.* touched, took
hold 126/10.
grounded, *pp.* founded 117/9;
grounded, *pp.* learned, versed
12/33.
groundes, *np.* foundation 56/7.
growen, *pp.* grown 68/22.
grucch, *v. i. inf.* grudge, murmur
50/10; grucch, *v. t. 2 s. imper.*
20/31; grucch, *v. i. 2 pl. pres.*
28/28; grucch, *v. i. 2 pl. imper.*
49/19; grucchid, *v. i. 3 pl. p.*
40/31; grucching, *pres. p.* mur-
muring, rebelling 15/8.
grucching, *adj.* grudging, complain-
ing, 41/1.
gruf, *adv.* prone, face downwards
124/12.
guttys, *np.* guts, intestines 128/26.

H

ha, a, *v. t. inf.* have 8/5, 57/17, 68/5,
69/6, 84/22, &c.; haue, *v. t. 2 pl.*
pres. 18/18; hatȝ, *v. t. 3 s. pres.*
hath 4/3, 19/28, 113/7; ha, had,
v. t. 3 s. p. 19/2, 145/8.
hald, *v. t. inf.* hold 17/10; held,
v. t. 3 pl. p. 74/13; hald, halden,
hold, holden, *pp.* held 44/28,
63/29, 89/14, 113/9, 128/9.
halidayes, *np.* holidays 28/29.
halowid, *pp.* hallowed 25/31.
halsyng, *n.* embracing 83/8; halsyngis, *np.* embraces 83/14.
hambyr, *n.* hammer 52/10.
hand, *n.* handwriting 4/3.
hard-hertid, *adj.* hard-hearted
54/20.

hast, *v. t. inf.* haste 16/17; hasted, *v. t.* 3 *pl. p.* 20/35.

hattest, *adj. sup.* hottest 2/16.

hatyd, *v. t.* 3 *s. p.* hated 47/19.

hayir, her, *n.* hair 48/27, 70/31; herys, *np.* hairs 47/7.

he, it, *pron.* it 19/33, 56/33; his, hise, *poss. pron.* his, its 5/19, 28/3, 36/15.

hed, heed, *n.* head 15/7, 25/4.

hed, *n.* heed, 18/6, 55/16.

heith, *n.* height 81/3, 56/32.

hele, *n.* health 127/27.

Helise, *n.* Elisha 102/9.

Hely, *n.* Elijah 38/30.

hem, *pron.* them 1/10, &c.

hemmys, *np.* hems, borders 107/25.

hepes, *n. p.* heaps 21/29.

her, herys, *see* hayir.

heȓ, here, *v. t. inf.* hear 14/14, 15; heȓ, here, *v.t.* 2 *s. imper.* 33/19, 21; herd, *v. t.* 3 *pl. p.* 4/14; herand, *pres. p.* 76/28.

heȓ, *adv.* here 5/5.

her, heȓ, here, *pron.* their 1/6, 4/11, 6/2, 9/3, 12/21, 108/12, &c.

herborowid, *pp.* harboured 84/9.

heremite, heremyte, *n.* hermit 20/25; hermytes, *np.* 28/16.

hereres, *np.* hearers 140/11.

heres, *np.* knights 147/16.

hert, *n.* heart 1/29.

hertly, *adv.* heartily 10/6, 45/15.

heruest, *n.* harvest 23/10.

herying, *n.* hearing 47/10.

Heseleschop, *n.* Hesaleskew Grange 103/23.

hethen, *adj.* 24/3.

heuene, *n.* heaven 1/5.

heuy, *adj.* heavy 10/14, 29/4.

hewe, *v. t. inf.* hew 17/33.

heyeȓ, *adv.* higher 66/6.

heyly, *adv.* highly 15/20, 43/14.

heyne, *v. t. inf.* exalt 68/17.

hie, *adj.* high 27/7; hyer, *adj. comp.* 107/4.

him-selue, hym-selue, his-selve, *pron.* himself 4/1, 54/18, 57/29.

hin, in, *n.* inn 13/26, 102/13.

hing, hyng, *v. i.* 3 *s. p.* hung 71/11, 120/8.

hipped, *v. i.* 3 *s. p.* hopped 118/18.

hir, hiȓ, hire, *pron.* her 1/16, 4/21, 13/28.

his, hise, *poss. pron.* his 5/19, 28/3, 36/15. *See* he.

hith, *v. i.* 3 *s. p.* hight, was called 4/20, 5/7, 81/9.

hoggis, *np.* hogs 9/11.

hol, hool, hole, *adj.* whole 34/11, 14, 99/27.

hold, holden, *see* hald.

holed, *pp.* healed 75/4.

holpe, *pp.* helped 37/33.

holsom, *adj.* wholesome 80/9, 118/2.

hom, *n.* home 11/9, 20/3.

homward, *adv.* homeward 20/36.

hony, *n.* honey 24/22.

hoot, hote, *adj.* hot 2/24, 47/16.

hopped, *v. i.* 3 *s. p.* leapt, hopped 16/9. *See also* hipped.

horribil, *adj.* horrible 21/6.

hors bere, *n.* horse-bier 131/20.

horsed, *pp.* set on horse 126/22.

hose, *n.* hose 118/30; hosen, hosyn, *np.* hose 45/17, 74/29.

hosill, *n.* housel 76/6.

Hostie, *n.* Ostia 31/31.

hothous, *n.* 4/27.

housyng, *n.* housing 17/29.

humores, *np.* humours 134/23.

huscher, *n.* usher 80/8.

hydyn, *v. t. inf.* hide 140/30.

I

I, *pron.* 89/14.

Iaphet, *n.* Japhet 3/8.

idus, *n.* ides 142/5.

iff, *conj.* if 6/8.

Ihesu, *n.* Jesus 1/5.

impetuosnesse, *n.* 103/21.

implicat, *pp.* implicated 50/7.

importably, *adv.* insupportably 66/10.

imprended, *v. t.* 3 *s. p.* imprinted 11/21.

in, hin, *n.* inn 13/26, 102/13.

inclinacion, *n.* inclination (of the sun) 20/35; inclynacion, *n.* 3/28.

inexpert, *adj.* 85/15.

infancia, *n.* infancy 7/3.

infect, *pp.* infected 27/17.

inflawmed, *v. t.* 3 *s. p.* inflamed 54/19.

I-now, *adv.* enough 35/13.

inqwired, *v. t.* 3 *s. p.* inquired 19/14.

inqwyet, *v. t. inf.* disturb 126/5.

insolens, *np.* insolent deeds 9/6.

instauns, *n.* instance 1/16.

interfered, *pp.* interposed 96/11.

interogaciones, *np.* 36/28.

interrupt, *pp.* interrupted 57/26.

intituled, *pp.* entitled 12/10.

intollerablely, *adv.* intolerably 14/4.

inuecciones, *np.* invections, inveighings 13/3.

inuent, *adj.* literary, artistically composed (?) 14/25.

inuisibil, *adj.* invisible 35/6.

iocunde, *adj.* jocund 12/32.

iocundnesse, *n.* jocundity 46/16.

Ion, *n.* St. John Baptist 38/30.

iornay, *n.* journey 16/5, 98/5.

ioye, *n.* joy 23/7.

ioynend, *v. t.* 3 *pl. p.* joined 108/18.

iȝ, ire, *n.* ire, anger 5/24, 30.

irous, *adj.* subject to ire 6/7.

issewe, *n.* issue 63/8.

it, *prom.* it, 65/16. *See also* he.

Itaile, *n.* Italy 8/21.

iteration, *n.* 19/19.

Iubiter, *n.* Jupiter 56/12.

Iude, *n.* Judea 3/14.

iuge, *n.* judge 66/4.

iunctuȝ, *n.* juncture 87/18.

iurates, *np.* sworn men 111/7.

K

kalende, *n.* calend 60/12.

kandel, *n.* candle 123/28.

kechyn, kychyn, *n.* kitchen 47/30, 123/12.

kende, *n.* kind 82/8.

kendly, *adv.* kindly, naturally 97/11.

kepand, *pres. p.* keeping 30/22.

kepeȝ, *n.* keeper 16/26.

kerchy, *n.* kerchief 91/22.

kirk, *see* Cherch.

kit, *v. t. inf.* cut 123/20.

knokkyng, *pres. p.* knocking 52/11.

knowest, knowist, *v. t.* 2 *s. pres.* 18/19, 33/13; knowe, *v. t.* 2 *s. imper.* 19/15; knew, *v. t.* 3 *s. p.* 18/8; knew, *v. t.* 3 *pl. p.* 68/28; know, knowyn, *pp.* 14/29, 87/26; a-knowe, I-knowe, *pp.* made known 47/5, 50/23. *See* a-knowe.

knowlech, *n.* knowledge 8/31, 52/3; knowlech, *n.* knowledge, acquaintance 6/1.

knyt, *pp.* knit 81/15.

knyte, *n.* knight 62/33 ; knytys, *n. gen.* 121/13; knytys, *np.* 38/29.

kyndeled, *v. t.* 3 *pl. p.* kindled 24/19.

kynred, kynrod, *n.* kindred 4/8, 36/9, 68/25.

kyrnel, *n.* kernel 85/11.

L

labourand, *pres. p.* labouring 50/5.

laboureres, *np.* laborers 4/10.

lak, *v. t.* 3 *pl. pres.* lack 7/12; lakkyn, *v. t.* 2 *pl. pres.* 46/22; lakkid, *pp.* 69/16.

lamentable, *adj.* 22/1.

Lammesse, *n.* Lammas 121/17.

languoȝ, *n.* 67/31.

laschid, *pp.* lashed 8/4.

Latyn, *n.* Latin 1/17.

laudes, *n.* lauds, the prayers following matins 71/23.

laumpe, *n.* lamp 82/24.

lay, *see* ly.

leccherie, leccherye, *n.* lechery 7/25, 95/3.

lech, leche, *n.* leech, doctor 34/11, 60/10.

lede, *v. t. inf.* lead 29/15; led, *v. t.* 1 *s. p.* 30/2; ledde, *pp.* led 2/35.

lederes, *np.* leaders 50/23.

ledir, *n.* leather 38/22.

leed, *n.* lead 17/32.

lefte, *v. t. inf.* lift 48/33; lyft, *v. t.* 3 *pl. p.* 32/6; lift, lyfte, *pp.* 108/28, 116/8.

lefully, *adv.* lawfully 67/21.

legge, *n.* leg 126/20.

lendes, *np.* loins 38/31, 120/2.

lened, *v. i.* 3 *s. p.* leant 122/20; lenyng, *pres. p.* leaning 32/2.

lenger, *adj. comp.* longer 51/16.

Lentoñ, *n.* Lent 70/13.

leones, *n. gen.* lion's 85/23.

leprosite, *n.* leprosy 133/27.

lerned, *pp.* taught 29/4.

lernyng, *n.* learning 4/14.

lese, *v. t. inf.* lose 51/10.

lesingis, *np.* lies 33/16.

lest, *v. i. inf.* last 93/9.

lestith, *v. i.* 3 *s. pres.* 7/22 ; lestid, *v. i.* 3 *s. p.* lasted 42/6.

lest, *adj.* least 61/3.

lette, *v. t. inf.* prevent, obstruct 98/15; lete, *v. t.* 3 *s. p.* let, allowed 101/22 ; lettid, lettyd, *pp.* hindered 13/15, 45/15.

lettered, letteryd, *pp.* lettered, learned 5/9, 40/26, 67/15.

letteris, *np.* letters 3/27.

letting, *n.* stop, cessation 11/10.

lettiruȝ, *n.* learning 1/9.

letuse, *n.* lettuce 47/12.

leue, lyue, *v. i. inf.* live 4/12, 20/33 ; leued, lyued, *v. i.* 3 *s. p.* lived 26/29, 98/2 ; leued, *v. i.* 3 *pl. p.* lived 6/17, 34/20; leuand, liuand, lyuand, lyuyng, *pres. p.* living 19/27, 28, 54/9, 130/11, 137/10.

leue, *n.* leave 45/31.
leue, *v. t. inf.* leave 23/8.
leuer, *adv.* liefer 73/4.
lewid, *adj.* lewd, unlearned 40/7.
ley, *v. t.* 2 *pl. imper.* lay! 32/23.
leyser, *n.* leisure 12/1, 21/31.
lich, *adv.* like 2/12, 28/20.
licorous, *adj.* voluptuous, gluttonous 47/30.
lif, lyue, *n.* life 1/17, 20/32, 62/33; lyues, *np.* 71/24.
lift, *see* lefte.
likly, *adv.* likely 13/24.
likne, *v. t. inf.* liken 145/heading; likned, *pp.* likened 2/10.
liknesse, *n.* likeness 19/12.
likour, *n.* liquor 125/11.
lippis, *np.* lips 33/15.
list, *v. i.* 2 *s. pres.* listest 28/30; list, *v. i.* 3 *s. p.* listed 66/5.
lith, *adj.* light, easy 27/28.
lith, *s.* light 9/25.
lithnesse, *n.* lightness 119/19.
litigious, *adj.* 17/25.
litil, *adv.* little 8/23.
litil, *n.* little (time) 32/29.
litly, *adv.* lightly 47/14.
liuand. *See* leue.
loggid, *pp.* lodged 89/19.
loke, *v. t. inf.* look 7/15, 17/34. 47/30; loke, *v. i.* 2 *pl. imper.* 38/25; lokid, *v. t.* 3 *s. p.* looked 32/21.
lond, *s.* land 16/5, 41/6.
londyd, *pp.* landed 104/10.
longith, *v. i.* 3 *s. pres.* belongeth 1/4; longid, *v. i.* 3 *pl. p.* belonged 34/19; longing, *pres. p.* belonging 6/32, 20/8.
lordchip, lordschip, *s.* lordship 2/7, 33/16.
lordis, *n. gen.* lord's 4/15.
losed, *pp.* loosed 33/2.
loth, *adj.* 18/28.
loue, *n.* love 1/28,
low, *v. i.* 3 *s. p.* laughed 8/28.
lowed, *v. t.* 3 *s. p.* humbled 68/17.
loy, *see* ly.
ly, *v. i. inf.* lie down 32/29, 71/7; liggest, *v. i.* 2 *s. pres.* 119/9; lith, *v. i.* 3 *s. pres.* 141/11; lay, loy, *v. i.* 3 *s. p.* 20/6, 51/15, 98/10.
Lyban, *n.* Lebanon 50/22.
lyft, *see* lefte.
lylyis, *np.* lilies 55/18.
lynand, *n.* linen 70/31, 123/32.
lyue, lyuand, *see* leue, lif.
lyuysch, *adj.* living 98/22.

M

magr, *prep.* maugre, *malgré*, in spite of, 15/7.
makith, *v. t.* 3 *s. pres.* maketh 7/13; mad, *pp.* 1/27, 20/37.
mal, *adj.* male 26/13.
malandrynes, *np.* highwaymen 109/8.
malencolie, *n.* melancholy 5/25.
Mandauria, *s.* Madaura 8/8.
maner, *n.* manner 6/8.
manhod, *s.* manhood 72/26.
Manicheis, Maniches, *np.* Manichaeans 9/27, 31/11.
mannes, *n. gen.* man's 5/4; mennys, *np. gen.* men's 66/19.
marchaunt, *n.* merchant 30/11.
marteres, *np.* martyrs 16/24.
masse, *s.* mass 117/14; messis, missis, *np.* 59/1.
matrimonial, *adj.* 6/9.
maydenes, *np.* maidens 6/26.
maydenhed, *s.* maidenhood 21/4.
maystires, *np.* masters, great authors 11/25.
mech, *adj.* much 18/31.
mede, *s.* reward 71/1.
medeled, *pp.* mingled, mixed 47/10, 63/10.
mediacion, *s.* 61/18.
medycyne, *n.* 33/21.
meked, *v. t.* 3 *s. p.* humbled 96/18.
meknesse, *s.* meekness 19/8.
mel, *s.* meal 47/20.
membres, *np.* members (of the body) 21/22.
mene, *adj.* mean, poor 46/33.
mene, *s.* mean, compromise 39/29; menes, *np.* means 10/7.
meny, *s.* company 30/28.
merciable, *adj.* capable of mercy 18/28.
merie, mery, myri, *adj.* merry 16/9, 13, 70/2.
mark, *s.* mark 6/5; merkys, *np.* marks 6/1.
merour, *s.* mirror 39/3.
meruayle, merveile, *s.* marvel 6/10, 68/28.
merueling, *pres. p.* marvelling 21/26; meruelyng, *pres. p.* marvelling, causing to marvel 12/4.
messageris, *np.* messengers 51/34.
messis, *see* masse.
mesurable, *adj.* measurable, moderate 46/21.
mette, *s.* measure 136/11.

meued, *v. t. 3 s. p.* moved, induced 1/15; meued, mevid, *pp.* moved 34/13, 44/13, 72/30.

mevyngis, *np.* movements 66/7.

meynteyn, *v. t. inf.* maintain 140/15.

meyr, *n.* mayor 14/23.

misellis, *np.* lepers 67/31.

moder, modir, modyr, *n.* mother 4/20, 5/3, 62/32; moderis, *n. gen.* 63/11.

molten, *pp.* molten, melted 48/3.

monasteriis, *np.* monasteries 64/20.

mony, *n.* money, coin 82/6.

moo, *adj.* more 24/11.

moost, *adv.* most 1/15.

mor, *adv.* more 1/11, 26/10.

morer, *n.* increaser, one who increases 1/6, 2/32.

moring, *n.* increasing 139/8.

mornyng, *n.* mourning 79/8. .

morow, *adj.* morrow 77/22.

morownyng, *n.* morning 71/21.

motiues, motyues, *np.* motives 12/25, 13/6.

mountes, *np.* mountains 112/14.

munkys, *np.* monks 29/22.

myddis, *n.* midst 37/26.

mydwey, *n.* midway 70/31.

myschef, *n.* trouble, harm 48/6.

myth, *v. i. 3 s. p.* might 4/16; myte, myth, *v. i. 3 pl. p.* 21/27, 67/13.

myte, *n.* might 116/19.

N

Nabugodonosor, *s.* Nebuchadnezzar 112/18.

namely, namelych, *adv.* specially 6/20, 36/34, 61/19.

narratyf, *n.* narrative, a form of writing 31/20.

nase, *n.* nose 105/29.

nawt, nowt, *adv.* not, naught 7/17, 9/11, 21/20.

ne, *conj.* nor 3/25.

negligense, *n.* negligence 66/18.

necys, *np.* nieces 50/13.

nedis, *adv.* needs 118/15.

neophites, *np.* 85/20.

ner, *adv.* nearly 2/7.

neuer-þe-lasse, neuyrþelasse, *conj.* nevertheless 3/25, 39/12.

neuly, *adv.* newly 20/12.

neuyr, *adv.* never 5/28.

nite, nyth, *n.* night 10/8, 27/25, 77/19.

nobil, *adj.* noble 42/20.

Noe, *n.* Noah, 3/5.

non, *pron.* none 6/5.

nonas, *np.* nones 141/33.

norche, *v. t. inf.* nourish 102/17; norchid, *pp.* 4/21.

norcher, *n.* nourisher 46/6.

norching, *n.* nourishing 6/32.

notwithstand, *conj.* notwithstanding, 6/6.

notyfied, *pp.* 61/5.

noueltes, *np.* novelties, 11/14; noueltes, *np.* news, new things 122/15.

nowle, *n.* navel 106/16.

nowt, *see* nawt.

noyhous, *adj.* hurtful 100/33.

Numedie, Numedye, *n.* Numidia 3/20.

Nussie, *n.* ? Russie *or* Tussie, *for* Russia *or* Tuscany 8/15

ny, *adv.* nearly 20/36, 52/29; ny, *adv.* nigh 10/1; ny, *prep.* nigh 18/1.

nyher, *adv. comp.* nigher 38/19, 44/12.

O

o, *adj.* one 6/12, 20/23.

o, *prep.* on 55/20.

obeyen, *v. t. 3 pl. pres.* 103/13.

obliuious, *adj.* oblivious 147/15.

off, *prep.* of 4/8, 19/30.

offense, *n.* 33/15.

oft-tyme, often-tyme, *adv.* 19/13, 14.

omelies, *np.* homilies 57/3.

on, *pron.* one 1/27, 19/10.

on = of them ? 7/7.

on-certeyn, *adj.* uncertain 23/25.

onclennesse, *n.* uncleanliness 7/25.

on-corupte, *adj.* uncorrupted 75/2.

on-defensed, *adj.* undefended 94/16.

ondirstood, *v. t. 3 s. p.* understood 11/30.

ongilty, *adj.* unguilty, innocent 18/13.

onknowe, on-knowyn, *adj.* unknown 20/19, 68/21.

onlerned, *adj.* unlearned 21/15, 68/1.

on-mouled, *adj.* unmouldered 75/2.

onresonable, *adj.* unreasonable 5/31.

onstabilnesse, *n.* unstableness 23/23.

onthrifty, *adj.* unthrifty 65/22.

on-to, *prep.* unto 18/17.

on-wetyng, *adj.* unknowing 52/23.

on-wise, *adj.* unwise 1/3.

ony, *adj.* any 1/21.

onyment, *n.* ointment 93/18.

onys, *adv.* once 60/30.

ope, *adj.* open 84/20.

opinyones, *np.* opinions 23/6.

opposicioñ, *n.* opposition 61/12.

or, *adv.* ere 16/14, 141/5.

or, *v. i.* 3 *pl. pres.* ought 7/7.

orarium, *n.* border (Latin. *See note,* p. 157) 91/24.

oratorie, *n.* oratory 13/29.

ordeyn, *v. t. inf.* ordain 27/28.

ordres, *np.* orders (religious) 34/23.

oth, *n.* oath 51/9; othis, *np.* 51/8.

oþir, *adj.* other 1/11, 20/23.

ouer-say, *v. t.* 3 *s. p.* revised 58/12.

ouŕ, *poss. pron.* ours 18/20.

ouŕ, *n.* hour 64/22.

ouyr-lokid, *v. t.* 3 *s.p.* revised 57/10.

ouyr-nyth, *adv.* overnight 97/5.

ouyrsailed, *v. t.* 3 *pl. p.* oversailed, passed at sea 185/18.

ouyrspred, *pp.* overspread 132/9.

owt, *n.* aught 18/19.

owt, *adv.* out 17/30, 40/7.

Oxenford, *n.* Oxford 99/12.

oyle, *n.* oil 82/25.

P

paciens, *n.* patience 6/17.

paganite, *n.* paganism 145/6.

palesye, *n.* palsy 73/17.

paleys, *n.* palace 19/34.

papate, *n.* papacy 142/14.

parceyue, *v. t. inf.* perceive 127/6.

parchemyn, *n.* parchment 60/5.

parfit, parfite, parfith, *adj.* perfect 29/24, 45/25, 66/14.

parfithly, *adv.* perfectly 16/8.

parfithnesse, *n.* perfection 29/18.

parischones, *np.* parishioners 65/28.

partie, partye, *n.* part 3/8, 31/4; parties, *np.* 2/31.

partye, *adv.* partly 95/27.

pase-tyme, *n.* Easter 25/30.

passe, *np.* paces 126/8.

passyng, *adj.* 25/22.

patrimonie, *n.* 37/32.

pauyment, *n.* pavement 120/23.

paynem, *adj.* pagan 4/30.

pencifnesse, *n.* pensiveness 147/24.

Pers, *n.* Persia, 3/13.

perseuering, *pres. p.* persevering 21/2.

perseyue, *v. t. inf.* perceive 89/3.

pertinent, *adj.* 62/29.

pes, *n.* peace 6/15, 24/30.

pesibily, *adv.* 37/12.

petites, *np.* little children 64/14.

petous, *adj.* piteous 129/21.

petycioñ, *np.* petitions 61/17.

peyre, *n.* pair 25/9.

peysed, *v. t.* 3 *s. p.* poised 53/29.

philisophŕ, *n.* philosopher 19/11.

pinsones, *np.* sort of thin shoes 99/25.

pipes, *np.* pipes, the trachea and gullet, 127/13.

pite, *n.* pity 125/3.

pitte, *n.* pit 62/4.

plat, *adv.* flat 101/17.

playes, *np.* games 64/17.

pleasauns, *n.* pleasance, 1/24.

pleneŕ, *adj.* plenary 75/25.

plente, *n.* plenty 37/31.

plenteuously, *adv.* plenteously 21/30.

plete, pleten, *v. i. inf.* plead 17/25, 28.

pley, pleye, *v. i. inf.* play 20/5, 31/15; played, *v. i.* 3 *pl. p.* 81/15.

plite, plith, *n.* plight 16/22, 122/25.

plowmen, *np.* 86/31.

podagra, *n.* podagra, gout 99/16.

Poncian, *n.* Pontitianus 19/30.

pored, *v. t.* 3 *s. p.* poured 69/2.

postcomun, *n.* post-communion 112/6.

postulacion, *n.* postulation, solicitation 138/14.

pouert, pouerte, *n.* poverty 30/2, 68/9, 77/8.

poynaunt, *adj.* poignant 93/22.

practik, *n.* practice 42/3.

praisen, *v. t.* 2 *pl. imper.* praise 77/22.

preamble, *n.* 62/24.

prechid, *v. i.* 3 *s. p.* preached 27/24.

prees, pres, *n.* press, crowd 32/3, 43/32.

preest, *n.* priest 5/4; prestis, *np.* 34/24.

preisable, *adj.* to be praised, praiseworthy 136/18.

prerogatif, *n.* prerogative 68/28.

presens, *n.* presence 27/7.

pressuŕ, *n.* 128/1.

presthod, *n.* priesthood 65/11.

presumpcioñ, *n.* 80/32.

preuylegis, *np.* privileges 38/7.

prey, *v. i. inf.* pray 23/17.

prikkid, *pp.* pricked 118/22.

priuyth, *v. t.* 3 *s. pres.* depriveth 99/18.

proferen, *v. t.* 3 *pl. pres.* proffer 7/16; profered, *v. t.* 3 *s. p.* 30/16.

profete, *n.* prophet 74/21.

profiten, *v. i. inf.* 88/22.

profith, *n.* profit 66/19.

progenie, *n.* 78/26.

progenitouris, *np.* progenitors 4/8.
propicius, *adj.* propitious 75/11.
propirly, *adv.* 54/33.
proporcioned, *v. t.* 3 *s. p.* 10/24.
prouentis, *np.* revenues 66/31.
proues, *np.* proofs 95/20.
prouost, *n.* 113/5 ; prouostis, *np.* 76/19.
prouynces, *np.* provinces 3/14.
prys, *n.* price 33/27.
pryse, *n.* price, value 40/31.
pryuy, *adj.* privy 15/13.
pryuyly, *adv.* privily 31/7.
psalmys, *np. gen.* 72/11.
puericia, *n.* boyhood 7/21, 22.
puple, *n.* people 2/18.
puplysch, *v. t. inf.* publish 107/23.
pupplicacion, *n.* publication 107/26.
purpos, *n.* purpose 20/37.
purpos, *v. t. inf.* propose 11/8 ; purpose, *v. t.* 1 *s. pres.* purpose 20/29.
pursewed, *v. t.* 3 *s. p.* 52/8.
purveyid, *v. t.* 3 *s. p.* purveyed 36/18.
purueyed, *v. t.* 3 *pl. p.* 114/17.
puruyaunce, *n.* purveyance 86/27.
putte, *v. t. inf.* put 2/31.
pyned, *v.t.* 3 *s.p.* pined, wasted 97/21.

Q

qwaked, *v. i.* 3 *s. p.* quaked 73/16.
qwech, *pron.* which 12/17.
qweer, *n.* choir 106/14.
I-qwenchid, *pp.* quenched 9/25.
quod, *v. t.* 3 *s. p.* quoth, said 10/27.

R

ragyn, *n.* raging 64/2.
rankour, *n.* rancour 120/3.
rankyd, *pp.* became rank 126/21.
ransake, *v. t. inf.* ransack 66/2.
rase, *v. t. inf.* raze 47/26.
rauyschid, *pp.* ravished 32/8.
rawt, *see* rowt.
Rebaptizatores, *np.* Rebaptizers 52/30.
receyue, *v. t. inf.* receive 11/9 ; receyued, *v. t.* 1 *s. p.* received 1/14 ; receuyed, *v. t.* 2 *pl. p.* 2/24.
receynour, *n.* receiver 9/1.
receytis, *np.* receipts 50/1.
recors, *n.* recourse 28/15.
recure, *v. t.* 3 *pl. p.* recover 103/5.
recuryng, *n.* recovery 98/10.
red, *v. t. inf.* read 61/21 ; rede, *v. t.* 1 *s. pres.* 89/14 ; rede, *v. t.* 2 *pl. pres.* 3/26 ; redith, *v. t.* 3 *s. pres.* 54/20 ; red, *v. t.* 3 *s. p.* 11/29,

24/26 ; red, redde, *pp.* read 2/11, 11/27, 61/14.
redact, *v. t.* 3 *pl. p.* arranged in writing 79/29.
rederes, *np.* readers 33/30.
redyer, *adj.* readier 11/8.
redyly, *adv.* readily 29/33.
redyng, *n.* reading 11/11, 20/27.
refelle, *v. t.* 3 *s. p.* refel, refute 41/26.
refresch, *v. t. inf.* 20/5 ; refreschid, *pp.* 31/5.
reherse, *v. t. inf.* 33/24.
reise, *v.t. inf.* 33/1.
reles, *n.* release 122/22.
remissiones, *n.* remissions 66/4.
renne, *v. i. inf.* run 18/14, 36/17 ; rennyth, *v. i.* 3 *s. pres.* 31/32 ; ran, *v. i.* 3 *s. p.* 41/5 ; runne, *v. i.* 3 *pl. p.* 53/1 ; rennyng, *pres. p.* 85/2.
renneres, *np.* runners 38/27.
renounsid, *v. t.* 3 *s. p.* renounced 25/15.
repayr, *v. t. inf.* 100/5.
repe, *v. t. inf.* reap 81/17 ; repe, *v. i.* 3 *pl. pres.* 55/16.
replecchid, repleschid, *pp.* replenished 72/13, 145/18.
replet, *adj.* replete 76/28.
repreuyth, *v. t.* 3 *s. pres.* reproveth 56/20.
reprobat, *adj.* reprobate 62/19.
rered, *pp.* reared 19/17.
reson, reson, *n.* reason 2/32, 7/12.
rest, *pp.* wrested 76/29.
rethorician, *n.* rhetorician 19/11.
rethorik, *n.* rhetoric 8/21.
retorne, *v. i. inf.* return 72/19.
Retractaciones, *np.* Retractations (by Augustine) 31/27.
retribuciones, *np.* rewards 1/25.
reuel, *n.* revel 13/15.
reuers, *n.* reverse 7/8, 52/6.
reule, *v. t. inf.* rule 1/1 ; reule, *n.* rule, level board 10/18.
richesse, rychesse, *n.* riches 30/1, 68/11.
ripening, *adj.* 2/16.
risyn, *see* roos.
ritefulmen, *np.* rightful men 136/25.
rith, *adj.* level, flat 10/11 ; rith, *adj.* right 2/35, 29/1.
rith, *adv.* right, just 20/1.
rithwysnesse, *n.* righteousness 72/21.
rof, *n.* roof 115/26.
rood, *v. i.* 3 *s. p.* rode 8/24.
roop, *n.* rope 118/33.
roos, *v. i.* 3 *s. p.* rose 21/31 ; risyn, *pp.* risen 127/9.

rote, *n.* root 62/23.
roted, *pp.* grounded, learned 45/31.
roted, *pp.* rooted 68/9.
rotes, *np.* roots 87/24.
rowt, *v. i.* 3 *s. p.* raught 40/31; rawt,
   pp. 7/9.
rubrich, *n.* rubric; dedication of a
   book 5/12.
rudenesse, *n.* 74/28.
ryp, *adj.* ripe 24/26, 76/9.

S

Sabat-day, *n.* Sabbath-day 77/16.
saciat, *adj.* satiate 27/5.
sacramental, *adj.* 25/34.
sadeled, *pp.* saddled 104/1.
saf, *adj.* safe 52/22.
Sarsines, *np.* Saracens 147/13.
Sattirday, *n.* Saturday 77/15.
saue, *prep.* save, except 15/11,
   24/10.
sauely, *adv.* safely 1/11.
sauoured, *v. i.* 3 *s. p.* savoured, cared
   1/8.
say, sey, seyn, seyne, *v. t. inf.* say
   1/17,7/1,49/16,65/8,86/2, 87/25;
   seith, seyth, *v. t.* 3 *s. pres.* saith
   2/12, 35/8, 49/8; sey, *v. t.* 2 *pl.*
   pres. 7/7; sei, sey, seye, *v. t.* 3 *pl.*
   pres. say 2/28, 3/5, 99/16; seid,
   v. t. 1 *s. p.* 5/16; saide, seid, *v. t.*
   3 *s. p.* 1/6, 2/23, 19/21; saide,
   v. t. 1 *pl. p.* 5/5; sayde, *v. t.* 2 *pl. p.*
   61/14; saide, *v. t.* 3 *pl. p.* 9/27.
sayle, *v. i. inf.* sail 32/1.
scalis, *np.* scales, 134/26.
I-schake, *pp.* roused, moved 84/7.
schal, *v. aux.* 2 *s. pres.* shalt 11/11;
   schul, 2 *pl. pres.* shall 3/3; schal,
   schul, 3 *pl. pres.* 5/19,6/29; schul,
   1 *pl. pres.* 16/4; schulde, 3 *s. p.*
   should 19/24.
schalful, *adj.* 22/20. *See note* p. 152.
schape, *pp.* shapen 28/20.
scharp, *adv.* sharp 2/25.
schaue, *pp.* shaven 48/27.
sche, *pron.* she 1/20, 10/27.
schepis, *n. gen.* sheep's 85/22.
schew, *v. t. inf.* show 11/4; schewid,
   pp. 3/23.
schidis, *np.* strips of wood 80/28.
schipmen, *np.* sailors 16/2.
schippard, *n.* shepherd 79/11.
schippe, *v. i. inf.* ship 29/21.
schippis, *np.* 34/8.
schon, *np.* shoes 45/18.

schortly, *adv.* 74/13.
schrine, schryne, *n.* shrine 115/19, 34.
schryue, *v. i. inf.* shrive 41/10;
   schryuyth, *v. t.* 3 *s. pres.* shriveth
   9/5, 54/16; schryue, *pp.* shriven
   133/10.
schyne, *v. i. inf.* shine 74/16; schynyth, *v. i.* 3 *s. pres.* shineth 2/12;
   schone, schyned, *v. i.* 3 *s. p.* shon
   83/19.
sciens, *n.* science, learning 1/10,
   19/12; sciens, *np.* 3/26.
scisme, *n.* schism 75/28.
scorne, *n.* 19/18.
scrowes, *np.* scrolls 30/12.
se, see, *n.* sea 15/28, 29/20, 30/28.
se, *n.* see 58/2.
se, *v. t. inf.* see 11/11, 15/29; se,
   v. 1 *s. pres.* 19/17; se, *v. t.* 3 *pl.*
   pres. 18/3; say, sey, *v. t.* 3 *s. p.*
   6/33, 12/12, 19/27, 29/30; sey,
   v. t. 2 *pl. p.* 96/27; sey, *v. t.* 3 *pl. p.*
   20/34; seand, *pres. p.* seeing 76/27;
   sen, sene, seyn, *pp.* seen 6/19,
   65/27, 137/35, 138/1.
sealis, *np.* seals 139/5.
secretaries, *np.* 97/7.
secrete, *n.* secret, a prayer 112/5.
seculer, *adj.* secular 20/7.
sedes, *np.* seeds 81/17.
seid, seyn, *pp.* 7/8, 23/20; seying,
   pres. p. saying 16/26.
seke, *n.* sick 66/29.
sekenesse, *n.* sickness 8/11; seknesse, *np.* 75/5.
sekyng, *pres. p.* seeking 10/1.
seld, seldom, *adv.* 34/21, 47/12.
selle, *v. t. inf.* sell 81/10; seld, *v. t.*
   3 *s. p.* sold 76/33, 77/6.
selue, *n.* self 64/6.
semeth, *v. i.* 3 *s. pres.* seems 4/23;
   sempt, *v. i.* 3 *s. p.* seemed 65/19.
semly, *adv.* seemly 51/1.
sengil, *adj.* single, unmarried 26/6.
ser, *n.* sir 112/20; seres, *np.* 16/4.
sercle, *n.* circle 77/30.
sere, *adj.* sere 118/26.
sered, *pp.* sered 118/16.
seruage, *n.* servitude 63/19.
seruauntis, *np.* servants 6/21.
seruyse, *n.* service 6/14.
seruyse, *n.* dinner 51/10.
seruyseable, *adj.* serviceable 30/32.
sesed, *v. t.* 3 *s. p.* ceased 96/9.
se-side, *n.* sea-side 13/23.
sete, *n.* seat 77/32.
sette, *v. t.* 3 *s. p.* set 17/1; sette, *pp.*
   set 1/1, 19/27.

senene, *adj.* seven 7/22.
sewe, sewid, *v. t.* 3 *s. p.* pursued, followed, 26/9, 89/33.
sewirer, *adj. comp.* surer 90/7.
sexte, *adj.* sixth 35/3.
sextenesse, *n.* female sexton 121/1.
seying, *n.* seeing 67/14.
seyn, *n.* saint 17/1.
sikir, *adj.* certain 26/25.
sikirly, *adv.* certainly 13/23.
sikirnesse, sikyrnesse, *n.* certainty, safety 11/20, 35/11, 89/22.
silens, *n.* silence 20/20.
siluyr, *n.* silver 17/29, 100/2.
similitude, *n.* 82/2.
simpil, *adj.* simple 1/11.
sistir, *n.* sister 5/9.
sith, sithe, *adv.* since 15/17, 56/4.
sith, *n.* sight 21/28, 38/27, 73/21.
sithe, *n.* time 40/21.
Sithia, *n.* Scythia, 58/20.
sitte, *v. i. inf.* sit 21/27; satte, *v. i.* 3 *s. p.* sat 20/19; sat, soten, *v. i.* 3 *pl.* p. 21/26, 70/20.
skape, *v. t. inf.* escape 8/1; skaped, *v. t.* 3 *pl.* p. 134/31.
skil, *n.* reason, cause 57/27.
skole, *n.* school 4/13, 23/3.
skole mater, *n.* divinity, doctrine 56/4.
skoleres, skoleris, *np.* scholars 13/17, 23/10.
skoleward, *n.* schoolward 118/14.
slaundir, *n.* slaunder 16/35.
slauth, *n.* sloth 21/28.
slep, *n.* sleep 71/12.
slitte, *pp.* slit 34/12.
sluttynesse, *n.* sluttishness 46/23.
sly, *adj.* 53/7.
smale, *adj.* small 8/6.
smet, *pp.* smitten 95/32.
snybbe, *v. t. inf.* snub, rebuke 6/26.
snybbyng, *n.* rebuking 73/11.
sobbyng, *n.* 24/27.
sobir, *adj.* sober 21/14.
socour, *n.* succour 92/17.
sodeynly, *adv.* suddenly 7/9, 19/21.
soke, *n.* suck 89/36.
sokkys, *np.* socks 99/25.
solace, *n.* 27/10, 73/1.
solacious, *adj.* 70/3.
solemply, *adv.* solemnly 23/12.
solempne, *adj.* solemn 1/22.
solempnyȝed, *pp.* solemnized 80/4.
solitarie, *adj.* solitary 20/34.
solitarily, *adv.* 23/17.
somyr, *n.* summer 70/25.

sond, *n.* sending 118/10; sondes, *np.* messages 139/24.
sone, *adv.* soon 5/25.
soner, *adv. comp.* sooner 108/33.
sones, *np.* sons 3/6.
songe, songen, sunge, *pp.* 27/1, 27/13, 28/5.
sonner, *adv. comp.* sooner 49/28.
soo, *adv.* so 7/6, 19/21.
soor, *n.* sore 100/13.
sophisticacion, *n.* 10/31.
sor, *adv.* sorely 21/25.
sory, *adj.* sorry, worthless 8/26.
soten, *see* sitte.
soth, *n.* sooth, truth 95/6.
sotil, sotill, *adj.* subtle, delicate 9/25, 26/16, 35/12, 47/28.
sotilly, *adv.* subtly 26/19.
souered, *see* suffir.
souereynis, *np.* sovereigns 76/18.
soundeth, *v. i.* 3 *s. pres.* 23/25.
soute, *v. t.* 1 *s. p.* sought 36/23; soute, sowt, *v. t.* 3 *s. p.* 15/27, 37/2, 81/2; sout, *v. t.* 3 *pl.* p. 20/35; sout, *pp.* sought 4/24.
sowe, *v. t. inf.* sew 112/35; sowe, *v. t.* 2 *s. imper.* sew 113/10.
sowe, *v. t. inf.* sow 81/16; sowe, *v. i.* 3 *pl. pres.* 55/16; sowyn, *pp.* sown 81/22.
spatil, *n.* spittle 131/5.
specialte, *n.* speciality, importance 32/25.
speke, *v. i. inf.* speak 12/19, 20/15, 25/6; spekith, *v. i.* 3 *s. pres.* 28/24; spak, *v. i.* 3 *s. p.* 1/5, 12/14, 76/28.
sperd, *v. t.* 3 *s. p.* closed 83/5; sperd, *pp.* closed 67/10.
spirith, *n.* spirit 16/13.
sprad, *v. t.* 3 *s. p.* spread 134/16.
spryngin, *v. i.* 3 *pl. pres.* spring 56/30; sprange, *v. i.* 3 *pl.* p. 62/24.
spynne, *v. i.* 3 *pl. pres.* spin 55/18.
stabil, *adj.* stable 10/30.
stale, *see* stele.
stant, *v. i.* 3 *s. pres.* stands 3/18, 33/20, 37/15; stant, *v. i.* 3 *pl. pres.* stand 3/13; stant, stood, *v. i.* 3 *s. p.* stood 10/11, 114/9.
statua, *n.* statue. Used as a Latin word by Capgrave. Latin *statua* = image, statue 19/12.
stedfast, *adj.* steadfast 20/12.
stele, *v. t. inf.* steal 18/1; stelist, *v. t.* 2 *s. pres.* stealest 30/27; stale, *v. t.* 3 *pl.* p. stole 14/1.
steppis, *np.* steps 19/24.

step-modir, *n.* step-mother 55/29.
ster, *v. t. inf.* stir, incite 54/21;
  stered, *pp.* 6/16, 35/28.
sterres, *np.* stars 2/10, 77/23.
stert, stirt, *v. i. 3 s. p.* started 21/23,
  25, 47/30.
stewis, *np.* stews, brothels 8/26.
stile, *n.* style 25/23.
stille, *adv.* 21/2.
stilled, *v. i. 3 pl. p.* distilled 132/32.
stodie, *n.* study 11/11.
stodied, *v. i. 3 s. p.* studied 80/28;
  stodiand, stodying, *pres. p.* studying 17/23, 111/13.
stombeled, *v. i. 3 s. p.* stumbled
  123/13.
stood, *see* stant.
stoon, *n.* stone 118/24.
straungeris, *np.* strangers 36/34.
strawe, stre, *n.* straw 71/20, 111/22.
streit, streith, *adv.* straitly 34/4,
  95/24.
stretes, *np.* streets 101/6.
streyned, *v. i. 3 pl. p.* strained
  120/30.
streyt, *adj.* straight 67/18, 108/24.
strokis, strokys, *np.* strokes, blows
  53/2.
stuf, *n.* material 60/28.
stuffid, *pp.* stocked, filled 69/35.
stynkyng, *adj.* stinking 64/2.
suasiones, *np.* suasions 95/12.
subieccion, *n.* subjection 6/13.
substauns, *n.* substance 4/17.
subucula (Latin), undergarment
  125/30.
suffir, *v. t.* 1 *s. pres.* suffer 6/10;
  suffir, *v. t.* 2 *pl. pres.* 21/15;
  souered, *v. t. 3 s. p.* 33/21.
summe, *pron.* some 6/1.
sumtyme, *adv.* sometimes 5/32.
Sunamite, *n.* Shunammite 102/9.
sunne, *n.* sun 20/34.
supplanter, *n.* 145/3.
supplicacion, *n.* 25/7.
Surre, Surry, *n.* Syria 3/13, 109/12.
suspecte, *adj.* suspect 36/28.
suspense, *adj.* undecided, unbiased
  18/8; suspense, *adj.* raised up
  72/10.
sustentacle, *n.* sustainment 71/11.
swames, *np.* scales (Latin *squama*)
  134/25.
swech, *adj.* such 1/13, 20/14.
swem, *n.* swoon, sorrow 29/30.
swete, *adj.* sweet 2/18.
swete, *n.* sweat 132/30.
swetith, *v. i. 3 s. pres.* sweateth

132/31; swette, *v. i. 3 s. p.* sweated
  119/10.
swynesye, *n.* quinsy 127/10.
swynys, *n. gen.* swine's 94/9.
syluyr, *n.* silver 48/3.
synne, *n.* sin 21/9.

T

tables, *np.* written agreements 6/9.
Tagatenses, *n.* Tagaste 3/22.
tak, *v. t. inf.* take 85/23; take, *pp.*
  taken 21/12, 56/10.
talent, *n.* talent, piece of money
  87/17.
talkyng, *n.* 5/2.
tariing, tary, tarying, *n.* tarrying
  24/27, 113/16, 115/19.
tast, *v. t. inf.* taste 25/2.
teoches, *np.* characteristics 73/29.
tech, *v. t. inf.* teach 14/19; techith,
  v. t. 3 s. pres. 11/13; taute, *v. t.*
  3 *s. p.* 12/4; tawt, *v. i. 3 s. p.*
  23/26; taute, *v. t. 3 pl. p.* 27/23.
techer, *n.* teacher 63/34.
tedioua, *adj.* 63/10.
telle, *v. t. inf.* tell 1/15, 30/12; telle,
  v. 3 s. subj. pres. tell 4/24; telleth,
  tellith, tellit, tellz, *v. i. 3 s. pres.*
  4/26, 7/8, 16/31, 17/22, 26/16;
  teld, *v. t. 3 s. p.* told 19/5.
tempir, *v. t. inf.* temper 95/23; tempered, *v. t. 3 s. p.* tempered, mode-
  rated 51/37.
temporal, *adj.* 27/11.
teres, *np.* tears 11/20.
tete, *n.* teat 9/19; tetes, *np.* 89/35.
teth, *np.* teeth 7/16, 25/5.
tewnys, *np.* tunes 27/14.
Tewysday, *n.* Tuesday 78/28.
teyhid, *v. t. 3 s. p.* tied 118/33.
than, *adv.* then 1/22, 9/31.
theef, *n.* thief 17/31.
tho, thoo, *adv.* then 9/26, 20/14,
  21/13.
tilleres, *np.* tillers 63/16.
tilth, *n.* 101/5.
to-gidir, to-gidyr, *adv.* together
  2/31, 19/32.
tokne, *n.* token 87/6; toknes, tokenes, *np.* 30/13, 107/11.
tong, tonge, tunge, *n.* tongue 2/34,
  3/30, 21/21; tonge, *n.* tongue,
  used for nation or country 3/16;
  tongis, *np.* tongues 3/31.
too, *pron.* two 17/3, 20/24.
too, *adj.* two 3/12, 16/10.
toos, *np.* toes 118/29.

touchith, *v. t. 3 s. pres.* 33/9.

touȝ, *n.* tower 111/19.

tow, *adj.* tough 73/12.

trad, *v. i. 3 s. p.* trod 119/12.

translat, *v. t. 1 s. p.* translated 61/7; translat, translate, *pp.* translated 33/6, 80/6.

transumpoiones, *np.* transumptions 85/27.

trauase, *v. t. inf.* traverse 135/1.

trauayle, *v. i. inf.* travail, work 37/28; trauayled, *v. i. 3 s. p.* laboured, suffered 6/33.

trauns, *n.* trance 128/20.

trayled, *v. i. 3 s. p.* trailed 118/32.

tre, *n.* tree 10/11, 21/32; tre, *n.* wood 100/2.

tremel, *v. i. inf.* tremble 15/14; tremuled, *v. i. 3 pl. p.* trembled 94/27.

tresoȝ, tresouȝ, *n.* treasure 1/13, 50/3.

trespas, *n.* 33/22.

tretith, *v. i. 3 s. pres.* 23/31; tretith, *v. t. 3 s. pres.* treateth 25/21.

tretys, *n.* treatise 56/2.

treuly, *adv.* truly 1/17.

tribus, *np.* tribes 145/20.

trost, *n.* trust 15/19.

trostand, trosting, trostyng, *pres. p.* 90/32, 94/30, 99/4, 126/24.

trowe, *v. t. 1 s. pres.* trow 47/13.

Tussie, *s.* Tuscany 31/2.

tuycioȝ, *n.* tuition 27/26.

twyes, *adv.* twice 14/13.

tydannes, tydyngis, tytandis, *np.* tidings 35/27, 72/34, 115/4.

tyl, *adv.* till 17/18.

Tyrington, *n.* West Torrington 81/28.

þ

þai, *pron.* 48/19.

þan, þañ, þanne, *adv.* then 19/17, 20/28, 21/6.

þankyng, *s.* thanking, thanks 20/10; þankinggis, *np.* 137/2.

þankyng, *pres. p.* 21/1.

þat, *conj.* that 1/2.

þat, *rel. pron.* who 18/6.

þedir, þedyr, þidir, *adv.* thither 14/8, 31/13, 111/20.

þei, *pron.* they 6/17.

þem, *pron.* them 96/32.

þenne, *adv.* thence 102/21.

þeȝ, *adv.* there 5/18.

þese, *pron.* these 1/7.

þi, *pron.* thy 111/33.

þidir, *see* þedir.

þing, þingis, *np.* things, 1/27, 103/6.

þink, *v. t. inf.* 28/6.

þird, *adj.* third 1/29.

þirknesse, *n.* darkness 16/17, 77/27. (*Also* dirknes.)

þirled, *pp.* pierced 115/26.

þo, *adj.* those 16/32.

þoo, *pron.* those 9/17, 12/13.

þolyd, *pp.* endured 75/15.

þongis, *np.* thongs 38/30.

þorw, *prep.* through 11/14.

þorw-oute, *prep.* throughout 2/17, 15/3.

þouȝ, *conj.* though 80/31.

þouȝ, *v. t. 3 s. p.* thought 10/11, 36/8, 67/6, 88/27; þout, þouȝ, *v. t. 3 pl. p.* 32/9, 76/10.

þoutes, *np.* thoughts 15/13, 86/11.

þouȝ, *conj.* though 1/8.

þretis, *np.* threats 48/19.

þretyng, *n.* threatening 95/11.

þrew, *v. t. inf.* 21/32; þrew, *v. t. 3 s. p.* 81/7.

þries, *adv.* thrice 64/33.

þrote, *n.* throat 95/14.

V

vacaunt, *adj.* vacant, unemployed 61/21.

vanite, *n.* vanity 9/6; vanytees, *np.* 23/6.

venemhous, *adj.* venemous 27/17.

veniauns, *n.* vengeance 7/17.

vers, *n.* verse 24/28; vers, *np.* verses 47/21.

vertu, *np.* virtues 67/6.

very, *adj.* true 30/13.

veryly, *adv.* verily 1/20.

vexid, *pp.* vexed 49/2.

veyn, *adj.* vain 8/6, 14/14.

veynglorie, *n.* vainglory 70/33.

vhanne, *adv.* when 8/19.

viage, *n.* voyage 91/17, 135/20.

vikeȝ, vykeȝ, *n.* vicar 40/22, 90/30.

vis, *n.* vice 47/20; vices *np.* 47/19.

visite, *v. t. 3 s. p.* visited 31/4, 49/1.

vitaile, *n.* victuals 69/35.

vnce, *n.* ounce 82/7.

vnch, *np.* inches 132/19.

vndir-fote, *adv.* underfoot 81/7.

vndirtake, *v. t. inf.* take charge of 8/27.

vnkunnyng, *n.* ignorance 114/19.

vnneth, *adv.* scarcely 61/20.

vnsperd, *v. t.* 3 *s. p.* unclasped, opened 20/7.

vomyte, *n.* vomiting 133/22.

voyde, *v. t. inf.* dismiss 11/18.

voys, *n.* voice 21/14; voyses, *np.* cries 22/1.

up-hap, vphap, *adv.* 20/25, 46/32.

vset3, *v. t.* 3 *s. pres.* useth 88/19; vsed, *pp.* habituated 41/11.

vttyr, *v. t. inf.* utter 32/9; vttered, vttir, *v. t.* 3 *s. p.* 34/27, 43/11.

W

wallid, *pp.* walled 83/28.

wallis, *np.* walls 19/18.

Wandali, *np.* Vandals 58/18 (Latin *Vandali*).

war, *adj.* ware 48/15.

Wardon, *n.* Watton 109/17.

warned, *pp.* forbidden, refused 47/17.

was, wast, *see* be.

wasch, *pp.* washed 62/10.

wast, *n.* waste 47/28.

water, *v. t. inf.* wash 112/27.

watirside, *n.* 64/30.

wauntown, *adj.* wanton 8/25, 64/2.

wawe, *n.* wave, sea 103/21.

weoch, *n.* watch 27/28.

wecchid, *pp.* 121/20.

weddid, *pp.* 5/26, 21/3.

wedyr, *n.* weather 103/24.

welde, *v. t. inf.* possess, rule 83/21.

welfar, *n.* 20/2.

well, *adv.* well 3/28, 14/24, 43/31.

wenest, *v. t.* 2 *s. pres.* 105/12.

wenyng, *pres. p.* weening, causing to ween 42/28.

wengis, *np.* wings 85/23.

wepe, *v. i. inf.* weep 21/30.

wepun, *np.* weapons 53/2.

were, *v. t. inf.* wear 47/4; wered, *r. t.* 3 *s. p.* wore 46/19.

werk, *n.* work 1/23.

werre, *n.* war 50/31.

weuer, *n.* weaver 129/31.

weuyng, *n.* weaving 129/32.

wex, *v. i.* 3 *s. p.* waxed, grew 96/2.

weye, *n.* way 2/35.

weyk, *adj.* weak 34/12.

whan, *adv.* when 4/13.

whech, *pron.* which, who 1/6, 16/2, &c.

wheither, *conj.* whether 15/2.

whens, *adv.* whence 32/34.

wher-so-euyr, *adv.* wheresoever 17/1.

whil, whill, *adv.* while 4/30, 16/23.

while, *n.* 32/9.

who, *adv.* how 5/18.

wicchis, *np.* witches 137/30.

widowis, *np.* 66/29.

wil, *n.* will 1/20.

wildyrnesse, *n.* wilderness 20/16.

wilful, *adj.* voluntary 80/2.

wite, *v. t. inf.* blame 51/5.

withdrawe, *v. t. inf.* diminish 45/16; with-drow, *v. t.* 3 *s. p.* withdrew 39/19.

withinne, *prep.* within 19/17.

with-outen, *conj.* without 4/16: wit3-outen, *prep.* 99/22.

witnes, *n.* evidence 113/24; witnesseres, *np.* witnesses 110/9.

witte, *n.* wit, understanding 26/15; wittes, wittis, *np.* wits 32/20, 93/27.

wit3, *prep.* with 10/7, 112/24.

wode, *adj.* mad 128/15.

wode, *n.* wood 20/23; wodes, wodis, *np.* woods 20/22, 31/2.

wodnesse, *n.* madness 79/20.

womannes, *n. gen.* woman's 15/31.

womennes, *np. gen.* 86/27.

wone, *adj.* wont 21/20.

wonyng, *n.* dwelling 122/28.

wook, *v. i.* 3 *s. p.* woke 66/10.

worchep, worchip, *n.* worship 1/23, 74/22.

worchipid, *v. t.* 3 *s. p.* worshipt 19/2.

wordes, wordis, wordys, *np.* words 2/24, 10/28, 11/19.

wortes, wortys, *np.* worts, herbs, roots 47/12, 70/14.

wot, wote, *v. t.* 1 *s. pres.* know 4/3, 32/13; wist, woot, *v. t.* 3 *s. p.* 14/5, 29/13.

wounde, wounden, woundyn, *pp.* wound 116/7, 117/15, 18.

wrastillingis, *np.* wrestlings 65/22.

wrecched, *adj.* wretched 46/21.

wrestiling, *pres. p.* wrestling 53/17.

wroth, *adj.* 30/19.

wrout, *v. t.* 3 *s. p.* wrought 34/33; wroute, *v. t.* 3 *pl. p.* 17/30.

wrytith, *v. i.* 3 *s. pres.* writeth 28/26; wroot, wrot, *v. t.* 3 *s. p.* wrote 25/10, 60/21; wrytyn, *v. i.* 3 *pl. p.* 95/5; wretyn, writin, writyn, wrytin, *pp.* written 5/12, 7/26, 135/27, 136/7.

wyis, *adj.* wise 50/19.

wyndown, wyndown, *n.* window 32/2, 84/1.

wynne, *v. t.* 3 *pl. p.* win 21/16.

Wyntir, *n.* Winter 70/24.

12

wyte, *n.* imposition, burden 90/10.
wyues, wyuys, *np.* wives 6/12, 26/9.

Y

ydiotes, ydiotis, *np.* unlearned, ignorant people 1/4, 85/16.
ydropesey, *n.* dropsy 122/10.
ylde, *n.* island 76/5.
ympne, *n.* hymne 25/34; ympnis, ympnys, *np.* 27/1, 11; ympnis, *np. gen.* 72/11.
Ynde, *n.* India 3/13.
Ynglond, *n.* England 3/17, 68/21.
Ypone, *n.* Hippo 3/21.
Ytaile, *n.* Italy 3/16.

ȝ

ȝa, *adv.* yes 18/19.
ȝald, *v. t.* 3 *s. p.* yielded 60/15.
ȝe, *pron.* ye 6/8.
ȝel, *n.* zeal 65/10.

ȝelow, *adj.* yellow 132/32.
ȝere, *n.* year 33/2; ȝer, ȝere, *np.* years 7/6, 8/19, 33/5, 75/2; ȝeris, *n. gen.* year's 49/36.
ȝet, ȝit, *adv.* yet 1/9, 111/9.
ȝeue, *v. t. inf.* 16/27, 46/24; ȝeueth, *v. t.* 3 *s. pres.* 26/28; ȝyue, *v. t.* 3 *s. pres. subj.* 46/27; gaf, ȝaue, *v. t.* 3 *s. p.* 14/12, 18/17, 19/8, 50/1; ȝoue, *v. t.* 3 *pl. p.* gave 13/13; ȝeuyng, *pres. p.* giving 46/10; goue, ȝoue, ȝouen, *pp.* 2/4, 13/17, 20/14, 56/21, 136/14.
ȝeueres, *np.* givers 88/15.
ȝeugis, *n.* Zeugitana 3/13.
ȝiftis, *np.* gifts 68/8.
ȝok, *n.* yoke 90/19.
ȝondir, *adv.* yonder 105/14.
ȝong, *adj.* young 6/20, 21/3.
ȝonger, *adj. comp.* younger 49/20.
ȝou, ȝow, *pron.* you 8/23, 6/9, 29/1, 37/29.
ȝour, *pron.* your 6/8.

SUBJECT INDEX

A

Achademia, explanation of 23/25.
Achaia 3/15.
Acharius, abbot of Peterborough 79/28, 142/9.
Adeodatus, son of Augustine, baptized with him 26/4; cause of *de Quantitate Animae* 26/26, 31/17.
Ad fratres in heremo, a sermon 146/22.
Africa 3/10.
Ages, the seven 7/4.
Alans 58/18.
Albyne, a canon of St. Gilbert's 98/4.
Alexander, Bishop of Lincoln, 83/32, 87/34.
Alypius, goes to Augustine 17/4; convicted of theft 17/20; goes to Africa with Augustine 29/20, 37/6.
Anagnia 111/2, 142/3.
Anastasius, a monk of Augustine's 30/3, 37/7.
Ancelme, a priest 135/5.
Anna 89/32.
Antichrist 137/31.
Antioch, Council of 43/21.
Apollo 56/12.
Apostolus Petrus, a sermon 49/13.
Arabia 3/13.
Arian heresy 27/16.
Arillus, a monk 30/4.
Aristotle, his *Categories* 4/2, 11/27.
Asher 147/3.
Asia 3/8.
Augustine, his life translated from Latin at the request of a gentle woman 1/15; virtues of his name 1/26; significance of his name 2/25; born at Tagaste 3/22; hated Greek 3/27; knew both Greek and Latin 3/31; translated Aristotle's *Categories* 4/2; position of his parents 4/9; goes to school at Carthage 4/13; born on St. Brice's day 4/28; his brother, Navigius

5/6; his monasteries 5/16; his childhood 7/3; at school 7/27; studies Scripture unprofitably 9/21; at Madaura 8/8; study at Carthage 8/20, 11/25; robe an apple-tree 9/7; reads Cicero 9/12; becomes a Manichaean 9/27; teaching rhetoric at Carthage 12/7; doubts the Manichaean heresy 12/20; writes against Manichaean heresy 12/18; argues with Faustus 12/30; goes to Rome 13/11; goes to Milan to teach rhetoric 14/21; meets St. Ambrose 14/28; converted by the preaching of St. Ambrose 15/12; goes to Simplicianus 18/25; Simplicianus and 19/24; Pontitianus visits him 19/30; hears a voice: 'Take up and read!' 22/8; leaves Milan 23/17; lives in a field (villa) belonging to Verecundus 23/19; asks advice of St. Ambrose 25/14; helps Ambrose compose *Te Deum* 25/35; adopts a habit from Simplicianus 28/11; gets twelve hermits from Simplicianus 29/8; names of his first monks 30/3; goes to Ostia 30/28, 31/31; goes to Rome 31/1; writes against Manichaeans 31/9, 34/32; communes with Monica 32/4; goes to Carthage 34/1; returns to his heritage at Tagaste 34/19; goes to Hippo 36/5; builds a monastery near Hippo 36/30; elected priest 39/4; his second monastery 40/2; preaching under Valerius 40/29; argues with Fortunatus 41/20; chosen bishop 42/23; his third monastery 43/29; increase of his order 46/2; his manner at table 47/8; casts out spirits 49/2; conduct of worldly affairs 50/2; in danger from heretics 52/16; writes his *Retractations* 57/18; in the siege of Hippo 58/16; miracle before death 59/21; death 60/15; rule of 67/23; St. Jerome and

OXFORD: HORACE HART
PRINTER TO THE UNIVERSITY

CPSIA information can be obtained at www.ICGtesting.com
Printed in the USA
244648LV00007B/11/A